Second Edition

CRIMINAL LAW

in Maryland

CASES, CONCEPTS AND CRITICAL ANALYSIS

Robyn S. Brown
Kelly A. Koermer
Anne Arundel Community College

Kendall Hunt
publishing company

Cover Copyright © Shutterstock, Inc.

Kendall Hunt
publishing company

www.kendallhunt.com
Send all inquiries to:
4050 Westmark Drive
Dubuque, IA 52004-1840

Printed in the United States of America
10 9 8 7 6 5 4 3 2

IN LOVING MEMORY,
William & Maryruth Scheina
ROBYN S. BROWN

IN LOVING MEMORY,
Robert C. Koermer
KELLY A. KOERMER

Contents

Introduction

Welcome to the second edition of *Criminal Law in Maryland; Cases, Concepts, and Critical Analysis*. Criminal law is undoubtedly a fascinating subject and one which we can't seem to escape. Turn on any television program, open any newspaper, navigate through any news website, and it's bound to hit you right in the face. Crime sells. However, not only does crime sell, but it also *provides*. Provides what, you ask? It provides lots of jobs. With the public's fascination of criminal law comes job opportunities that tie in our interests and expertise with crime: police officers, homeland security officers, crime scene analysts, attorneys, computer analysts. The list is endless. Therefore, the importance of learning criminal law, *really* learning it, is very practical.

Before you jump into the contents of this workbook, you need to keep a few very important things in mind:

First, if you don't already, start paying attention to what's happening in the world around you. When you're listening to the news and you hear that Mr. Smith was just arrested for "second degree murder," stop and think for a minute. What, exactly, does that mean? Why is it murder and not manslaughter? Why second and not first-degree? The more you *apply* what you are learning to the crimes that occur every day all around us, the more you are truly mastering the subject.

Second, always keep in mind that one criminal episode will typically result in several crimes having been committed. We call this a "laundry list" of crimes so to speak. In other words, try to see beyond the one or two obvious crimes that jump out at you right away and analyze *all* possible crimes that have been committed. Consider the following example: Bob walks up to Tom, puts a gun to Tom's head, and Bob says "Give me all your money or I'll kill you." Tom hands over his wallet and Bob flees. Now, our guess is that you immediately said "Oh, Bob committed robbery," and you would be absolutely correct. Robbery is the one crime that jumps off the page. But, don't stop there. Bob has also committed a theft, false imprisonment, and an assault. The point of this little example? Be as thorough as possible when dissecting a scenario for possible crimes.

Third and finally, don't have tunnel vision when it comes to the crimes. More often than not we think we know everything about a crime because of its name, or what we've seen on television, or even what our friend has told us. But there is much more to any given crime than initially meets the eye. Take the time to learn the elements of each crime so you can break it down into its components and really analyze the offense. Don't make assumptions and don't try to reach a conclusion too quickly, or your conclusion will likely be wrong! This simple true/false quiz will help impress upon you that exact lesson. Take this quiz your first week of class as best you can without consulting anything and with your best guess only. Then, at the end of the semester, retake the quiz. You'll be amazed at how your answers change given the fact that you are now an expert on what criminal law is really all about.

We hope you enjoy studying criminal law as much as we have enjoyed writing this workbook!—R.B. & K.K.

CRIMINAL LAW QUIZ

Directions: In the space next to each number, write T if the statement is True, or F if the statement is False.

_____ 1. Brenda is shopping in a department store when she sees a young child mouthing off to his mother. Brenda, who has raised five children of her own and can't stand it when kids are disrespectful to their parents, walks up to the child and punches him so hard that he falls to the ground unconscious. Brenda is guilty of child abuse.

_____ 2. Mike breaks into Sally's house late one night and makes his way to her bedroom because he wants to kill Sally. Mike is guilty of burglary.

_____ 3. Anna takes nude photographs of her young children and posts them on the Internet. Anna has never touched her children in an inappropriate way. Anna is guilty of child abuse.

_____ 4. Carl is growing fifty marijuana plants in his back yard. Carl is guilty of manufacture of a controlled dangerous substance.

_____ 5. Roy is physically abusing his two young sons. Kim, Roy's wife, is aware of the abuse but chooses to do nothing about it because she doesn't want to see Roy get into trouble and she doesn't want their marriage jeopardized. Kim is guilty of child abuse.

_____ 6. Lynn is sitting in her vehicle in her driveway. Zachary walks up to Lynn, puts a gun to her head, and demands that she get out of the car. Zachary drives away for a "joy ride," and returns the vehicle to her driveway approximately one hour later. Zachary is guilty of carjacking.

_____ 7. Betty says to Fred, "If you kill my husband for me, I'll pay you $50,000." Fred responds, "What are you nuts? No way I'm committing any murder." Betty is guilty of a crime.

_____ 8. Steve robs a bank. The moment he pulls away from the bank in his car, he sees flashing lights and hears sirens. Steve takes off, driving 70 mph through busy city streets with the police in pursuit. About ten minutes after the bank robbery and about fifteen miles from the bank, Steve runs over and kills Emma, a pedestrian crossing in a crosswalk while he is still trying to lose the cops. The most Steve can be convicted of for Emma's death is manslaughter.

_____ 9. Matt, who is 25, goes to a bar Friday night. He must show his ID to get into the bar. While there he meets Courtney, who is dressed in a business suit. She tells Matt that she just graduated from law school and is working for a firm in Annapolis. One thing leads to another and they ultimately end up back at Matt's apartment where they have consensual sex. The next morning the police knock on his door and inform him that Courtney is really only 15 years old. Matt is guilty of rape.

_____ 10. Tommy is seated inside the passenger seat of a vehicle parked outside of a 7-11. William walks up to Tommy, pulls out a gun, and demands that Tommy get out of the car. Tommy complies, and William drives away. As it turns out, Tommy is only a 13-year-old boy. He was waiting in the car while his father ran into the store to buy something. William is guilty of carjacking.

_____ 11. Greg kisses Felicia without her permission. Greg is guilty of battery.

_____ 12. Bryan rings the doorbell of Jenny's home. Jenny answers, and Bryan explains that he is selling a new line of cosmetics that he'd like to show her. Jenny lets him inside and they both sit down on the couch to look at the products. All of a sudden Bryan begins coughing and asks Jenny for a glass of water. Jenny goes into the kitchen to get the water, and Bryan proceeds to steal valuables in Jenny's home. Bryan is guilty of a burglary.

_____ 13. Jerry is an expert pick-pocket. One day while walking along Main Street in Annapolis, he brushes past Tracey. Tracey doesn't even notice Jerry. Two hours later when Tracey reaches for her wallet in her pocket, she realizes it is gone. Jerry, meanwhile, is counting the cash in Tracey's wallet that he lifted from her pocket. Jerry is guilty of robbery.

_____ 14. Andrew is smoking a cigarette. When he's done he carelessly flicks it onto the porch of his neighbor's home. The porch ignites and the home burns to the ground. Andrew is guilty of arson.

_____ 15. Chris is applying to colleges, but his grades in high school weren't so great. So, he hacks into his high school's database and changes a few of his "D's" to "B's." Chris is guilty of forgery.

_____ 16. Cindy is looking outside of her second-story bedroom window when she sees Frank hotwire her car and drive away. Frank is guilty of carjacking.

_____ 17. Tom says to Nicole, "Hey, I'll sell you this bag of weed for $75." Nicole hands over the money and takes the bag. When Nicole gets home, she learns that the "weed" is really a bag of oregano. Nicole is guilty of the crime of possession of a controlled dangerous substance.

_____ 18. Barbara wakes up late one night because she hears a strange noise coming from downstairs. She grabs a handgun she keeps for protection and heads downstairs, where she sees a man dressed all in black and a ski mask standing in her living room. Barbara is legally allowed to use deadly force when defending her home.

_____ 19. Butch and Spike are long time rivals. Butch decides he wants to kill Spike. He plans out his crime and shoots Spike as Spike is leaving a bar late one night. After the shooting, Butch walks up to Spike's dead body and notices that Spike's wallet fell out of his pocket. As an afterthought, Butch takes Spike's wallet and runs. Butch is guilty of robbery.

_____ 20. Mark forces Adam at gunpoint to engage in anal sex with him. Mark is guilty of rape.

Parties to a Crime

Introduction

The first chapter of this book deals not with specific criminal offenses but, instead, with the criminal responsibility of individuals involved in the commission of a crime. Oftentimes, when crimes are committed more than one perpetrator is involved. The question then becomes, to what extent is each participant responsible for the crime or crimes committed? Do all perpetrators share equal criminal responsibility or do some carry greater responsibility for the offenses? The divisions of criminal responsibility discussed throughout this chapter will explain the different levels of criminal participation recognized in Maryland and the different degrees of criminal liability attached to each. As with each level of culpability, it is important to remember that a "target crime" is the main objective. A target crime is the ultimate goal the criminal venture seeks to accomplish.

Focus Crimes

Principal in the First Degree, *Pope v. State*, 284 Md. 309, 396 A.2d 1054 (1979).

Principal in the Second Degree (Aiding and Abetting), *Pope v. State*, 284 Md. 309, 396 A.2d 1054 (1979); MPJI-Cr. 6:01.

Accessory Before the Fact, *Lewis v. State*, 285 Md. 705, 404 A.2d 1073 (1979); MPJI-Cr. 6:00.

Accessory After the Fact, *State v. Hawkins*, 326 Md. 270, 604 A.2d 489 (1992); MPJI-Cr. 6:02.

Objectives

Upon completing this chapter you should be able to:

- ➲ Distinguish between principals and accessories generally;
- ➲ Distinguish between a principal in the first degree and a principal in the second degree;
- ➲ Distinguish between an accessory before the fact and an accessory after the fact;
- ➲ Analyze the concept of "constructive presence" at the scene of a crime and how it impacts potential criminal responsibility; and
- ➲ Recognize the different levels of culpability depending upon the degree of participation in a crime.

CASE LAW	*State v. Sowell*, 353 Md. 713, 728 A.2d 712 (1999)
	*See explanation at end of case for subsequent history.

Respondent Brian Lamont Sowell was convicted by a jury in the Circuit Court for Prince George's County of armed robbery, robbery, two counts of use of a handgun in the commission of a crime of violence, and first degree assault for his involvement along with three other men in the robbery of his employer, Recycling Incorporated. He appealed to the Court of Special Appeals. That court reversed respondent's convictions, holding that the evidence presented to the jury was not sufficient to support a finding that respondent was present at the scene of the crime, either constructively or actually. Therefore, under the common law rules relating to principals and accessories, that court held that the respondent should not have been convicted as a principal in the second degree.

We granted a writ of certiorari to consider whether the common law distinction between principals and accessories remains viable in Maryland. We hold that it does. Accordingly, we shall affirm.

I. Facts

On the date of the underlying crimes, October 17, 1995, respondent was employed by Recycling Incorporated. The company paid its employees' wages in cash, and the money normally was distributed by DeLisa Holmes, the office manager. Around 11:30 a.m., respondent called Recycling Incorporated's office to inquire when the payroll would be ready. Ms. Holmes told respondent the payroll would be ready at 12:00 p.m. Respondent then asked how the employees were going to be paid. Ms. Holmes replied that they would be paid in cash, to which respondent replied, "good." Respondent picked up his pay in cash at around 12:30 p.m.

About an hour later, three men wearing dark clothing and carrying guns entered the Recycling Incorporated office. One man walked directly to Brian Fowler, the vice-president of the company, and held a gun on him. A second man put a gun to Ms. Holmes' head and told her to get the cash. She placed all of the cash, $14,600, in a bag provided by one of the men and the three men left. Ms. Holmes testified that the man who held the gun to her head seemed familiar with the office and knew where the money was located.

Testimony by other witnesses indicated that respondent was the mastermind behind the robbery. Anthony Williams testified that prior to the robbery, respondent told Williams he knew where they could get some easy money and that he had it "all planned out." Respondent targeted the recycling company because it paid its employees in cash and he knew how someone could get in and out quickly. Williams further testified that respondent had a map of the recycling center detailing where the employees would be standing, who should be grabbed, and who might have a gun. Respondent told the others that the robbery should occur between 11:30 a.m. and 12:30 p.m. and that while the robbery was in process, he would be on his route for the recycling company. The men arranged to meet later to split up the money. Williams further testified that he saw the men involved in the robbery the next

day. Respondent said that "it was easy, just like he had planned."

II. Discussion and Analysis

A. Common Law Doctrine of Accessoryship

The question for which we issued the writ of certiorari and as phrased in the State's brief is: "Was the evidence sufficient to establish that [respondent] was an accomplice either because constructive presence is not required to establish accomplice liability or because he was constructively present?"

The underlying issue argued by both parties is whether Maryland should retain the common law distinction between principals and accessories before the fact. The Court of Special Appeals, although criticizing the long-standing Maryland common law rule that distinguishes an accessory before the fact from a principal in the second degree by the requirement that the principal be actually or constructively present, nonetheless reversed respondent's convictions as a principal in the second degree. That court held: There is, of course, a major legal hurdle regarding the State's request [to dispense with the distinction between accessories before the fact and principals]. The argument, in *Lewis* [*v. State*, 285 Md. 705, 404 A.2d 1073 (1979)], to change the rule mandating that an accessory cannot be tried before the principal is sentenced, was presented to the Maryland Court of Appeals, the State court of last resort authorized to set policy. It may well be that that Court would be favorably disposed to dispense with the distinction between accessories and principals, particularly principals in the second degree. Until and unless the Court of Appeals effectuates such a change, we hold that the evidence before the jury neither directly nor inferentially permitted a finding that [respondent] was constructively or actually present at the scene of the crime. Therefore, he could have been convicted only of being an accessory before the fact, rather than a principal in the second degree. Accordingly, we must reverse the judgements of conviction of [respondent] Sowell. *Sowell v. State*, 122 Md.App. 222, 238, 712 A.2d 96, 103-04 (1998).

This Court described the common law distinction between principals and accessories in *State v. Ward*, 284 Md. 189, 197, 396 A.2d 1041, 1046-47 (1978):

A principal in the first degree is one who actually commits a crime, either by his own hand, or by an inanimate agency, or by an innocent human agent. A principal in the second degree is one who is guilty of felony by reason of having aided, counseled, commanded or encouraged the commission thereof in his presence, either actual or constructive. An accessory before the fact is one who is guilty of felony by reason of having aided, counseled, commanded or encouraged the commission thereof, without having been present either actually or constructively at the moment of perpetration. An accessory after the fact is one who, with knowledge of the other's guilt, renders assistance to a felon in the effort to hinder his detection, arrest, trial or punishment.

The main difference between an accessory before the fact and a principal in the second degree is that the latter must be actually or constructively present at the scene of the crime.

As noted by the Court of Special Appeals in its opinion below, the distinction has not been without criticism. In *State v. Williamson*, 282 Md. 100, 112-14, 382 A.2d 588, 594-95 (1978), Judge Levine, concurring, took issue with the majority's failure to abandon the accessory before the fact distinction:

> Since accessories and principals at common law were deemed to be equally culpable and therefore subject to the same punishment, *Agresti v. State*, 2 Md.App. at 281, [234 A.2d 284]; 1 J. Chitty, A Practical Treatise on the Criminal Law *267 (1819); Clark & Marshall, A Treatise on the Law of Crimes § 8.05, at 522 (7th ed.1967), the classification of parties as principals and accessories had little, if any, substantive significance.

On the other hand, the common law doctrines of accessoryship did give rise to several highly technical procedural rules which, as one recent commentator has stated, "tended to shield accessories from punishment notwithstanding overwhelming evidence of their criminal assistance." W. LaFave & A. Scott, Handbook on Criminal Law § 63, at 498-99 (1972)····
····

The reason for the development of these rules is obscure at best. Professor Perkins has speculated that they were devised by 14th and 15th century English common law courts as a means of alleviating the harshness of the death penalty in felony cases. R. Perkins, Criminal Law 669 (2d ed.1969); and see W. LaFave & A. Scott, Handbook on Criminal Law § 63, at 499 (1972). If this theory of the historical provenience of the common law categories and procedures be correct, it is now beyond question that the rules have outlived their purpose, in light of the universal rejection of capital punishment for any but the most heinous felonies and the manifold constitutional restrictions placed upon application of the death penalty in recent years. *See, e.g., Gregg v. Georgia*, 428 U.S. 153, 96 S.Ct. 2909, 49 L.Ed.2d 859 (1976); *Furman v. Georgia*, 408 U.S. 238, 92 S.Ct. 2726, 33 L.Ed.2d 346 (1972).

The common law principles of accomplicity and their procedural counterparts, in my opinion, have injected a most undesirable hypertechnicality into the law of accomplice responsibility, which not infrequently operates to thwart justice and reduce judicial efficiency. See Note, 19 Wash. & Lee L.Rev. 96 (1962). As this Court candidly stated in *Watson v. State*, 208 Md. at 218, [117 A.2d 549]:

> "'This distinguishing of the accessory before the fact from the principal is a pure technicality. It has no existence either in natural reason or the ordinary doctrines of the law. For in natural reason the procurer of a crime is not chargeable differently from the doer; and a familiar rule of the common law is that what one does through another's agency is regarded as done by himself···· Likewise in morals, there are circumstances wherein we attach more blame to the accessory before the fact than to his principal;····'" (Quoting 1 J. Bishop, Criminal Law § 673, at 486-87 (9th ed.1923)).

The time has come in my opinion to discard the common law distinction between principals and accessories before the fact and to replace these categories with an all-encompassing doctrine which would treat all those who knowingly procure, command, counsel, encourage, aid or abet a felon in the commission of a crime as principals regardless of whether the aider or abettor was actually or constructively present at the scene of the crime.

* * *

Tellingly, the Legislature has not, since the 1906 Act relating only to homicide, attempted to abrogate the common law doctrine of accessoryship for any other crime. In fact, as recently as 1994, the Committee Note to 1994 Maryland Laws, Chapter 712 indicated with regard to the revision of the burglary and related offenses provision: "Current [statutory] provisions referring to an 'accessory before the fact' or to 'causing', 'aiding', or 'counselling' a burglary offense have been repealed. The Committee believes that the common law on accomplice liability adequately covers these types of actions." The Legislature thus chose to continue to allow the law of accessoryship to be controlled by the common law with its enactment of Chapter 712. It did so despite several opinions by this Court limiting the doctrine's technical rules and expressing some disagreement with the restrictions of the common law. The Legislature is presumed to be aware of this Court's holdings. *See Wiegmann*, 350 Md. at 606, 714 A.2d at 851.

As petitioner notes and as we readily have admitted, several opinions written by this Court over the course of the last twenty years have abrogated certain requirements relating to accessoryship, such as the requirement that a principal must be convicted before the accessory. *See Lewis*, 285 Md. at 716, 404 A.2d at 1079. What is important to note is that these opinions abrogated merely the "technical procedural rules accompanying the common law doctrine of accessoryship." *Id.* at 715, 404 A.2d at 1079. For instance, the procedural rule rejected in Lewis related to when the accessory may be tried, not the doctrine of accessoryship itself. Similarly, in *Jones*, 302 Md. at 160-61, 486 A.2d at 188, we held an accessory before the fact may be convicted of a greater crime than the principal, noting that

> [m]erely because the evidence in the principal's trial may have been different, or the principal may have agreed to a favorable plea bargain arrangement, or the jury in the principal's trial may have arrived at a compromise verdict, is not a good reason for allowing the accessory to escape the consequences of having committed a particular offense.

Id. at 161, 486 A.2d at 188. In Jones we only abrogated a procedural aspect of the doctrine of accessoryship, not the doctrine.

Finally, as we mentioned, supra, although Maryland apparently is the only jurisdiction that has not rejected the common law distinctions between principals and accessories, the majority of the other jurisdictions rejecting the distinctions have done so legislatively. Given the relative importance in completely abrogating an ancient and historic common law doctrine such as accessoryship, we believe such a task is generally better left to the legislative body of this State. *See, e.g., Wiegmann*, 350 Md. at 607, 714 A.2d at 851-52 (declining to abolish the common law rule permitting persons to resist illegal arrests). We decline, at this time, to abrogate the doctrine by judicial action.

B. Constructive Presence

Because we decline to abolish the common law distinctions between principals and accessories, we must address whether the Court of Special Appeals erred in holding "the evidence before the jury neither directly nor inferentially permitted a finding that [respondent] was constructively or actually present at the scene of the crime." *Sowell*, 122 Md.App. at 238, 712 A.2d at 104.

* * *

Before this Court, the parties do not dispute that respondent was not actually present during the commission of the robbery and concede the only issue is whether he was constructively present. In *Ward*, 284 Md. at 197, 396 A.2d at 1046-47, we explained that

> [a] principal in the second degree is one who is guilty of felony by reason of having aided, counseled, commanded or encouraged the commission thereof in his presence, either actual or constructive. An accessory before the fact is one who is guilty of felony by reason of having aided, counseled, commanded or encouraged the commission thereof, without having been present either actually or constructively at the moment of perpetration.

We further described in detail the distinction between principals in the second degree and accessories before the fact in *Williamson*, 282 Md. at 103-04, 382 A.2d at 590 (quoting 4 W. Blackstone, Commentaries):

> "A principal in the ⋯ second degree ⋯ is who is present, aiding and abetting the fact to be done. Which presence need not always be an actual immediate standing by, within sight or hearing of the fact; but there may be also a constructive presence, as when one commits a robbery or murder and another keeps watch or guard at some convenient distance." *Id.* 282 Md. at 103, 382 A.2d at 590. (Emphasis in original.) (Footnotes omitted.)

> "As to the second point, who may be an accessory before the fact; Sir Matthew Hale defines him to be one who, being absent at the time of the crime committed, doth yet procure, counsel, or command another to commit a crime. Herein absence is necessary to make him an accessary; for if such procurer, or the like, be present, he is guilty of the crime as principal."

The concept of constructive presence is fairly broad, as one need not be in sight or hearing of the crime being committed to be a principal in the second degree. The test is not whether the alleged principal in the second degree could see the scene of the crime, but whether he or she could render assistance to the actual perpetrator. *See Williamson*, 282 Md. at 105, 382 A.2d at 591 ("A person is regarded as constructively present, within the rules relating to parties in criminal cases, whenever he is cooperating with the perpetrator and is so situated as to be able to aid him, with a view known to the other, to insure success in the accomplishment of the common purpose." (quotations and citation omitted)); *McBryde*, 30 Md.App. at 360, 352 A.2d at 326 ("A person is constructively present, hence guilty as a principal, if he is acting with the person who actually commits the deed in pursuance of a common design, and is aiding his associate, either by keeping watch or otherwise or is so situated as to be able to aid him, with a view, known to the other, to insure success in the accomplishment of the common enterprise." (citation omitted)). In *Williamson*, for example, even though the defendant was physically close enough to the scene of her husband's murder to render assistance to the killer, there was no evidence that she in fact was present in order to render aid of any kind; thus she could not, even though nearby, be convicted as a principal in the second degree. *Williamson*, 282 Md. at 105, 382 A.2d at 591. By contrast, the defendants in *McBryde*, although not within sight of the scene of the crime, were waiting nearby to aid the principal in the first degree in his escape after he robbed a convenience store and thus were principals in the second degree. *McBryde*, 30 Md.App. at 360, 352 A.2d at 326-27. The common element in constructive presence for the purpose of proving a defendant was a principal in the second degree, therefore, is the ability, desire, and design to render any necessary aid to the principal in the first degree during the commission of the crime.

* * *

Turning to the case at hand, the evidence tended to show that respondent went to Recycling Incorporated to pick up his wages at approximately 12:30 p.m. About an hour later, the three men who ultimately committed the robbery and other crimes entered Recycling Incorporated's offices and took the cash. Respondent was not present on the premises or nearby when the crimes took place. One witness testified that prior to the commission of the crimes, respondent drove to the area where the actors were waiting in parked cars and told them to go ahead. The witness testified:

A. He pulls up to the car, his side of the car in the front.
Q. And then drives off?
A. He says go ahead.
Q. You drive off and [respondent] drives off?
A. Yes.
Q. Their car is there, your car is there, Smoot's car is there, and [respondent] goes off in a different direction?
A. Yes.
Q. He drives his car off, and he's out of sight, right?
A. Yes.

Another witness testified as to the following:

Q. .... [W]hat, if anything, did [respondent] say about where he would be when the robbery took place?

....

THE WITNESS: He said he was going to go out on his route so it wouldn't look like he had anything to do with it, and that he would meet them back around Tuley Street right after everything happened, and then they would split the money up. [Emphasis added.]

There was no evidence presented that respondent waited as a lookout or in a getaway car during the robbery. In fact, the evidence showed that respondent purposefully absented himself from the scene of the crime to avoid suspicion about his involvement. That he "scouted out" the situation before the robbery and signaled to the actors to "go ahead" with their plan, although making him an accessory before the fact, does not render respondent actually or constructively present during the crime for purposes of principal in the second degree liability. There was no evidence that respondent had the ability to render aid to the principals during the actual commission of the crimes. Although the evidence tended to show that respondent was the mastermind of the robbery and planned the crimes from beginning to end, the simple fact is that he was not present, either actually or constructively, during the commission of these crimes. Accordingly, we hold there was not sufficient evidence from which to convict respondent as a principal in the second degree.

III. Conclusion

We hold that until the Legislature provides otherwise, Maryland retains the common law distinction between principals and accessories. Respondent was tried only as a principal in the second degree, which requires presence, not as an accessory before the fact, which does not require presence. Accordingly, we must affirm the Court of Special Appeals and reverse respondent's convictions because there was not sufficient evidence to find that he was present, actually or constructively, at the scene of the crime.

JUDGMENT OF THE COURT OF SPECIAL APPEALS AFFIRMED; COSTS TO BE PAID BY PRINCE GEORGE'S COUNTY.

CASE END

Case Questions
State v. Sowell

1. Why was Sowell's conviction as a principal in the second degree problematic in this case?

2. Why did the state want Sowell to be held responsible as a principal in the second degree rather than an accessory before the fact?

3. What did the court ultimately determine with respect to Sowell's criminal responsibility as a principal in the second degree? Do you agree with the court's holding? Explain.

A Note to the Reader

The Maryland General Assembly's enactment of Md. Code Ann., Crim. Pro. § 4-204 provides an excellent example of legislative action in direct response to a judicial decision. Section 4-204 was designed specifically to overrule *Sowell* and change the law with respect to the presence at the scene of a crime. It reads:

(a) In this section, the words "accessory before the fact" and "principal" have their judicially determined meanings.

(b) Except for a sentencing proceeding under § 2-303 or § 2-304 of the Criminal Law Article:
    (1) the distinction between an accessory before the fact and a principal is abrogated; and
    (2) an accessory before the fact may be charged, tried, convicted, and sentenced as a principal.

(c) An accessory before the fact may be charged, tried, convicted, and sentenced for a crime regardless of whether a principal in the crime has been:
    (1) charged with the crime;
    (2) acquitted of the crime; or
    (3) convicted of a lesser or different crime.

(d) If a crime is committed in the State, an accessory before the fact may be charged, tried and convicted, and sentenced in a county where:
    (1) an act of accessoryship was committed; or
    (2) a principal in the crime may be charged, tried and convicted, and sentenced.

Additional Crimes to Consult

Maryland only recognizes the four types of criminal responsibility discussed throughout this Chapter. However, it should be noted that Maryland law treats an individual who employs another to commit a murder for hire (*i.e.,* a contract murder) as a principal in the first-degree to first-degree murder even though that individual is not the actual killer. *See Gary v. State*, 341 Md. 513, 520, 671 A.2d 495 (1996). The individual who procures such a murder is also eligible for the death penalty pursuant to Md. Code Ann., Crim. Law § 2-303(g)(1)(vii) (West 2002).

HYPOTHETICAL #1

Best friends Jane and Katie share a two-bedroom apartment in downtown Baltimore. Katie has recently begun dating Trevor and it appears to be getting serious, but Jane doesn't approve of the relationship. Although Trevor is a caring and genuine person, Jane is jealous that Trevor is taking Katie away from her. Jane is convinced that in the very near future Trevor is going to ask Katie to marry him. She is also convinced that Katie will accept the marriage proposal and will then move out of the apartment the two roommates share. The last thing Jane wants is to live a lonely and miserable life, so Jane decides she has to act quickly. One afternoon, Trevor is at their apartment taking a nap in Katie's bedroom. Jane decides this is her best opportunity. "Hey Katie," Jane says, "My car ran out of gas last night and I need a can of gas, could you do me a favor and run to the gas station and fill up this can?" Jane hands Katie a tin can. "Sure," says Katie, "no problem. I'll do it now and be right back." Within ten minutes Katie returns with the full can of gasoline. "Thanks a million," Jane says, "Now why don't you fix us all a nice dinner and I'll get my car started." "Sounds great," answers Katie. She grabs her purse and heads to the local grocery store to pick up food for dinner that evening. Meanwhile, instead of making her way out to her car, Jane sneaks into the bedroom where Trevor was sound asleep. With an evil grin on her face, Jane douses the bed in gasoline, lights a match, and POOF! The entire bed is an inferno. Trevor is dead within moments. Katie, who was at the grocery store while the entire crime unfolded, doesn't realize what has happened until she returns home and sees fire trucks and an ambulance out front of her apartment complex. She is devastated.

MAIN ISSUE

Was Katie an Accessory Before the Fact to Murder?

ISSUE	THESIS	RULE	ANALYSIS	CONCLUSION
Was a felony committed by another WHEN Jane set the bed on fire, intentionally killing Trevor?	A felony was committed WHEN Jane set the bed on fire, intentionally killing Trevor.	An accessory before the fact must aid prior to the commission of a FELONY in order to have criminal culpability.	The felony of first-degree premeditated murder was committed BECAUSE Jane intentionally and with premeditation killed Trevor.	A felony was committed by Jane.
Did Katie aid in the commission of the felony before it was committed WHEN she purchased the gasoline that was used as the murder weapon?	Katie aided in the commission of the felony before it was committed WHEN she purchased the gasoline that was used as the murder weapon.	An accessory before the fact must in some way have AIDED, COUNSELED, COMMANDED OR ENCOURAGED the commission of the felony before the completion of the crime.	Katie aided in the commission of the murder BECAUSE she purchased the gasoline that was used by Jane to set Trevor's bed on fire and murder him.	Katie rendered aid prior to the commission of the felony.
Did Katie render aid in the commission of the felony with the intent to make the crime succeed WHEN she gave Jane the gasoline which Jane used to set the bed on fire?	Katie did not render aid in the commission of the felony with the intent to make the crime succeed WHEN she gave Jane the gasoline which Jane used to set the bed on fire.	An accessory before the fact must have rendered any aid WITH THE INTENT TO MAKE THE CRIME SUCCEED.	Katie did not render aid with the intent to make the crime succeed BECAUSE she had no knowledge that Jane was going to kill Trevor: Jane said it was to fill her car up with gas, Katie loved Trevor and did not want him dead.	Katie did not render aid with the intent to make the felony succeed.

CONCLUSION

Katie was not an accessory before the fact to murder when she bought the gasoline used to set Trevor's bed on fire and kill him because she did not have the intent to help make the crime succeed.

HYPOTHETICAL #2

Tom and Jerry decide they are going to rob a bank. Tom purchases the guns while Jerry buys masks to wear as a disguise. They plan exactly how and when they will commit the robbery for at least a week. On the day of the robbery, they get into their car and are on their way to the bank when they see their long-time buddy, Buddy, on the street. They stop and get to talking, and they eventually tell Buddy of their plans. Buddy says "Hey, let me come too—I'll help out and you will only have to give me 10% of the take." So, they bring Buddy along. They get to the bank and the following occurs . . .

Buddy waits in the car as the "get away" driver with the engine running and ready to speed away as soon as the other two hop in. Tom and Jerry enter the bank. Tom holds the gun on the customers and the bank tellers while Jerry collects the money. As soon as they have their loot they run out of the bank, jump into the car and shout "Go! Go! Go!" Buddy drives as fast as he can, headed for the house of their other long-time friend whom they hadn't seen in years, Junior. Once at Junior's house, they fill Junior in on everything that recently transpired, and they also tell him that the cops are probably after them. Junior agrees to hide them at his place until things quiet down. The four men then relax and share a pint of whiskey.

➲ List the criminal responsibility of each defendant based on the conspiracy to rob the bank and the robbery.

DEFENDANT	CRIME	CRIMINAL RESPONSIBILITY: PRINCIPAL IN THE FIRST DEGREE? ACCOMPLICE? ACCESSORY BEFORE THE FACT OR AFTER THE FACT?
Tom	Conspiracy	
Tom	Robbery	
Jerry	Conspiracy	
Jerry	Robbery	
Buddy	Conspiracy	
Buddy	Robbery	
Junior	Conspiracy	
Junior	Robbery	

➲ For EACH defendant, complete an Analysis Chart assessing the possibility of conviction.

DISCUSSION QUESTIONS

1. Other than knowingly harboring a fugitive, what examples can you think of that would render someone an accessory after the fact to a felony?

2. Do you agree with the Court's opinion in *Sowell* that the respondent, who masterminded the entire robbery scheme, could not be held equally responsible as the men who committed the robbery merely because Sowell was not present when the crime was committed?

3. Based on the Court's description in *Sowell* of a principal in the second degree, in which of the following examples would the individual be held accountable as a principal in the second degree: (a) A look-out standing immediately inside the bank but who does nothing other than stand there because no one attempts to stop the robbery; (b) the getaway driver waiting on the curb during a bank robbery; (c) someone positioned on top of a building across the street from the bank with binoculars and a two-way radio, ready to warn the robbers of any potential danger; (d) someone ten blocks away from the bank posted in front of the police station with a cell phone ready to call the robbers if there is a sudden rush of officers out of the station.

4. How could crimes committed via the Internet present unique problems in determining the criminal participation in a crime and accomplice liability? Explain.

5. One evening, Jack unexpectedly shows up at Jill's house. Jack explained that he needed someplace to stay because his house was being fumigated for termites. Jill thought nothing of it and she let Jack spend the night at her house. The next morning, while Jack is still asleep, Jill turns on the local news and sees that Jack is wanted for murder. She immediately wakes Jack up and tells him to get out of her house. Is Jill an accessory after the fact to murder? What if Jill called the police the second that Jack left and informed them he had just left her house, would your answer change? Why or why not?

6. Do you think a principal in the first degree, principal in the second degree, accessory before the fact, and accessory after the fact should all share the same criminal responsibility for the commission of a crime, or do you think one or more deserves a greater punishment than the others? Explain.

7. Bobby is at a liquor store one evening purchasing beer for a party he's about to have, when two masked men walk into the store, put a gun to the cashier's head, and demand all of the money in the cash register. After collecting the money, the two masked men run out of the store and the cashier runs after them with a loaded shotgun. Bobby, who is standing by the front door, never liked the cashier because he was a grumpy old man. So, Bobby thinks it would be funny to trip the cashier. Bobby sticks his foot out, the cashier goes flying through the air, and the two masked men get away. Is Bobby a principal in the second degree? Explain.

TEST BANK

True/False

_____ 1. In order to be an accessory after the fact, an individual must have knowledge that a felony had just been committed.

_____ 2. A principal in the second degree must have either direct or indirect knowledge that a crime is being committed.

_____ 3. Serving as a lookout during the commission of a crime would be an example of an accessory before the fact.

_____ 4. It is not possible for an individual to be both an accessory before the fact and a principal in the second degree.

_____ 5. There may never be more than one principal in the first degree to the commission of a crime.

MULTIPLE CHOICE

6. Bart holds Lisa's arms down while Homer has forcible and nonconsensual sexual intercourse with Lisa. Bart and Homer would most likely have the following criminal liability:

   A. Bart principal in the second degree to rape; Homer principal in the first degree to rape

   B. Bart principal in the first degree to rape; Homer principal in the second degree to rape

   C. Bart nothing; Homer principal in the first degree to rape

   D. Bart accessory before the fact to rape; Homer principal in the second degree to rape

7. Which of the following statements about a principal in the second degree is FALSE:

   A. A principal in the second degree has a lesser liability for the underlying criminal offense than the principal in the first degree

   B. A principal in the second degree is present at the time of the underlying criminal offense or close enough to render immediate aid or assistance

   C. A principal in the second degree is also commonly referred to as an "accomplice"

   D. A principal in the second degree must know that he or she is assisting in a criminal offense in order for liability to attach

8. Which of the following elements do a principal in the second degree, accessory before the fact, and accessory after the fact all share?

   A. Presence at the scene of the crime

   B. Knowledge that a felony has been committed

   C. Action to elude authorities

   D. All of the above

9. Which of the following would be an example of an accessory before the fact to the burglary of a home:

   A. An individual who obtains floor plans of the home

   B. An individual who obtains the code to the home's burglar alarm

   C. An individual who gives the guard dog of the home a potent sleeping tablet the day before the burglary

   D. All of the above

10. With regard to an accessory before the fact and an accessory after the fact, what does the phrase "the fact" refer to?

    A. The target crime

    B. The arrest

    C. The commencement of prosecution

    D. The conspiracy

Inchoate Offenses

Introduction

Inchoate offenses are sometimes referred to as incomplete crimes. Inchoate offenses include attempt, solicitation and conspiracy. For each of these crimes, the underlying substantive offense, commonly called the "target crime," need not be completed. Inchoate offenses originated in common law, and Maryland still applies these common law principles. Maryland's legislature has also codified some inchoate offenses with respect to certain underlying substantive crimes, such as murder or sexual offenses.

Focus Crimes

Attempt—*Grill v. State*, 337 Md. 91, 651 A.2d 856 (1995); MPJI-Cr. 4:02.

Solicitation—*Gardner v. State*, 286 Md. 520, 408 A.2d 1317 (1979); MPJI-Cr. 4:31.

Conspiracy—*Gardner v. State*, 286 Md. 520, 408 A.2d 1317 (1979); MPJI-Cr. 4:08.

Objectives

Upon completing this chapter your should be able to:

- ➲ Identify and analyze the elements of attempt;
- ➲ Identify and analyze the elements of conspiracy; and
- ➲ Identify and analyze the elements of solicitation.

CASE LAW

Smallwood v. State, 343 Md. 97, 680 A.2d 512 (1996)

In this case, we examine the use of circumstantial evidence to infer that a defendant possessed the intent to kill needed for a conviction of attempted murder or assault with intent to murder. We conclude that such an inference is not supportable under the facts of this case.

I

A

On August 29, 1991, Dwight Ralph Smallwood was diagnosed as being infected with the Human Immunodeficiency Virus (HIV). According to medical records from the Prince George's County Detention Center, he had been informed of his HIV-positive status by September 25, 1991. In February 1992, a social worker made Smallwood aware of the necessity of practicing "safe sex" in order to avoid transmitting the virus to his sexual partners, and in July 1993, Smallwood told health care providers at Children's Hospital that he had only one sexual partner and that they always used condoms. Smallwood again tested positive for HIV in February and March of 1994.

On September 26, 1993, Smallwood and an accomplice robbed a woman at gunpoint, and forced her into a grove of trees where each man alternately placed a gun to her head while the other one raped her. On September 28, 1993, Smallwood and an accomplice robbed a second woman at gunpoint and took her to a secluded location, where Smallwood inserted his penis into her with "slight penetration." On September 30, 1993, Smallwood and an accomplice robbed yet a third woman, also at gunpoint, and took her to a local school where she was forced to perform oral sex on Smallwood and was raped by him. In each of these episodes, Smallwood threatened to kill his victims if they did not cooperate or to return and shoot them if they reported his crimes. Smallwood did not wear a condom during any of these criminal episodes.

Based upon his attack on September 28, 1993, Smallwood was charged with, among other crimes, attempted first-degree rape, robbery with a deadly weapon, assault with intent to murder, and reckless endangerment. In separate indictments, Smallwood was also charged with the attempted second-degree murder of each of his three victims. On October 11, 1994, Smallwood pled guilty in the Circuit Court for Prince George's County to attempted first-degree rape and robbery with a deadly weapon. The circuit court (Nichols, J.) also convicted Smallwood of assault with intent to murder and reckless endangerment based upon his September 28, 1993 attack, and convicted Smallwood of all three counts of attempted second-degree murder.

Following his conviction, Smallwood was sentenced to concurrent sentences of life imprisonment for attempted rape, twenty years imprisonment for robbery with a deadly weapon, thirty years imprisonment for assault with intent to murder, and five years imprisonment for reckless endangerment. The circuit court also imposed a concurrent thirty-year sentence for each of the three counts of attempted second-degree murder. The circuit court's judgments were affirmed in part and reversed in part by the Court of Special Appeals. In *Smallwood v. State,* 106 Md.App. 1, 661 A.2d 747 (1995), the intermediate appellate court found that the evidence was sufficient for the trial court to conclude that Smallwood intended to kill his victims and upheld all of his convictions. Upon Smallwood's petition, we granted certiorari to consider whether the trial court could properly conclude that Smallwood possessed the requisite intent to support his convictions of attempted second-degree murder and assault with intent to murder.

B

Smallwood asserts that the trial court lacked sufficient evidence to support its conclusion that Smallwood intended to kill his three victims. Smallwood argues that the fact that he engaged in unprotected sexual inter-

course, even though he knew that he carried HIV, is insufficient to infer an intent to kill. The most that can reasonably be inferred, Smallwood contends, is that he is guilty of recklessly endangering his victims by exposing them to the risk that they would become infected themselves. The State disagrees, arguing that the facts of this case are sufficient to infer an intent to kill. The State likens Smallwood's HIV-positive status to a deadly weapon and argues that engaging in unprotected sex when one is knowingly infected with HIV is equivalent to firing a loaded firearm at that person.

II

A

In *Faya v. Almaraz,* 329 Md. 435, 438-440, 620 A.2d 327 (1993), we discussed HIV and the Acquired Immune Deficiency Syndrome (AIDS) in detail. There, we described HIV as a retrovirus that attacks the human immune system, weakening it, and ultimately destroying the body's capacity to ward off disease. We also noted that

[t]he virus may reside latently in the body for periods as long as ten years or more, during which time the infected person will manifest no symptoms of illness and function normally. HIV typically spreads via genital fluids or blood transmitted from one person to another through sexual contact, the sharing of needles in intravenous drug use, blood transfusions, infiltration into wounds, or from mother to child during pregnancy or birth.

Id. at 439, 620 A.2d 327. In *Faya,* we also described AIDS and its relationship to HIV:

AIDS, in turn, is the condition that eventually results from an immune system gravely impaired by HIV. Medical studies have indicated that most people who carry the virus will progress to AIDS. AIDS patients by definition are profoundly immunocompromised; that is, they are prone to any number of diseases and opportunistic infections that a person with a healthy immune system might otherwise resist. AIDS is thus the acute clinical phase of immune dysfunction···· AIDS is invariably fatal.

Id. at 439-40, 620 A.2d 327. In this case, we must determine what legal inferences may be drawn when an individual infected with the HIV virus knowingly exposes another to the risk of HIV-infection, and the resulting risk of death by AIDS.

B

As we have previously stated, "[t]he required intent in the crimes of assault with intent to murder and attempted murder is the specific intent to murder, i.e., the specific intent to kill under circumstances that would not legally justify or excuse the killing or mitigate it to manslaughter." *State v. Earp,* 319 Md. 156, 167, 571 A.2d 1227 (1990). *See also State v. Jenkins,* 307 Md. 501, 515, 515 A.2d 465 (1986) ("[T]he intent element of assault with intent to murder requires proof of a specific intent to kill under circumstances such that if the victim had died, the offense would be murder."); *Franklin v. State,* 319 Md. 116, 126, 571 A.2d 1208 (1990). Smallwood has not argued that his actions were performed under mitigating circumstances or that he was legally justified in attacking the three women. He was properly found guilty of attempted murder and assault with intent to murder only if there was sufficient evidence from which the trier of fact could reasonably have concluded that Smallwood possessed a specific intent to kill at the time he assaulted each of the three women.

To evaluate the sufficiency of the evidence in a non-jury trial, we must review the case on both the law and the evidence. *Wilson v. State,* 319 Md. 530, 535, 573 A.2d 831 (1990); *West v. State,* 312 Md. 197, 207, 539 A.2d 231 (1988). In making this inquiry, we will not set aside the trial court's findings of fact unless they are clearly erroneous. *Wilson, supra,* 319 Md. at 535, 573 A.2d 831; Maryland Rule 8-131(c). We must determine "whether the evidence shows directly or supports a rational inference of the facts to be proved, from which the trier of fact could fairly be convinced beyond a reasonable doubt of the defendant's guilt of the offense charged." *Wilson, supra,* 319 Md. at 535-36, 573 A.2d 831.

An intent to kill may be proved by circumstantial evidence. "[S]ince intent is subjective and, without the cooperation of the accused, cannot be directly and objectively proven, its presence must be shown by established facts which permit a proper inference of its existence." *Earp, supra,* 319 Md. at 167, 571 A.2d 1227 (quoting *Davis v. State,* 204 Md. 44, 51, 102 A.2d 816 (1954)). Therefore, the trier of fact may infer the existence of the required intent from surrounding circumstances such as "the accused's acts, conduct and words." *State v. Raines,* 326 Md. 582, 591, 606 A.2d 265 (1992); *Earp, supra,* 319 Md. at 167, 571 A.2d 1227. As we have repeatedly stated, "under the proper circumstances, an intent to kill may be inferred from the use of a deadly weapon directed at a vital part of the human body." *Raines, supra,* 326 Md. at 591, 606 A.2d 265; *Jenkins, supra,* 307 Md. at 513, 515 A.2d 465 ("Numerous cases make it clear that evidence showing a design to commit grievous bodily injury, such as using a deadly weapon directed at a vital part of the body, is sufficient because it gives rise to an evidentiary *inference* of an intent to murder.") (emphasis in original).

In *Raines, supra,* we upheld the use of such an inference. In that case, Raines and a friend were traveling on a highway when the defendant fired a pistol into the driver's side window of a tractor trailer in an adjacent lane. *Raines, supra,* 326 Md. at 586-87, 606 A.2d 265. The shot killed the driver of the tractor trailer, and Raines was convicted of first degree murder. *Id.* The evidence in the case showed that Raines shot at the driver's window of the truck, knowing that the truck driver was immediately behind the window. *Id.* at 592, 606 A.2d 265. We concluded that "Raines's actions in directing the gun at the window, and therefore at the driver's head on the other side of the window, permitted an inference that Raines shot the gun with the intent to kill." *Id.* at 592-93, 606 A.2d 265.

The State argues that our analysis in *Raines* rested upon two elements: (1) Raines knew that his weapon was deadly, and (2) Raines knew that he was firing it at someone's head. The State argues that Smallwood similarly knew that HIV infection ultimately leads to death, and that he knew that he would be exposing his victims to the risk of HIV transmission by engaging in unprotected sex with them. Therefore, the State argues, a permissible inference can be drawn that Smallwood intended to kill each of his three victims. The State's analysis, however, ignores several factors.

C

First, we must consider the magnitude of the risk to which the victim is knowingly exposed. The inference drawn in *Raines, supra,* rests upon the rule that "[i]t is permissible to infer that 'one intends the natural and probable consequences of his act.' " *Ford v. State,* 330 Md. 682, 704, 625 A.2d 984 (1993) (quoting *Davis v. State,* 204 Md. 44, 51, 102 A.2d 816 (1954)). Before an intent to kill may be inferred based solely upon the defendant's exposure of a victim to a risk of death, it must be shown that the victim's death would have been a natural and probable result of the defendant's conduct. It is for this reason that a trier of fact may infer that a defendant possessed an intent to kill when firing a *deadly* weapon at a *vital* part of the human body. *Raines, supra,* 326 Md. at 591, 606 A.2d 265; *Jenkins, supra,* 307 Md. at 513, 515 A.2d 465. When a deadly weapon has been fired at a vital part of a victim's body, the risk of killing the victim is so high that it becomes reasonable to assume that the defendant intended the victim to die as a natural and probable consequence of the defendant's actions.

Death by AIDS is clearly one *natural* possible consequence of exposing someone to a risk of HIV infection, even on a single occasion. It is less clear that death by AIDS from that single exposure is a sufficiently *probable* result to provide the sole support for an inference that the person causing the exposure intended to kill the person who was exposed. While the risk to which Smallwood exposed his victims when he forced them to engage in unprotected sexual activity must not be minimized, the State has presented no evidence from which it can reasonably be concluded that death by AIDS is a probable result of Smallwood's actions to the same extent that death is the probable result of firing a deadly weapon at a vital part of someone's body. Without such evidence, it cannot fairly be concluded that death by AIDS was sufficiently probable to support an inference that Smallwood intended to kill his victims in the absence of other evidence indicative of an intent to kill.

D

In this case, we find no additional evidence from which to infer an intent to kill. Smallwood's actions are wholly explained by an intent to commit rape and armed robbery, the crimes for which he has already pled guilty. For this reason, his actions fail to provide evidence that he also had an intent to kill. As one commentator noted, in discussing a criminal case involving similar circumstances, "[b]ecause virus transmission occurs simultaneously with the act of rape, that act alone would not provide evidence of intent to transmit the virus. Some additional evidence, such as an explicit statement, would be necessary to demonstrate the actor's specific intent." Note, *Criminal Liability for Transmission of AIDS: Some Evidentiary Problems,* 10 Crim. Just. J. 69, 78 (1994). Smallwood's knowledge of his HIV-infected status provides the only evidence in this case supporting a conclusion that he intended anything beyond the rapes and robberies for which he has been convicted.

The cases cited by the State demonstrate the sort of additional evidence needed to support an inference that Smallwood intended to kill his victims. The defendants in these cases have either made explicit statements demonstrating an intent to infect their victims or have taken specific actions demonstrating such an intent and tending to exclude other possible intents. In *State v. Hinkhouse,* 139 Or.App. 446, 912 P.2d 921 (1996), for example, the defendant engaged in unprotected sex with a number of women while knowing that he was HIV positive. The defendant had also actively concealed his HIV-positive status from these

women, had lied to several of them by stating that he was not HIV-positive, and had refused the women's requests that he wear condoms. *Id.* 912 P.2d at 923-24. There was also evidence that he had told at least one of his sexual partners that "if he were [HIV] positive, he would spread the virus to other people." *Id.* at 924. The Oregon Court of Appeals found this evidence to be sufficient to demonstrate an intent to kill, and upheld the defendant's convictions for attempted murder.

In *State v. Caine,* 652 So.2d 611 (La.App.), *cert. denied,* 661 So.2d 1358 (La.1995), a conviction for attempted second degree murder was upheld where the defendant had jabbed a used syringe into a victim's arm while shouting "I'll give you AIDS." *Id.* at 616. The defendant in *Weeks v. State,* 834 S.W.2d 559 (Tex.App. 1992), made similar statements, and was convicted of attempted murder after he spat on a prison guard. In that case, the defendant knew that he was HIV-positive, and the appellate court found that "the record reflects that [Weeks] thought he could kill the guard by spitting his HIV-infected saliva at him." *Id.* at 562. There was also evidence that at the time of the spitting incident, Weeks had stated that he was "going to take someone with him when he went, that he was 'medical now,' and that he was 'HIV-4.'"

The evidence in *State v. Haines,* 545 N.E.2d 834 (Ind.App.1989), contained both statements by the defendant demonstrating intent and actions solely explainable as attempts to spread HIV. There, the defendant's convictions for attempted murder were upheld where the defendant slashed his wrists and sprayed blood from them on a police officer and two paramedics, splashing blood in their faces and eyes. *Id.* at 835. Haines attempted to scratch and bite them and attempted to force blood-soaked objects into their faces. During this altercation, the defendant told the officer that he should be left to die because he had AIDS, that he wanted to "give it to him," and that he would "use his wounds" to spray the officer with blood. *Id.* Haines also "repeatedly yelled that he had AIDS, that he could not deal with it and that he was going to make [the officer] deal with it." *Id.*

Scroggins v. State, 198 Ga.App. 29, 401 S.E.2d 13, 15 (1990), presents a similar scenario, where the defendant made noises with his mouth as if bringing up spittle and then bit a police officer hard enough to break the skin. Immediately after this incident he informed a nurse that he was HIV-positive and laughed when the police officer asked him if he had AIDS. *Id.* The Georgia Court of Appeals found that evidence showing that the defendant "sucked up excess sputum" before biting the officer was "evidence of a deliberate, thinking act" and that in conjunction with the defendant's laughter when asked about AIDS, it provided sufficient evidence of intent to support Scroggins's conviction for assault with intent to kill *Id.,* 401 S.E.2d at 18.

In contrast with these cases, the State in this case would allow the trier of fact to infer an intent to kill based solely upon the fact that Smallwood exposed his victims to the risk that they might contract HIV. With-

out evidence showing that such a result is sufficiently probable to support this inference, we conclude that Smallwood's convictions for attempted murder and assault with intent to murder must be reversed.

JUDGMENTS FOR ATTEMPTED MURDER IN THE SECOND DEGREE AND ASSAULT WITH INTENT TO MURDER REVERSED; COSTS TO BE PAID BY THE RESPONDENT.

CASE END

 CASE LAW *Meyer v. State*, 47 Md.App. 679, 425 A.2d 664, *cert. denied*, 454 U.S. 865 (1981)

On April 26, 1978, a jury in the Circuit Court for Prince George's County found appellant guilty of the first degree murder of Carol Lewis and the second degree murder of Heather Lewis. The victims were, respectively, the wife and infant daughter of one Lon Alec Lewis; and it was alleged that the murders were committed pursuant to an agreement with Mr. Lewis that they were, in colloquial terms, "contract murders." Appellant ultimately was sentenced to consecutive terms of life and thirty years imprisonment for those crimes, and the convictions were affirmed on appeal. *See Meyer v. State*, 43 Md.App. 427, 406 A.2d 427 (1979), *cert. den.*, 286 Md. 750, *cert. den.*, 446 U.S. 938, 100 S.Ct. 2159, 64 L.Ed.2d 792 (1980). Lewis was also tried and convicted for his complicity. *See Lewis v. State*, 285 Md. 705, 404 A.2d 1073 (1979).

Appellant was not sentenced on April 26. The court deferred sentencing pending (possibly among other things) receipt of a presentence investigation report; and appellant was lodged at the Prince George's County Detention Center during the interim.

While at the Center awaiting sentencing, appellant attempted to set in motion a plan for four more killings. Specifically, according to the record before us, he sought to arrange for the killing of his wife, Mr. Lewis, and two police officers who had investigated the Lewis killings and succeeded in extracting a confession from him (Detectives Hatfield and Morrissette). Fortunately for the intended victims, but unfortunately for appellant, the person he solicited to carry out or arrange for these executions was an undercover State policeman, Frank Mazzone, who recorded the two conversations he had with appellant pertaining to this scheme.

By reason of these activities, appellant was charged with four counts of solicitation of murder—one count for each intended victim. He was convicted on all four counts, given four consecutive sentences of twenty

years each (consecutive to the life plus thirty already being served), and now appeals. He claims:

"1. The Trial Judge Erred In Denying Appellant's Motion For Judgment Of Acquittal Where The Evidence Indicated That The Appellant Solicited Mazzone Not To Murder The Intended Victim As Charged But Rather To Solicit Others To Carry Out The Intended Murder And In Instructing The Jury That The Appellant Should Be Found Guilty If It Was Proven That He Solicited Mazzone To Have The Murders Committed.

"2. The Trial Judge Erred In Imposing Four (4) Consecutive Twenty (20) Year Sentences Upon The Appellant Where The Criminal Act Of The Appellant Was One Continuous Series of Conversations Wherein He Made The Solicitation."

* * *

We find no merit in any of these contentions.

Appellant's initial contact with regard to his plan was with Joseph Walker, a co-inmate at the Detention Center. He asked whether Walker knew "anyone who did contract killings or hits." Walker responded in the affirmative, whereupon, according to Walker, appellant "asked me if I could arrange for a killing." He did not tell Walker who the victim or victims were to be. Walker passed this information on to a Prince George's County policeman, for whom he had served as an informant. With the concurrence of the State's Attorney's Office, it was arranged for Captain Mazzone, of the State Police, to play the role of Vince Rinaldo, an agent for two "hit men" and, wearing a secret transmitter, to meet with appellant at the Detention Center and find out more about what he had in mind.

Two meetings took place, and in both instances the conversation was recorded and transcribed. At the first meeting, on May 8, 1978, appellant very clearly imported Mazzone to kill, or to arrange for others to kill, appellant's wife. At the second conversation, on May 15, 1978, there was further discussion about the liquidation of the wife and additional importunings of Mazzone to kill, or to arrange for others to kill, the two police officers and Lon Alec Lewis. The conversations tended to ramble a bit, but what essentially came through was this:

(1) As to the wife, appellant explained that he was upset with her because she failed to testify in his behalf. She was then living in Puerto Rico, and, in order to facilitate the execution, appellant told Mazzone in some detail what her living arrangements were. He described his wife's appearance and also made arrangements for Mazzone to obtain a picture of her from appellant's apartment.

(2) There was a great deal of discussion about the fee for murdering the wife, the parties finally agreeing on $40,000. Appellant promised a deposit of $1,000 "up front," to be taken from an existing bank account in Minnesota, with the balance to be paid from the proceeds of a $100,000 insurance policy on the wife's life. Indeed, as that policy was about to lapse because of nonpayment of premiums, appellant insisted that the killing take place before May 15. He told Mazzone that he didn't care what method was used, but would leave that up to the actual executioner. Appellant did, in fact, later procure a $1,000 money order payable to Vince Rinaldo which he caused to be sent to Mazzone.

(3) The scheme to kill the two officers and Lewis came up in the second conversation, which was initially prompted by the fact that Mazzone had not yet received the $1,000 deposit. After some discussion about that and some further conversation about the execution of the wife, appellant broached the subject of killing the two officers. He told Mazzone that he didn't want them around as witnesses in the event of a second trial. There was no rush about doing away with the officers; as appellant put it, "I suppose anytime, they say a year before the appeal, so anytime within the next year, so its (sic) not really pushing it." Notwithstanding the permissible delay in implementation, appellant and Mazzone did arrive at a definite agreement as to their ultimate disposition. Appellant gave Mazzone the names of the officers and told him where they worked. They agreed on a fee of $80,000 for the two officers, over and above the $40,000 for the wife.

(4) Lewis was almost an afterthought. Near the end of the second conversation, appellant indicated a desire to be rid of him as well. This part of the conversation is most relevant:

FRANK (MAZZONE): All right, what do you want to do with him?

GENE (APPELLANT): Um, same thing with Hatfield or Morrisette (the two officers) if that's . . . .

FRANK: Is he on the street right now.

GENE: No, he's up here second floor.

FRANK: Does he know your (sic, you're) here?

GENE: Disappears or if he dies, people collect _____ people ask too many questions here.

FRANK: You, you do want him dead, or you don't.

GENE: I do.

Ultimately, it was agreed that Mazzone should wait until Lewis was transferred from the Detention Center to the State prison where the killing would be easier to accomplish. Appellant promised an additional fee of $9,000 for Lewis.

Walker had told appellant that Mazzone was a "legal representative of . . . two professional hitmen." Mazzone never represented himself as a lawyer, and in fact never made clear to appellant what his supposed relationship was with whomever was to commit the murders. Indeed, there is nothing in the transcript of the conversations to foreclose the possibility that Mazzone himself would be the actual "hitman." Throughout the conversations, when referring to the killings, Mazzone used the plural pronoun "we" "Then we do the job," "if we got to go to Puerto Rico . . . ," "what do you want to show that we did the job? We bring you something back?" "we got a standard way we do things." By way of contrast, when referring to things he individually would do, such as retrieve the picture of appellant's wife from his apartment, Mazzone used the singular pronoun, "I." In short, although he said nothing directly to dispel any notion that he was merely an agent for others, Mazzone, in his own conversations with appellant, clearly portrayed himself as an integral part of a group willing to carry out contract murders, without indicating who would actually "do the job."

Q. Did you in your activities and conversations with Meyer lead him to believe that you were in fact an attorney?

A. Well, I guess I can't really say what he believed but I led him to believe that I would commit a murder for him. If he felt that I was an attorney, I couldn't say.

Q. That you would commit a murder or that you would get someone to commit a murder?

A. Well, again, I guess I don't know what he was thinking, but probably that I would do it or I would have someone to do it. I don't know which way he was taking it.

Q. You do not know which way he was taking it?

A. No, sir.

Q. Well, you did note on your prior testimony then that you would appear for him to other people as an attorney to seek their services?

A. I never said anything about being an attorney to Mr. Meyer.

With this background, we may dispose of appellant's complaints.

(1)

Appellant's first challenge, both as to the sufficiency of the evidence and the jury instructions, rests upon the premise that Mazzone was acting solely as an agent for others rather than as the "hitman" himself, and that his entreaties to Mazzone were made upon that understanding. His argument is a technical one, proceeding from this syllogism: (i) In Maryland, the common law crime of solicitation requires as its object the commission of a felony; (ii) the evidence here establishes at best (or worst) an importuning of Mazzone to enter into a conspiracy to have other persons commit the murders and not to commit the murders himself; (iii) the entering into a conspiracy in Maryland is a misdemeanor; (iv) ergo, as the sole object of his entreaties to Mazzone was the commission of a misdemeanor, he cannot be adjudged guilty of common law solicitation.

We need not examine in any detail the correctness of appellant's asserted legal propositions because his factual predicate for them is incorrect. For one thing, Mazzone's testimony and the transcript of the conversations with appellant permit a fair and reasonable inference that Mazzone/Rinaldo was negotiating as a potential "hitman" himself or as one who would not only arrange the killings but be present at the scene of their commission. Even accepting appellant's view that Mazzone was merely an agent not intending to commit the murders (or be present at their commission), he nevertheless would clearly have been an accessory before the fact had the murders actually been committed by his "clients." At the very least, Mazzone/Rinaldo's role was to aid, counsel, command, or encourage the commission of the killings. In either case, whether his role was that of actual participant or accessory before the fact, he would have been culpable as a principal had the

murders been committed by reason of his efforts. *See State v. Ward,* 284 Md. 189, 396 A.2d 1041 (1978).

It is clear, therefore, that the object of appellant's solicitation was for Mazzone to commit murder, a felony; and thus, even under the Cherry dicta, the evidence sufficed to establish the crime of criminal solicitation.

(2)

Appellant next asserts, in a somewhat confused fashion, that the imposition of four consecutive sentences was inappropriate since, at best (or worst) only one criminal solicitation was involved. The object or thrust of his argument is clear he seeks to vacate at least three of the sentences but the argument itself is ambiguous in terms of both the precise nature of the complaint and the legal theory offered in support of it.

The contention is initially framed in his brief, and was expounded at oral argument, as an attack only upon the multiple sentences and not upon the underlying multiple convictions. Yet the basis of his complaint is the assertion that only one criminal act occurred, which, if true, would impact as much, if not more, upon the validity of the several convictions as upon the sentences imposed on them. In laying out his theory, he weaves back and forth between the argument that only one incitement took place and the contention that the doctrine of merger, as laid down in *Newton v. State,* 280 Md. 260, 373 A.2d 262 (1977), is applicable, which presupposes the existence of separate crimes that, under common law, or Constitutional double jeopardy strictures, have to be merged one into the other.

In order to address the issue, we first have to define it. Ordinarily, if an appellant limits his attack to the sentence, we will not consider any non-jurisdictional defect in the underlying conviction. Maryland Rule 1085. Here, however, given the nature of appellant's complaint, it would be impossible for us to consider his objection solely in the context of the multiple sentences; it so obviously relates to the multiple convictions as well that we must, of necessity, consider and resolve the broader question of whether it was proper to charge, convict, and sentence appellant on four separate counts of solicitation upon the evidence in this case. Consecutive sentences are permissible only for distinct violations of law. *Kaylor v. State,* 285 Md. 66, 400 A.2d 419 (1979).

Having set the question for review, we turn to the legal issue which, as we have observed, is also a bit muddled. Appellant's most elemental position is that the gist of a criminal solicitation is the incitement, and that the evidence here established but one such incitement, notwithstanding that multiple victims were involved. He draws an analogy in this regard to the crime of conspiracy, the gist of which is the unlawful agreement among the conspirators; and, pointing to cases such as *Braverman v. United States*, 317 U.S. 49, 63 S.Ct. 99, 87 L.Ed. 23 (1942), he argues that a single agreement to commit more than one unlawful act is still but one conspiracy for which but one punishment may be imposed. The same rule, he claims, applies to a criminal solicitation.

This does seem to be the real issue here not whether there are separate crimes that should be merged, but whether there were, in the first place, separate crimes established by the evidence. If, assuming arguendo the validity of appellant's analogy to the crime of conspiracy, the evidence showed only one act of incitement, there would arise only one act of criminal solicitation and thus nothing to merge. If, on the other hand, the evidence sufficed to establish separate and distinct acts of incitement, there would arise several acts of solicitation, and they would not be mergable under the concepts enunciated in *Newton, supra*. Each solicitation would stand entirely on its own under the "required evidence" or any other cognizable test. The issue, then, is not one of merger, but of evidentiary sufficiency in light of the nature of the crime of criminal solicitation.

We are, to some extent, in truly virgin territory. We have been neither directed to nor able to locate any reported decision in the United States or in the common law nations of the British Commonwealth precisely on point determining whether an entreaty to kill more than one person constitutes distinct incitements and thus permits conviction and punishment for more than one act of criminal solicitation. *Compare State v. Furr*, 292 N.C. 711, 235 S.E.2d 193 (1977), *cert. denied*, 434 U.S. 924, 98 S.Ct. 402, 54 L.Ed.2d 281, in which the issue was mentioned but not decided, and *see also Regina v. Most*, 7 Q.B.D. 244 (1881), involving a converse situation a solicitation placed in a newspaper (i.e., a solicitation of many people to perform one act).

We start with the nature of the crime itself. As we pointed out in *Cherry v. State, supra*, quoting from Clark and Marshall, Law of Crimes (7th Ed., 1967), the forbidden act in a criminal solicitation is "the accused person's parol or written efforts to activate another to commit a criminal offense." 18 Md.App. at 258, 306 A.2d 634. See *also In Re Appeal No. 180*, Sept. Term 1976, 278 Md. 443, 365 A.2d 540 (1976). We see no reason why, on the one hand, in a single conversation (much less in two separate conversations as occurred here), a person cannot make successive and distinct incitements, each having a separate object; and we therefore reject the notion that merely because there is but one solicitor, one solicitee, and one conversation, only one solicitation can arise. We similarly reject, however, as being equally simplistic, the "per capita" theory that there are necessarily as many solicitations as there are victims.

Accepting the analogy (although not precisely appellant's interpretation of it) to the allied crime of conspiracy and to the view of it set forth in *Braverman v. United States, supra*, the question of whether there is but one solicitation or several depends upon the circumstances. What, in other words, is the solicitor asking the solicitee to do?

Braverman involved a collaboration among several people, extending over a continuing period of time, to unlawfully manufacture, transport, and distribute distilled spirits. Their agreement was to carry on that activity. It so happened that that activity contravened a number of different Federal tax laws, and the conspirators were charged, convicted, and sentenced for multiple conspiracies, one for each specific statute violated. The Court reversed, holding, in effect, that if there is a single agreement, there can be but one conspiracy, even if the overt acts done pursuant to it violate several laws. "The single agreement," said the Court at p. 54 of 317 U.S., at p. 102 of 63 S.Ct., "is the prohibited conspiracy, and however diverse its objects it violates but a single statute . . . ."

Braverman, of course, but begs the question here. At best, it reinforces the requirement that we focus on the number of incitements and not solely on the number of victims. The number of victims is important only as it may be evidence of the number of incitements. By way of example, an entreaty made by a solicitor to blow up a building in the hope that two or more particular persons may be killed in the blast could be characterized as one solicitation, notwithstanding that implementation of the scheme might violate several different laws or, because of multiple victims, constitute separate violations of the same law. The multiple criminality of the implementation would not, in that instance, pluralize the incitement, which was singular. That is the thrust of *Braverman*. But that is quite different from the situation in which the solicitee is being importuned directly to commit separate and distinct acts of murder to kill, individually, several different specified victims possibly at different times and places and by different means and executioners. In the latter case, there is not a single incitement but multiple ones, each punishable on its own.

That is the framework within which we must judge this case; and, from the record before us, we find the evidence sufficient to show four separate criminal solicitations based upon four distinct incitements. In point of time, at least three of the incitements were clearly distinct. The deal for the wife was made on May 8; that for Lewis and the two officers was made a week later but in different parts of the conversation. The executions were to occur at different times and places, and possibly by different means and executioners; different (and cumulative) fees were to be paid for these acts. Different motives were involved. Even as between the two officers, the evidence permitted a fair inference that most of these distinguishing attributes were present. In short, the evidence sufficed to permit a finding that it was not a "lump sum" singular deal, but separate and independent incitements to commit four separate and distinct acts of murder against specific named individuals; and thus, neither the separate convictions nor the separate and consecutive sentences were inappropriate.

* * *

JUDGMENTS AFFIRMED; APPELLANT TO PAY THE COSTS.

_____**CASE END**

Case Questions
Smallwood v. State

1. According to the court's decision in this case, could a person who is infected with HIV or AIDS *ever* be convicted of attempted murder based on having unprotected sex with a victim? Why or why not?

2. What argument did the state make that Smallwood was properly convicted of attempted murder? What problems did the court have with the state's argument?

3. What examples did the court give of cases from other states where there was sufficient evidence of an intent to kill when attempting to inflict a victim with HIV or AIDS? How did the *Smallwood* case compare to those other cases?

Meyer v. State

1. What was the second issue that Meyer raised on appeal? What was the court's response to that issue?

2. Do you agree with the court's outcome in this case? Why or why not?

Additional Crimes to Consult

In addition to the common law crimes of attempt, conspiracy, and solicitation, the Maryland legislature has specifically prohibited attempt, solicitation and conspiracy of certain substantive crimes. The legislature has prohibited the attempt of several violent crimes, such as attempted murder and sexual offenses, found in Titles 2 and 3 of the Criminal Law Article of the Maryland Annotated Code. Legislation related to attempt and conspiracy is frequently found in Title 5 (drug offenses), Title 8 (fraud related offenses, such as bribes and kickbacks), Title 9 (crimes against public administration, such as juror intimidation) and Title 11 (morality crimes, such as prostitution).

HYPOTHETICAL #1

Vincent could not deal with his messy roommate, Susan, any longer. Vincent suspected that Nancy, their other roommate, felt the same way. So one day while Susan was out and Vincent and Nancy were knocking back a few beers, Vincent disclosed to Nancy a detailed plan to make Susan "disappear" in a local reservoir. After spelling out the plan that required two people to make Susan "disappear," Vincent somberly queried, "So are you in?" Nancy mulled the question over for a second, laughed and said "You are so funny. I can't believe you have such a great imagination. I daydream of knocking Susan off too." Nancy poured another beer, threw in a DVD, sat back and relaxed. Vincent did not discuss his plan with Nancy ever again and Susan continued to drive them both crazy.

MAIN ISSUE

Did Vincent Solicit Nancy to Commit Murder?

ISSUE	THESIS	RULE	ANALYSIS	CONCLUSION
Did Vincent urge, advise, induce, encourage, request or command Nancy to commit murder WHEN Vincent told Nancy of a plot to make Susan "disappear" and asked Nancy if she was in?	Vincent most likely urged, induced, encouraged or requested Nancy to commit murder WHEN he told Nancy of a plot to make Susan "disappear" and asked Nancy if she was in.	The defendant URGED, ADVISED, INDUCED, ENCOURAGED, REQUESTED OR COMMANDED ANOTHER PERSON TO COMMIT A FELONY OR BREACH OF THE PEACE MISDEMEANOR.	It is possible that the prosecution can prove that Vincent urged, induced, encouraged, or requested that Nancy murder Susan BECAUSE Vincent told Nancy of a detailed plot of making Susan disappear in a reservoir. The plot required two people, so it would be reasonable that Vincent would need assistance from Nancy. Specifically, after telling Nancy of the plot, he asked Nancy "Are you in?"	Vincent most likely asked Nancy to help murder Susan.
Did Vincent intend for the felony of murder to be committed WHEN he told Nancy of his plot to make Susan "disappear" when Vincent was tired of his sloppy roommate Susan?	Vincent may not have had the necessary intent that Susan's murder actually be committed WHEN he told Nancy about the plot and queried if she was in.	At the time the defendant made the oral or written efforts to persuade another person to commit a felony or breach of the peace misdemeanor, THE DEFENDANT INTENDED THAT THE FELONY OR BREACH OF THE PEACE MISDEMEANOR BE COMMITTED.	While Vincent may have had the motive to murder Susan because she was sloppy, motive does not equal intent. It may be difficult to prove that Vincent was serious and intended for Susan's murder to occur BECAUSE Nancy would most likely testify that she thought Vincent was joking with her and was drinking beer at the time he told her of his plot.	Vincent may not have actually intended that Nancy murder Susan.

CONCLUSION

It is very possible that Vincent will be found not guilty of soliciting Nancy for Susan's murder because it will be very difficult to prove Vincent intended for Susan to be murdered at the time he told Nancy of the plot and asked her if she was in.

HYPOTHETICAL #2

Ronald and Roy were the founders and CEOs of two of America's most popular fast food chains. Ronald specialized in beefy burgers and Roy got raves about his roast beef sandwiches. But one day out of nowhere a red-headed woman named Wendy appeared on the scene. She opened her own joint, and her burgers were meatier than Ronald's, her chicken was crispier than Roy's, and soon her restaurant was world famous.

Ronald wasn't about to let Wendy steal all of his business, so he decided to call Roy. "Hey Roy," Ron said, "why don't you and me figure out some way to run Wendy out of town. Ya know, get her to close up shop *for good*." Roy, who seemed a little confused, just chuckled. "Yeah, whatever Ron," he replied. Nothing more was said about the phone conversation until two weeks later when they met at a fast food convention. Once again Ronald approached Roy. "Look Roy," Ronald said in a very serious tone, "We gotta do something about Wendy." "What are you saying?" asked Roy. "What I'm sayin' is that we should sabotage her food chain. Put poison in the potatoes or soap in the soup." "You serious?" Roy asked. "No," Ronald said as he rolled his eyes and winked, "I'm only kidding. So, you in?" Roy never said a word in reply but smiled slyly and walked away.

Later that week the men concocted what they thought was a perfect plan, and they soon put that plan into action . . . Ronald and Roy visited Wendy's restaurant one night, telling her that they just *had* to taste her world-famous chili (but of course they had another plan in mind!) Wendy gladly invited them in. Once Wendy was gone the two men snuck into the kitchen, and when the cooks weren't looking Ronald dumped a huge bottle of laxatives into the chili pot. Roy, meanwhile, put about a pound of extra-hot pepper into the burger mixture. Both men quickly went back to their seats and watched for the next hour as the customers became horribly ill, one after another. Ronald and Roy just sat back and chuckled (and of course, they didn't touch the chili they had ordered!)

Within only a few days Wendy's chili had become more notorious than famous—her once packed restaurant barely had two customers in an entire day. And Wendy knew just who was responsible! So she decided she would devise her own plan. She invited the men back to her restaurant to try one of her new recipies of meatloaf. Not realizing that Wendy knew exactly what was going on, Ronald and Roy gladly accepted. But little did they know she had put rat poisoning in the meatloaf. Wendy watched from the kitchen as the men quickly gobbled the delectable meatloaf down in seconds. But much to Wendy's surprise, when they were finished their meal they were absolutely fine! Wendy couldn't figure out what had happened. But soon enough she knew, because a young woman sitting two tables down with a half-full plate of meat loaf began choking violently and slumped over her seat. The woman was dead! It turned out that Wendy had mistakenly switched plates and gave the woman the poisoned meatloaf while giving Ronald and Roy plates that were perfectly fine.

Not surprisingly, all three fast-food chains quickly hit rock bottom when an investigation revealed that Ronald, Roy and Wendy had been involved in plots to sabotage each others. That left only Colonel Sanders in the fast food world, whose crispy fried chicken became the most popular food in America!

⮕ List the crimes with which each defendant may be charged.

DEFENDANT	CRIMES
Ronald	
Roy	
Wendy	

⮕ For EACH crime identified, complete an Analysis Chart assessing the possibility of conviction of each defendant.

DISCUSSION QUESTIONS

1. Karen and Eric are married. Nerissa hits on Eric and asks him to have sex with her. Eric agrees. Has there been a conspiracy to commit adultery. Why or why not?

2. Officer Don busted a known drug dealer named "Pistol." Officer Don confiscated Pistol's pager and called a number on the pager's display. The officer spoke with a woman who identified herself as Peggy and asked for Pistol. The officer posed as Pistol's associate and told her that he was responding to Pistol's calls. Peggy said she wanted "china white," which was the street name for heroin. The officer set up a meeting and Peggy arrived at the appointed time and place. Peggy gave Officer Don, who was undercover, a twenty dollar bill and Officer Don gave Peggy a Ziploc bag with a white powdery substance that looked like heroin. Peggy drove away and was stopped by police several blocks away. Her car was searched and the look-alike heroin was seized. Peggy was charged with attempted possession of a controlled dangerous substance. Will Peggy be convicted of attempted possession. Why or why not?

3. Does conspiracy merge into the substantive offense? Does solicitation merge into the substantive offense? Does attempt merge into the substantive offense?

4. Lynn asks Dana to kill Ann. Dana agrees, so Lynn and Dana proceed to plan out how the murder will be committed. Unbeknownst to both women, however, at the exact moment they are plotting their evil deed, Ann is killed in a car accident. Is Lynn still guilty of solicitation? Are Lynn and Dana still guilty of conspiracy? Explain.

5. Could nonverbal conduct ever suffice for the "meeting of the minds" required to have a criminal conspiracy? If so, what examples of nonverbal conduct would suffice to show a conspiracy?

6. What is a "wheel conspiracy"? What is a "chain conspiracy?" See *Bolden v. State*, 44 Md.App. 643, 410 A.2d 1085, *cert. denied*, 287 Md. 750 (1980).

7. Are there any crimes you could not "attempt" to commit? If so, what crimes or types of crimes could not have an attempted version and why?

8. Blake, a grown man, tries to engage in forcible sexual intercourse with Paige, a six-year-old child. He is unable to penetrate her due to her small size. Blake is charged with and convicted of attempted second-degree rape. If Blake had been successful in his penetration, he would have been convicted of second-degree rape, which carries a maximum potential penalty of 20 years imprisonment (See also Chapter 4). For his conviction of attempted second-degree rape, what do you think his maximum potential penalty should be? Why?

TEST BANK

True/False

_____ 1. In solicitation, the crime is in the asking and the underlying substantive offense need not even be attempted.

_____ 2. Conspiracy always required one more person than is necessary to complete the underlying substantive offense.

_____ 3. John asked Marsha to rob a bank with him. John fully intended to rob the bank but had not yet made any specific plans as to how to carry the robbery out. When Marsha said no to John's request, John abandoned his plans. John would most likely be found guilty of attempted robbery.

_____ 4. John asked Marsha to rob a bank with him. John fully intended to rob the bank, but had not yet made any specific plans as to how to carry the robbery out. When Marsha said no to John's request, John abandoned his plans. John would most likely be found guilty of conspiracy.

_____ 5. At least one party to a conspiracy must take a substantial step toward completing the target crime in order for the prosecution to secure a guilty verdict for conspiracy.

MULTIPLE CHOICE

The multiple choice questions are based upon the following scenario:

"The Mayor" was the head of a local organized crime ring that was very active in the town of Daybury. To make money, the Mayor would digitally record TV shows from premium cable channels. One day, the Mayor approached Lisa Lovely, an honest townsperson who owned the Simple Pleasures craft store on Main Street. The Mayor asked Lisa if she would sell DVDs but did not inform Lisa of how the DVDs were made. The Mayor suggested that Lisa sell the DVDs for $15 each and that Lisa would keep $5. Lisa sold the DVDs as promised. The police discovered that the DVDs were pirated and arrested Lisa Lovely, who told the police she had received the DVDs from the Mayor. The police then arrested the Mayor.

6. With regard to conspiracy,
   A. The Mayor may be guilty of conspiracy to sell pirated material.
   B. The Mayor would not be guilty of conspiracy because, although Lisa agreed to sell the DVDs, Lisa did not agree to commit a crime because she did not actually know they were pirated.
   C. None of the above.

7. With regard to solicitation,
   A. The Mayor may be guilty of solicitation to sell pirated material.
   B. The Mayor would not be guilty of solicitation because, although the Mayor asked, Lisa agreed to sell the DVDs. Lisa did not know she was being asked to commit a crime.
   C. None of the above.

8. With regard to conspiracy,
   A. Lisa may be guilty of conspiracy to sell pirated material.
   B. Lisa would not be guilty of conspiracy because, although Lisa agreed to sell the DVDs, she did not agree to commit a crime because she did not actually know they were pirated and did not intend to commit a crime.
   C. None of the above.

9. With regard to solicitation,
   A. Lisa may be guilty of solicitation to sell pirated material based upon her agreement with the Mayor.
   B. Lisa would not be guilty of solicitation because, although the Mayor asked, Lisa agreed to sell the DVDs. She did not know she was agreeing to commit a crime.
   C. Lisa may be guilty of solicitation because she asked the public to buy the CDs.
   D. None of the above.

10. With regard to attempt,
    A. The Mayor may be guilty of one count of attempt to sell pirated material for all of the DVDs that remained unsold.
    B. If 10 DVDs remained unsold, the Mayor may be guilty of one count of attempt to sell pirated material for each unsold DVD, for a total of 10 counts of attempt.
    C. Lisa will be guilty of attempted piracy for each DVD she sold.
    D. None of the above.

chapter three

Homicide

Introduction

The term "homicide" is defined as "the killing of one human being by the act, procurement, or omission of another." Black's Law Dictionary 734 (6th ed. 1990). Given that broad definition, homicide is very much an umbrella term, encompassing within it various classifications depending on whether the perpetrator acted with malice, whether the death was intentional or unintentional, or whether the homicidal act was premeditated. There is no such thing as a quick and simple look at homicide. Therefore, this chapter will consider a variety of homicide offenses and how they are distinguished from one another.

Focus Crimes

First-Degree Premeditated Murder, Md. Code Ann., Crim. Law § 2-201 (West 2002); MPJI-Cr. 4:17.

First-Degree Felony Murder, Md. Code Ann., Crim. Law § 2-201 (West 2002); MPJI-Cr. 4:17.7.

Second-Degree Specific Intent Murder, Md. Code Ann., Crim. Law § 2-204 (West 2002); MPJI-Cr. 4:17.

Second-Degree Depraved Heart Murder, Md. Code Ann., Crim. Law § 2-204 (West 2002); MPJI-Cr. 4:17.8.

Manslaughter (Voluntary or Involuntary), Md. Code Ann., Crim. Law § 2-207 (West 2002); MPJI-Cr. 4:17.

Objectives

Upon completing this chapter you should be able to:

- Distinguish between murder and manslaughter;
- Distinguish between intentional and unintentional homicides;
- Analyze and explain the causal connection necessary between the homicidal act and the resultant death of the victim;
- Analyze the criminal responsibility of various participants in a felony murder;
- Explain the concept of transferred intent;
- Analyze the possibility of charging someone with the homicide of a fetus; and
- Recognize what constitutes legally adequate provocation to mitigate murder to manslaughter.

Homicide in Maryland*

	INTENTIONAL	UNINTENTIONAL
Murder	First-Degree Premeditated Murder	First-Degree Felony Murder
	Second-Degree Specific Intent to Kill Murder	Second-Degree Depraved Heart Murder
Manslaughter	Voluntary Manslaughter: 1. Hot Blooded Response to Legally Adequate Provocation 2. Partial Self-Defense or Defense of Others 3. Duress	Involuntary Manslaughter: 1. Grossly Negligent or Unlawful Act 2. Manslaughter by Motor Vehicle or Vessel 3. Homicide by Motor Vehicle or Vessel while Impaired or Under the Influence

Not Guilty	1. Complete Self-Defense or Defense of Others
	2. Justified Homicide:
	   a. Killing an enemy at war
	   b. Killing under a valid death sentence
		Not Applicable

*For a detailed discussion of how defenses affect the various levels of homicide, see Chapters 10 and 11 dealing with Criminal Defenses.

CASE LAW

Stewart v. State, 65 Md. App. 372, 500 A.2d 676 (1985)

This case principally concerns the criminal responsibility of an assailant under the felony-murder doctrine for the fright-induced death of a robbery victim. Our focus of attention on this issue will be whether the evidence was sufficient to prove a causative relationship between the robbery and the victim's death from heart failure approximately two hours later.

Facts

At approximately 11:15 during the evening of November 19, 1983, two men entered the In-Town Motor Hotel in Montgomery County while two others remained in a nearby car. One of the men handed the desk clerk, 60-year-old Pearl Pizzamiglio, a paper bag with a note attached which read "Don't say a word. Put all the money in this bag and no one will get hurt!" Mrs. Pizzamiglio placed $176.00 in the bag and the two men fled to their waiting vehicle and drove off. Mrs. Pizzamiglio immediately called the police and within minutes the four suspects were apprehended.

Montgomery County Police Officer Nancy Calder arrived at the motel at 11:21 p.m. and spoke with Mrs. Pizzamiglio in the motel lobby for approximately 35 to 40 minutes. Officer Calder reported that Mrs. Pizzamiglio, who was pale, nervous, and jittery, related that although she did not know if the individual who handed her the note had a weapon, she described him as "scary mean looking." Officer Calder further testified that while in the process of transporting Mrs. Pizzamiglio to the police station in an effort to see if she could identify the individuals who had just been arrested, the officer noticed that Mrs. Pizzamiglio began holding her

chest and developed difficulty in breathing. Officer Calder immediately summoned the Rescue Squad which arrived within minutes. Upon administering oxygen, the Rescue Squad transported Mrs. Pizzamiglio to Suburban Hospital, where she arrived at 12:30 a.m. Soon after she arrived at the hospital, Mrs. Pizzamiglio experienced cardiac arrest and, after attempts at treatment proved unsuccessful, expired at 1:28 a.m.

The appellant, Michael Stewart, concedes that he was the person who had handed the bag and attached note to Mrs. Pizzamiglio. At the trial the State presented evidence that the appellant was competent to stand trial and that Mrs. Pizzamiglio had been frightened to death by the robbery. The court determined that the appellant was competent to stand trial and the jury found that Mrs. Pizzamiglio's death was a direct result of the robbery. Stewart was convicted of felony-murder and robbery and found to be responsible at the time of the commission of the offense. The robbery charge was merged into the felony-murder count and Stewart was sentenced to life imprisonment, with all but fifteen years suspended.

The appellant presents the following issues for our review: . . . Whether the evidence was legally sufficient to sustain a conviction of felony-murder when the underlying offense was an unarmed robbery and the victim died some two hours later of heart failure.

* * *

The thrust of appellant's position is that the evidence was legally insufficient to sustain a conviction of felony-murder. Although he does not contest that Mrs. Pizzamiglio's death occurred subsequent to the robbery that he committed, he argues that his acts were not the legal cause of her death as "death is not a probable and natural consequence of an *unarmed* robbery." (Emphasis supplied.) In support of his theory, the appellant relies on *Campbell v. State,* 293 Md. 438, 444 A.2d 1034 (1980).

The Court of Appeals in *Campbell* was concerned with the responsibility of felons for the lethal acts of others. More particularly, whether under the felony-murder doctrine, the killing of a co-felon during an armed robbery, either by a police officer attempting to apprehend him, or by a victim resisting the armed robbery, constituted murder in the first degree on the part of the surviving felon. The Court determined that as the killing of the co-felon had been committed to thwart a felony rather than to further it, the surviving felon was not guilty of murder. Writing on behalf of the Court, Judge Davidson stated:

> We now hold that ordinarily, under the felony-murder doctrine, criminal culpability shall continue to be imposed for lethal acts committed by a felon or an accomplice acting in furtherance of a common design. However, criminal culpability ordinarily shall not be imposed for lethal acts of non-felons that are not committed in furtherance of a common design.

Clearly, the thrust of the inquiry under *Campbell,* whether the lethal acts of a non-felon should constitute felony-murder on the part of a surviving felon, is inappropriate to the analysis in the case *sub judice* where the appellant's own conduct and its link to the death of his robbery victim is at issue. We therefore must determine whether the evidence was legally sufficient to establish that Mrs. Pizzamiglio's death was a natural consequence of the appellant's unlawful act.

At early common law physical injury was required before criminal responsibility was imposed for homicide. *In re Heigho,* 18 Idaho 566, 110 P. 1029 (1910). The modern trend, however, is to determine criminality according to the degree of causative relationship between the unlawful act of the accused and the death of the victim. Annot., 47 A.L.R.2d 1072. To warrant a conviction for homicide it must be established that the act of the accused was a proximate cause of death. "If the act of accused was the cause of the cause of death, no more is required." 40 C.J.S. *Homicide* § 11. The appellant's attempts to distinguish various cases which hold an accused criminally responsible for the death of a victim by fright are not persuasive.

The appellant argues that *State v. Spates,* 176 Conn. 227, 405 A.2d 656 (1978) is inapplicable to the present case because in *Spates* the defendant used a gun to rob the victim, tied his hands and legs, and abandoned

him despite the victim's pleas for a doctor because he was having a heart attack. The appellant contends that the State's case on causation is much weaker in the instant case. Weaker, however, is not the standard. As noted above, if a direct causal link between the accused's actions and the victim's death can be established, no more is required.

The appellant further argues that neither *State v. Luther,* 285 N.C. 570, 206 S.E.2d 238 (1974) nor *State v. Edwards,* 136 Ariz. 177, 665 P.2d 59 (1983) is applicable to the instant matter. He claims that in both cases there was displayed a deadly weapon which, in one instance, was used. In the instant case no weapon was displayed or used. Furthermore, in *Luther* and *Edwards* the victim died during or immediately following the crime. In the present case the victim expired more than two hours after the incident. As a result, the appellant claims that the causal link between Mrs. Pizzamiglio's death and his unlawful act is not as direct as in *Luther* and *Edwards.*

In *State v. Luther, supra,* the accused struck the victim with a lead pipe. The victim died and an autopsy determined that there had been "a hardening of the arteries of the heart and no traumatic injury sufficient to cause death ···" *Luther,* 285 N.C. at 575, 206 S.E.2d 238. However, it was further determined that "the increased cardiac demand" occasioned by the altercation could have been the cause of death. The Court concluded that if the victim's "death came about as a result of the conjunction of his heart disease with either the violence or excitement and shock of defendant's assault it was still brought about by defendant's unlawful act, for the consequences of which he would be answerable." *Id.*

The accused in *State v. Edwards, supra,* had robbed bar patrons at gunpoint. In the course of the robbery a gun was placed against the neck of the proprietor who was ordered to open a safe. Suddenly, the victim's face went blank as he "slumped in a chair and began making a snoring sound." When the police arrived at the store, the proprietor was dead. The doctor who performed an autopsy on the victim testified that the cause of death had been due to a heart attack caused by the "fright-flight-fight syndrome." *Edwards,* 136 Ariz. at 186, 665 P.2d 59. He explained:

> [W]hen a person is faced with a stressful or frightening situation, his body will manifest certain reactions. Adrenalin will start to flow and the heart will begin to pound hard, supplying the higher requirement of increased blood to the muscles, preparing the person to fight or flee.

Id. Even though the victim suffered from a pre-existing heart disease and "a coronary attack could have been prompted by other causes completely independent of the robbery" the examining doctor maintained that the victim's heart attack and death had been "caused by the anxiety of the robbery." *Id.* From this testimony the Court concluded that "there was sufficient evidence before the jury to support the finding that the attack was caused by the robbery." *Id.*

Despite the factual differences pointed out by the appellant between the case *sub judice* and those above, the similar applications of the law render them indistinguishable. In each of the three cases, criminal responsibility for the victim's death was based on whether the "cause of the cause of death" was the illegal act of the accused. Other cases which turn on this point include *Ohio v. Losey,* No. 84 AP-768 slip op. (Ohio, June 25, 1985); *Durden v. State,* 250 Ga. 325, 297 S.E.2d 237 (1982); *State v. McKeiver,* 89 N.J.Super. 52, 213 A.2d 320 (1965); and *In re Heigho,* 18 Idaho 566, 110 P. 1029 (1910).

In *Ohio v. Losey, supra,* the defendant Losey approached a house late at night and knocked on the door. After receiving no response from within, he forced the door open and attempted to remove a bicycle. A friend outside warned of a car approaching slowly and the defendant left the bike beside the door and fled, leaving the front door open. The homeowner testified that he heard a noise and soon thereafter his mother, who shared the residence, came to his bedroom because she too had heard a noise. Together they went to the living room whereupon they discovered the front door open and the bicycle near the door. The son testified that his mother was very upset upon discovering the burglary and that he had never seen her that upset. Soon thereafter she collapsed. The emergency squad was called and after attempting to revive her for almost an hour the mother was pronounced dead. The coroner opined that the cause of death was coronary thrombosis brought on by the emotion of discovering the burglary. The trial court found the defendant criminally responsible for the death of the woman and he appealed.

The Ohio Court of Appeals upheld the conviction of involuntary manslaughter and concluded that:

> It is not necessary that the accused be in a position to foresee the precise consequence of his conduct; only that the consequence be foreseeable in the sense that what actually transpired was natural and logical in that it was within the scope of the risk created by his conduct.

The accused in *Durden, supra,* was convicted of felony-murder. The evidence at his trial revealed that the defendant entered a store from the roof and activated a "movement-sensitive" alarm in the owner's home behind the store. The owner notified the police and then went to the store to investigate. Shots were exchanged between the store owner and the defendant. Although the store owner was not wounded, within minutes after the police arrived, he suffered a heart attack and expired. The victim suffered from arteriosclerotic cardiovascular disease. The medical examiner testified that the victim's death was the result of small coronary arteries and stress from the events preceding his death.

On appeal *Durden* argued that the evidence was insufficient to establish that his actions were the proximate cause of the victim's death. In upholding the conviction, the Supreme Court of Georgia stated that:

> Where one commits a felony upon another, such felony is to be accounted as the efficient, proximate cause of death whenever it shall be made to appear either that the felony directly and materially contributed to the happening of a subsequent accruing immediate cause of death, or that the injury materially accelerated the death, although proximately occasioned by a pre-existing cause.

Durden, **250 Ga. at 329, 297 S.E.2d 237.**

In *McKeiver, supra,* the defendant, who had been charged with murder, moved to dismiss the indictment on the theory that his acts did not substantiate a charge for felony-murder because he had not had any direct contact with the victim. The facts revealed that McKeiver entered a tavern, fired a shot in the ceiling, and ordered the bartender and the patrons to one end of the bar while he took approximately $90 from the cash register. He then ordered everyone to walk toward the front door. One of the patrons fell to the floor and the defendant fled the scene. Despite being administered first aid, the fallen patron died. An autopsy revealed that the victim's death was "due to fright during hold-up in tavern: cardiac arrest; occlusive arteriosclerotic coronary artery disease." The New Jersey Superior Court denied McKeiver's motion and stated:

> Fright, or other "mental force" as it had been called, 1 Bishop, New Criminal Law, (8th ed.1892), sec. 562, will receive judicial recognition if it is accompanied by physical force. Physical force does not necessitate physical contact, because one can exert physical force over another by "working upon the fancy of another or treating him harshly or unkindly," as by certain actions which might cause him to "die of fear or grief." 1 HALE P.C. 429; 1 East P.C. 225.

McKeiver, **89 N.J.Super. at 57, 213 A.2d 320.**

The accused in *Heigho, supra,* while wearing a gun in plain view, went to the home of a person named Barton. An argument between the defendant and Barton ensued and during the altercation Barton's mother-in-law, Mrs. Rigleman, became upset and excited. Shortly thereafter, Mrs. Rigleman died. An attending physician made a post-mortem examination and determined that the death was attributable to an aneurysm of the ascending aorta. The physician stated that excitement was one of the three principal causes that produce such a result.

The Supreme Court of Idaho pursuant to a petition for habeas corpus, as to whether a charge of manslaughter could be brought under the circumstances, determined that:

> [I]t would be unsafe, unreasonable and often unjust for a court to hold as a matter of law that under no state of facts should a prosecution for manslaughter be sustained where death was caused by fright, fear or terror alone, even though no hostile demonstration or overt act was directed at the person of the deceased. Many examples might be called to mind where it would be possible for the death of a person to be accomplished through fright, nervous shock or terror as effectually as the same could be done with a knife or gun.

* * *

> It would seem that in some instances force or violence may be applied to the mind or nervous system as effectually as to the body.

<center>*Heigho*, 18 Idaho at 576, 110 P. 1029.</center>

Against this legal background the evidence in the case *sub judice* must be analyzed. The test on review of the sufficiency of the evidence is whether any rational trier of fact could have found beyond a reasonable doubt that the appellant's felonious acts caused Mrs. Pizzamiglio's death. *State v. Rusk,* 289 Md. 230, 240, 424 A.2d 720 (1981), citing *Jackson v. Virginia,* 443 U.S. 307, 319, 99 S.Ct. 2781, 2789, 61 L.Ed.2d 560 (1979).

The evidence before the jury was that Mrs. Pizzamiglio had been robbed by the appellant shortly after she began the all-night desk shift at the In-Town Motor Hotel. She called the police at 11:21 p.m. Officer Nancy Calder arrived shortly thereafter. Upon arrival, the officer observed that the victim was pale and nervous, which she had not been when Officer Calder had seen her the previous evening. The victim related that a man, whom she described, handed her a bag which had a note on it instructing her to put all the money in the bag and she would not be hurt. As she did so, the man told her he was watching her actions in a mirror behind her. The victim stated that she did not know if the man had a gun but that he appeared to be "scary

mean looking." Officer Calder stated that she and the victim remained at the scene approximately 35–40 minutes, during which time the victim's physical symptoms continued. When Mrs. Pizzamiglio entered Officer Calder's police car to be driven to the police station, the victim indicated that she was having difficulty in breathing and held her upper chest. She exited the police car and sat down on the curb. Officer Calder called the rescue squad, which arrived within a few minutes. The victim appeared nauseated, and unable to breathe or to talk. She was given oxygen and taken to the hospital.

Officer Calder testified that prior to these events, while still in the hotel, Mrs. Pizzamiglio had agreed to go to the police station to identify the apprehended suspects, but was most reluctant to do so. The news itself, however, that an identification would be needed did not seem to cause a visible change in her condition, according to the officer.

James Resnick was the paramedic who responded with a crew in a "cardiac unit" ambulance. He arrived at the hotel at 12:17 a.m. He observed that the victim had labored, "gurgly" breathing. In the ambulance, her vital signs were monitored. Her breathing was three to four times faster than normal and her heart beat was extremely fast. She was ashen, cold, and sweaty and had fluid in her lung. While en route to the hospital the victim began having premature ventricular contractions, which Resnick described as a very dangerous condition of irregular heart beat.

Upon arrival at the hospital at 12:30 a.m. Mrs. Pizzamiglio was taken to the "code blue" room for cardiac arrest patients. Dr. Douglas Koth was the treating emergency room physician. He testified that she had acute respiratory distress, rapid heart beat, and was semiconscious. She then went into respiratory failure and full cardiac arrest. Her heart continued to beat in a disorganized irregular fashion and would not respond to the medications applied by the emergency room staff. Mrs. Pizzamiglio was pronounced dead at 1:28 a.m.

The most crucial evidence presented by the State was given by two cardiologists, Drs. Gerald Scugol and Robert S. Elliot. Dr. Scugol, a physician specializing in cardiovascular diseases, concluded that the cause of Mrs. Pizzamiglio's death was that the acute emotional stress she had been subjected to set into motion a chain of events that resulted in acute heart failure. He further concluded that the fact that two hours had elapsed prior to death did not change his opinion, as the victim had symptoms of heart failure near the precipitating event, and it took two hours beyond that event for her to expire.

Dr. Robert Elliot, a leading national cardiologist, reviewed all records pertaining to Mrs. Pizzamiglio, and most particularly, microscopic slides of her heart muscle. His conclusion as to the cause of her death was as follows:

> The changes I saw were the most extreme I have ever seen in any example in which the effects of adrenaline-like substances caused the heart to overcontract and within a matter of five minutes in our studies what happens is when that heart overcontracts and these little muscle fibers overcontract individually, they can no longer function again. The changes that one sees under a microscope are an absolute hallmark of this kind of stress-induced death; death of heart muscle; which is brought on by huge amounts of adrenaline dumped into the system causing the heart muscle to react like a horse that has been whipped to the point where it collapses.

The doctor went on to conclude that:

> [T]he insult that she experienced and the fear that she experienced in the robbery was the critical event that tipped this over from the medical [to] the police records. I don't know of anything else that could have done it.

We believe that the evidence was sufficient to support the jury's finding that fright or shock of the robbery committed by the appellant had caused Mrs. Pizzamiglio's adrenaline induced heart failure. We conclude that any rational trier of fact could have found beyond a reasonable doubt, from the evidence, that the surge of adrenaline was in response to the fear Mrs. Pizzamiglio encountered as a result of having been placed in fear and robbed by the appellant. We, therefore, hold that under the facts and circumstances of this case, the evidence was sufficient to sustain the felony-murder conviction.

JUDGMENT AFFIRMED.

CASE END

 CASE LAW   *Girouard v. State*, 321 Md. 532, 583 A.2d 718 (1991)

In this case we are asked to reconsider whether the types of provocation sufficient to mitigate the crime of murder to manslaughter should be limited to the categories we have heretofore recognized, or whether the sufficiency of the provocation should be decided by the factfinder on a case-by-case basis. Specifically, we must determine whether words alone are provocation adequate to justify a conviction of manslaughter rather than one of second degree murder. The Petitioner, Steven S. Girouard, and the deceased, Joyce M. Girouard, had been married for about two months on October 28, 1987, the night of Joyce's death. Both parties, who met while working in the same building, were in the army. They married after having known each other for approximately three months. The evidence at trial indicated that the marriage was often tense and strained, and there was some evidence that after marrying Steven, Joyce had resumed a relationship with her old boyfriend, Wayne.

On the night of Joyce's death, Steven overheard her talking on the telephone to her friend, whereupon she told the friend that she had asked her first sergeant for a hardship discharge because her husband did not love her anymore. Steven went into the living room where Joyce was on the phone and asked her what she meant by her comments; she responded, "nothing." Angered by her lack of response, Steven kicked away the plate of food Joyce had in front of her. He then went to lie down in the bedroom.

Joyce followed him into the bedroom, stepped up onto the bed and onto Steven's back, pulled his hair and said, "What are you going to do, hit me?" She continued to taunt him by saying, "I never did want to marry you and you are a lousy fuck and you remind me of my dad." The barrage of insults continued with her telling Steven that she wanted a divorce, that the marriage had been a mistake and that she had never wanted to marry him. She also told him she had seen his commanding officer and filed charges against him for abuse. She then asked Steven, "What are you going to do?" Receiving no response, she continued her verbal attack. She added that she had filed charges against him in the Judge Advocate General's Office (JAG) and that he would probably be court martialed. When she was through, Steven asked her if she had really done all those things, and she responded in the affirmative. He left the bedroom with his pillow in his arms and proceeded to the kitchen where he procured a long handled kitchen knife. He returned to Joyce in the bedroom with the knife behind the pillow. He testified that he was enraged and that he kept waiting for Joyce to say she was kidding, but Joyce continued talking. She said she had learned a lot from the marriage and that it had been a mistake. She also told him she would remain in their apartment after he moved out. When he questioned how she would afford it, she told him she would claim her brain-damaged sister as a dependent and have the sister move in. Joyce reiterated that the marriage was a big mistake, that she did not love him and that the divorce would be better for her.

After pausing for a moment, Joyce asked what Steven was going to do. What he did was lunge at her with the kitchen knife he had hidden behind the pillow and stab her 19 times. Realizing what he had done, he dropped the knife and went to the bathroom to shower off Joyce's blood. Feeling like he wanted to die, Steven went back to the kitchen and found two steak knives with which he slit his own wrists. He lay down on the bed waiting to die, but when he realized that he would not die from his self-inflicted wounds, he got up and called the police, telling the dispatcher that he had just murdered his wife.

When the police arrived they found Steven wandering around outside his apartment building. Steven was despondent and tearful and seemed detached, according to police officers who had been at the scene. He was unconcerned about his own wounds, talking only about how much he loved his wife and how he could not believe what he had done. Joyce Girouard was pronounced dead at the scene.

At trial, defense witness, psychologist, Dr. William Stejskal, testified that Steven was out of touch with his own capacity to experience anger or express hostility. He stated that the events of October 28, 1987, were entirely consistent with Steven's personality, that Steven had "basically reach[ed] the limit of his ability to swallow his anger, to rationalize his wife's behavior, to tolerate, or actually to remain in a passive mode with that. He essentially went over the limit of his ability to bottle up those strong emotions. What ensued was a very extreme explosion of rage that was intermingled with a great deal of panic." Another defense witness, psychiatrist, Thomas Goldman, testified that Joyce had a "compulsive need to provoke jealousy so that she's always asking for love and at the same time destroying and undermining any chance that she really might have to establish any kind of mature love with anybody."

Steven Girouard was convicted, at a court trial in the Circuit Court for Montgomery County, of second degree murder and was sentenced to 22 years incarceration, 10 of which were suspended. Upon his release, Petitioner is to be on probation for five years, two years supervised and three years unsupervised. The Court of Special Appeals affirmed the judgment of the circuit court in an unreported opinion. We granted certiorari to determine whether the circumstances of the case presented provocation adequate to mitigate the second degree murder charge to manslaughter.

Petitioner relies primarily on out of state cases to provide support for his argument that the provocation to mitigate murder to manslaughter should not be limited only to the traditional circumstances of: extreme assault or battery upon the defendant; mutual combat; defendant's illegal arrest; injury or serious abuse of a close relative of the defendant's; or the sudden discovery of a spouse's adultery. Petitioner argues that manslaughter is a catchall for homicides which are criminal but that lack the malice essential for a conviction of murder. Steven argues that the trial judge did find provocation (although he held it inadequate to mitigate murder) and that the categories of provocation adequate to mitigate should be broadened to include factual situations such as this one.

The State counters by stating that although there is no finite list of legally adequate provocations, the common law has developed to a point at which it may be said there are some concededly provocative acts that society is not prepared to recognize as reasonable. Words spoken by the victim, no matter how abusive or taunting, fall into a category society should not accept as adequate provocation. According to the State, if abusive words alone could mitigate murder to manslaughter, nearly every domestic argument ending in the death of one party could be mitigated to manslaughter. This, the State avers, is not an acceptable outcome. Thus, the State argues that the courts below were correct in holding that the taunting words by Joyce Girouard were not provocation adequate to reduce Steven's second degree murder charge to voluntary manslaughter.

Initially, we note that the difference between murder and manslaughter is the presence or absence of malice. *State v. Faulkner*, 301 Md. 482, 485, 483 A.2d 759 (1984); *State v. Ward*, 284 Md. 189, 195, 396 A.2d 1041 (1978); *Davis v. State*, 39 Md. 355 (1874). Voluntary manslaughter has been defined as "an *intentional* homicide, done in a sudden heat of passion, caused by adequate provocation, before there has been a reasonable opportunity for the passion to cool" (Emphasis in original). *Cox v. State*, 311 Md. 326, 331, 534 A.2d 1333 (1988). *See also, State v. Faulkner, supra; State v. Ward, supra; Whitehead v. State*, 9 Md.App. 7, 262 A.2d 316 (1970).

There are certain facts that may mitigate what would normally be murder to manslaughter. For example, we have recognized as falling into that group: (1) discovering one's spouse in the act of sexual intercourse with another; (2) mutual combat; (3) assault and battery. *See State v. Faulkner,* 301 Md. at 486, 483 A.2d 759. There is also authority recognizing injury to one of the defendant's relatives or to a third party, and death resulting from resistance of an illegal arrest as adequate provocation for mitigation to manslaughter. *See, e.g.,* 40 C.J.S. *Homicide* § 48 at 913 (1944) and 40 C.J.S. *Homicide* § 50 at 915-16 (1944). Those acts mitigate homicide to manslaughter because they create passion in the defendant and are not considered the product of free will. *State v. Faulkner,* 301 Md. at 486, 483 A.2d 759.

In order to determine whether murder should be mitigated to manslaughter we look to the circumstances surrounding the homicide and try to discover if it was provoked by the victim. Over the facts of the case we lay the template of the so-called "Rule of Provocation." The courts of this State have repeatedly set forth the requirements of the Rule of Provocation:

1. There must have been adequate provocation;
2. The killing must have been in the heat of passion;
3. It must have been a sudden heat of passion—that is, the killing must have followed the provocation before there had been a reasonable opportunity for the passion to cool;
4. There must have been a causal connection between the provocation, the passion, and the fatal act.

Sims v. State, 319 Md. 540, 551, 573 A.2d 1317 (1990); *Glenn v. State,* 68 Md.App. 379, 406, 511 A.2d 1110, *cert. denied,* 307 Md. 599, 516 A.2d 569 (1986); *Carter v. State,* 66 Md.App. 567, 571, 505 A.2d 545 (1986); *Tripp v. State,* 36 Md.App. 459, 466, 374 A.2d 384 (1977); *Whitehead v. State,* 9 Md.App. at 11, 262 A.2d 316.

We shall assume without deciding that the second, third, and fourth of the criteria listed above were met in this case. We focus our attention on an examination of the ultimate issue in this case, that is, whether the provocation of Steven by Joyce was enough in the eyes of the law so that the murder charge against Steven should have been mitigated to voluntary manslaughter. For provocation to be "adequate," it must be " 'calculated to inflame the passion of a reasonable man and tend to cause him to act for the moment from passion rather than reason.' " *Carter v. State,* 66 Md.App. at 572, 505 A.2d 545 quoting R. Perkins, *Perkins on Criminal Law* at p. 56 (2d ed. 1969). The issue we must resolve, then, is whether the taunting words uttered by Joyce were enough to inflame the passion of a *reasonable* man so that that man would be sufficiently infuriated so as to strike out in hot-blooded blind passion to kill

her. Although we agree with the trial judge that there was needless provocation by Joyce, we also agree with him that the provocation was not adequate to mitigate second degree murder to voluntary manslaughter.

Although there are few Maryland cases discussing the issue at bar, those that do hold that words alone are not adequate provocation. Most recently, in *Sims v. State,* 319 Md. 540, 573 A.2d 1317, we held that "[i]nsulting words or gestures, no matter how opprobrious, do not amount to an affray, and standing alone, do not constitute adequate provocation." *Id.* at 552, 573 A.2d 1317. That case involved the flinging of racial slurs and derogatory comments by the victim at the defendant. That conduct did not constitute adequate provocation.

In *Lang v. State,* 6 Md.App. 128, 250 A.2d 276, *cert. denied,* 396 U.S. 971, 90 S.Ct. 457, 24 L.Ed.2d 438 (1969), the Court of Special Appeals stated that it is "generally held that mere words, threats, menaces or gestures, however offensive and insulting, do not constitute adequate provocation." *Id.* at 132, 250 A.2d 276. Before the shooting, the victim had called the appellant "a chump" and "a chicken," dared the appellant to fight, shouted obscenities at him and shook his fist at him. *Id.* The provocation, again, was not enough to mitigate murder.

The court in *Lang* did note, however, that words can constitute adequate provocation if they are accompanied by conduct indicating a present intention and ability to cause the defendant bodily harm. *Id.* Clearly, no such conduct was exhibited by Joyce in this case. While Joyce did step on Steven's back and pull his hair, he could not reasonably have feared bodily harm at her hands. This, to us, is certain based on Steven's testimony at trial that Joyce was about 5'1" tall and weighed 115 pounds, while he was 6'2" tall, weighing over 200 pounds. Joyce simply did not have the size or strength to cause Steven to fear for his bodily safety. Thus, since there was no ability on the part of Joyce to cause Steven harm, the words she hurled at him could not, under the analysis in *Lang,* constitute legally sufficient provocation.

Other jurisdictions overwhelmingly agree with our cases and hold that words alone are not adequate provocation. *See, e.g., State v. Doss,* 116 Ariz. 156, 568 P.2d 1054 (1977); *West v. United States,* 499 A.2d 860 (D.C.App.1985); *Nicholson v. United States,* 368 A.2d 561 (D.C.App.1977); *Hill v. State,* 236 Ga. 703, 224 S.E.2d 907 (1976); *Cox v. State,* 512 N.E.2d 1099 (Ind.1987); *State v. Guebara,* 236 Kan. 791, 696 P.2d 381 (1985); *State v. Hilliker,* 327 A.2d 860 (Me.1974); *Commonwealth v. Bermudez,* 370 Mass. 438, 348 N.E.2d 802 (1976);

Gates v. State, 484 So.2d 1002 (Miss.1986); *State v. Milosovich,* 42 Nev. 263, 175 P. 139 (1918); *State v. Mauricio,* 117 N.J. 402, 568 A.2d 879 (1990); *State v. Castro,* 92 N.M. 585, 592 P.2d 185 (1979); *State v. Best,* 79 N.C.App. 734, 340 S.E.2d 524 (1986); *State v. Butler,* 277 S.C. 452, 290 S.E.2d 1 (1982). One jurisdiction that does allow provocation brought about by prolonged stress, anger and hostility caused by marital problems to provide grounds for a verdict of voluntary manslaughter rather than murder is Pennsylvania. *See Commonwealth v. Nelson,* 514 Pa. 262, 523 A.2d 728, 733-34 (1987). The Pennsylvania court left the determination of the weight and credibility of the testimony regarding the marital stress and arguments to the trier of fact.

We are unpersuaded by that one case awash in a sea of opposite holdings, especially since a Maryland case counters *Nelson* by stating that "the long-smoldering grudge ⋯ may be psychologically just as compelling a force as the sudden impulse but it, unlike the impulse, is a telltale characteristic of premeditation." *Tripp v. State,* 36 Md.App. at 471-72, 374 A.2d 384. Aside from the cases, recognized legal authority in the form of treatises supports our holding. *Perkins on Criminal Law,* at p. 62, states that it is "with remarkable uniformity that even words generally regarded as 'fighting words' in the community have no recognition as adequate provocation in the eyes of the law." It is noted that

> mere words or gestures, however offensive, insulting, or abusive they may be, are not, according to the great weight of authority, adequate to reduce a homicide, although committed in a passion provoked by them, from murder to manslaughter, especially when

the homicide was intentionally committed with a deadly weapon[.] (Footnotes omitted)

40 C.J.S. *Homicide* § 47, at 909 (1944).
See also, 40 Am.Jur.2d *Homicide* § 64, at 357 (1968).

Thus, with no reservation, we hold that the provocation in this case was not enough to cause a reasonable man to stab his provoker 19 times. Although a psychologist testified to Steven's mental problems and his need for acceptance and love, we agree with the Court of Special Appeals speaking through Judge Moylan that "there must be not simply provocation in psychological fact, but one of certain fairly well-defined classes of provocation recognized as being adequate as a matter of law." *Tripp v. State,* 36 Md.App. at 473, 374 A.2d 384. The standard is one of reasonableness; it does not and should not focus on the peculiar frailties of mind of the Petitioner. That standard of reasonableness has not been met here. We cannot in good conscience countenance holding that a verbal domestic argument ending in the death of one spouse can result in a conviction of manslaughter. We agree with the trial judge that social necessity dictates our holding. Domestic arguments easily escalate into furious fights. We perceive no reason for a holding in favor of those who find the easiest way to end a domestic dispute is by killing the offending spouse.

We will leave to another day the possibility of expansion of the categories of adequate provocation to mitigate murder to manslaughter. The facts of this case do not warrant the broadening of the categories recognized thus far.

JUDGMENT AFFIRMED.

CASE END

Case Questions

Stewart v. States

1. What was Stewart's primary argument that he should not have been convicted of felony murder?

2. If the same crime had happened at common law, do you think the outcome of the case would have been the same? Explain.

3. What other examples of similar cases from throughout the country did the court cite to? What were the outcomes of those cases?

4. What facts of the case did the court use to support its ultimate decision as to whether Stewart's conviction for felony murder could stand? Do you agree with the court's conclusion? Explain.

Girourard v. State

1. What is the "Rule of Provocation"? Which specific element of that rule was at issue in this case?

2. What were some other examples given by the court of when words alone were insufficient to mitigate murder to manslaughter?

3. Do *all* states hold that words can never suffice to mitigate murder to manslaughter? Explain.

A Note to the Reader

In 2002 the Legislature enacted § 2-207(b), which states: "The discovery of one's spouse engaged in sexual intercourse with another does not constitute legally adequate provocation for the purpose of mitigating a killing from the crimes of murder to voluntary manslaughter even though the killing was provoked by that discovery." Notwithstanding that provision, the crux of the Court's opinion in *Girouard* that words alone can never serve as adequate provocation to mitigate murder to manslaughter still remains in full force and effect.

Additional Crimes to Consult

As discussed in the introduction to this Chapter, homicide is an extraordinarily complex subject and the Maryland Legislature has enacted numerous provisions in addition to the ones discussed in detail herein. For example, Md. Code Ann., Crim. Law § 2-209 proscribes manslaughter by vehicle or vessel. Within Title 2 of the Maryland Annotated Code, generally called "Homicide," appears Subtitle 3, which deals with specific guidelines for trials and sentencings for homicides, Subtitle 4, which is devoted to the death penalty, and Subtitle 5, which is devoted to Homicide by Motor Vehicle or Vessel While Impaired or Under the Influence.

HYPOTHETICAL #1

One day, Devious Dan decided he needed some extra cash and the best way to get that cash would be the illegal way. So, he planned to rob the America First bank in town. He planned his robbery very carefully—he loaded his handgun (just to scare the teller, you see Dan was actually very opposed to violence and had no desire to actually use the gun), he wrote the note that he would hand to the teller demanding money, and he got his ski cap and gloves together as his disguise. The next afternoon, Dan made his way into the America First bank. He walked up to Tammy the teller, raised his gun and pointed it at her head. He handed Tammy the note and an empty sack while whispering to her "Don't make a move honey and no one gets hurt, got that?" Tammy, obviously frightened, quickly began dumping all of the cash in her drawer into the sack. Unbeknownst to Dan, however, while putting the money in the bag Tammy also hit a panic button which silently alerted the bank security guard that a crime was in progress. Before Dan realized what was going on, Sam the security guard came running toward Dan with his weapon drawn shouting at Dan to drop his gun. At that point, all hell broke loose with the eruption of gunfire. When the smoke cleared, Sam and Tammy both lay still on the floor. Sam was dead, and Tammy was wounded. Dan was apprehended by police attempting to flee the bank. Ballistics testing revealed that Sam was killed by a bullet fired by Dan's gun, and Tammy was struck by a bullet fired by Sam's gun.

MAIN ISSUE

Did Dan Commit Felony Murder of Sam the Security Guard?

ISSUE	THESIS	RULE	ANALYSIS	CONCLUSION
Did Dan commit a felony WHEN he robbed the bank?	Dan committed a felony WHEN he robbed the bank.	In order to be charged with felony murder, the suspect must have committed an inherently dangerous FELONY with a substantial degree of risk of serious bodily harm.	Dan committed a felony when he robbed the bank BECAUSE robbery is an inherently dangerous felony subjected to felony murder according to the Maryland Legislature.	Dan committed a felony.
Did Dan kill Sam WHEN Dan shot him with the handgun?	Dan killed Sam WHEN Dan shot him with the handgun.	For felony murder, one of the felons must have actually CAUSED the death of the victim.	Dan caused Sam's death BECAUSE Dan shot Sam with his handgun.	Dan killed Sam.
Did Dan kill Sam during the commission or escape from the scene of the felony WHEN Dan shot Sam as Sam tried to prevent Dan from leaving the bank?	Dan killed Sam during the commission or escape from the scene of a felony WHEN Dan shot Sam as Sam tried to prevent Dan from leaving the bank.	For felony murder, the killing must occur either DURING THE COMMISSION or attempted commission of the felony or during the immediate escape therefrom.	Dan killed Sam during the commission of the robbery BECAUSE Dan was still in the bank and Sam attempted to prevent Dan from fleeing, thus the robbery was still in progress.	Dan killed Sam during the commission of a felony.

CONCLUSION

Dan committed felony murder of Sam when he killed Sam during the course of the bank robbery.

HYPOTHETICAL #2

Kim and Jeremy had been dating for several years, but they also had a very rocky relationship. They could never agree on whether to marry, whether to start a family, or where to live. So, their relationship was often very turbulent. One day, Kim informed Jeremy that she was pregnant with his child. Unbeknownst to Kim, Jeremy had secretly begun seeing someone new, so the last thing he needed was a baby on the way. Jeremy decided that he would literally "kill two birds with one stone." The next night when Jeremy was having dinner over Kim's apartment, he slipped some rat poisoning in Kim's iced tea. Kim immediately became violently ill and ran into the bathroom. In fact, she became so ill that she had to be taken to the hospital and was in intensive care for a week. Kim survived the incident but her unborn child did not. Kim was nine weeks pregnant at the time, and the obstetrician confirmed that the death of the fetus was due to the rat poisoning. Kim, completely distraught that she had lost her child, began having nightmares. Soon after, she had a nervous breakdown, she began drinking and then taking drugs. One day, approximately six months after that fateful night when Jeremy poisoned her iced tea, Kim overdosed on prescription pain killers and died. A note by her bedside read "I can't think about life without my child and I am going to be with my baby forever."

⊃   List the crimes with which Jeremy may be charged.

DEFENDANT	VICTIM	CRIMES
Jeremy	Kim	
Jeremy	Fetus	

⊃   For EACH crime identified, complete an Analysis Chart assessing the possibility of conviction.

DISCUSSION QUESTIONS

1. Revisit hypothetical #1. Suppose Tammy died as a result of her gunshot wound. In your opinion, do you think Dan should be charged with the felony murder of Tammy? What arguments support charging Dan with felony murder? What arguments go against charging Dan with felony murder? *See Campbell v. State*, 293 Md. 438, 444 A.2d 1034 (1982).

2. Still revisiting hypothetical #1, suppose that Dan did not rob the bank alone but instead with his partner Dave. While Dan approached the teller, Dave stood by the front door of the bank as a look-out, ready to warn Dan of any impending danger. Could Dave be charged with the felony murder of Sam even though Dan was the one who fired the bullet which killed Dave? Explain.

3. Is the individual who carries out a State sanctioned execution guilty of first-degree premeditated murder? Why or why not?

4. Bonnie and Clyde are two well known burglars in Maryland who have a very specific method of operation—they target single family homes during the day when no one is home, steal money and jewels, and leave without a trace. The pair have been committing these burglaries for several months. One day, they break into a house while ostensibly no one is home. Bonnie goes into the basement to look for valuables. Clyde heads to the second story bedrooms to do the same, but he notices a woman asleep in bed. Unbeknownst to Bonnie, Clyde rapes the woman and during the course of the struggle Clyde strangles the woman to death. Can Bonnie be charged with felony murder for the woman's death? *See Mumford v. State*, 19 Md.App. 640, 313 A.2d 563 (1974).

5. Tom had been stalking his ex-wife Sally for days threatening to harm her. One day, Tom approached Sally with a gun drawn and said "Now you're finally going to get what you've got coming!" Tom fired the gun, aiming directly at Sally's head. But, the bullet only grazed Sally's ear and subsequently struck Sam in the head, who was standing directly behind Sally. Sam was killed instantly. Tom wasn't even aware that Sam was standing there at the time. You are the prosecutor assigned to the case, what type of homicide would you charge Tom with and why? *See Poe v. State*, 341 Md. 523, 671 A.2d 501 (1996).

6. Ben intentionally shoots Jessica in the abdomen in an attempt to kill Jessica. Jessica is nine months pregnant at the time. Jessica dies immediately, but due to heroic efforts on the part of rescue personnel, her fetus is delivered by an emergency Cesarian section and survives for two days before eventually dying due to injuries sustained during the shooting. Can Ben be charged with the murder of the fetus? What if the fetus had been killed instantly, would your answer change? What if Jessica had been nine weeks pregnant rather than nine months pregnant at the time of the shooting? What if Ben had been unaware that Jessica was pregnant in any of the above scenarios, would your answer change? *See Williams v. State*, 77 Md.App. 411, 550 A.2d 722 (1988), and Md. Code Ann., Crim. Law § 2-103 (West Supp. 2009).

7. Larry intentionally runs over Harry with his car while Harry is walking down the street. Harry is severely injured and lapses into a coma due to his extensive injuries. Harry remains in a coma for over four years and then dies. Can Larry be charged with the murder of Harry? *See* Md. Code Ann., Crim. Law § 2-102 (West 2002).

8. Russell robs a bank while Rick waits outside the bank as the getaway driver. After the robbery, Russell jumps into the car, shouts "Go!" and Rick speeds away with the police in immediate pursuit. The police chase lasts for approximately fifteen minutes, and during the entire chase the police cruiser has its sirens blaring and lights flashing. Both vehicles reach speeds in excess of 90 miles per hour. All of a sudden, Edna, an elderly woman, crosses the street in front of Rick's speeding vehicle. Rick runs over Edna and kills her. What type of homicide could Rick be charged with? What type of homicide would Russell be charged with? Explain.

9. What examples of real life situations can you think of that would constitute depraved heart murder? *See, e.g., Alston v. State*, 101 Md.App. 47, 643 A.2d 468 (1994), *aff'd*, 339 Md. 306, 662 A.2d 247 (1995).

10. Charlie is suspected of poisoning his wife Charlotte and dumping her body in the Chesapeake Bay. Despite extensive search efforts, Charlotte's body is never recovered. Can Charlie be charged with Charlotte's murder despite the lack of a corpse? *See Riggins v. State*, 155 Md.App. 181, 843 A.2d 115 (2004).

11. In Maryland, which homicide offenses are subjected to the death penalty as a possible punishment? *See* Md. Code Ann., Crim. Law § 2-201(b)(1) (West 2002).

12. Marty, who lives in Montana, makes a bomb, wraps it up in a package, and mails it to Mitchell, who lives in Maryland. When Mitchell retrieves his mail from the post office he takes the package, brings it back to his house and opens it. The package explodes and Mitchell suffers severe burns. Mitchell is transported by helicopter to the nearest hospital, which is in Delaware. Mitchell dies from his injuries while in the hospital. Which State has jurisdiction to prosecute Marty for the murder of Mitchell? Does federal jurisdiction also exist? Explain. *See Stout v. State*, 76 Md. 317, 25 A. 299 (1892).

13. If a prosecutor charges the defendant with first-degree murder, is the defendant entitled to a second-degree murder or manslaughter instruction and could she be convicted of the lesser murder or manslaughter offense? Explain.

TEST BANK

True/False

_____ 1. Second-degree depraved heart murder is an intentional homicide.

_____ 2. A contract murder (i.e., murder for hire) is an example of first-degree premeditated murder.

_____ 3. Every type of murder has malice as the intent of the perpetrator.

_____ 4. Words alone can never serve as legally adequate provocation to mitigate murder to manslaughter.

_____ 5. The difference between first-degree premeditated murder and first-degree felony murder is that the former is intentional while the latter is unintentional.

MULTIPLE CHOICE

6. In order to commit the crime of first-degree murder, which of the following WOULD NOT be a sufficient amount of time to think about committing the crime in advance to constitute "premeditation":

   A. An hour

   B. Fifteen minutes

   C. 45 seconds

   D. Any of the previous answers could be a sufficient amount of time to form premeditation

7. Jennifer and Wanda are long time rivals. One day while at a fair, the two start a fist fight—both are punching each other, pulling hair, and screaming. Out of nowhere, Jennifer pulls a knife from her pocket and stabs Wanda in the neck. Wanda bleeds to death within seconds. In Maryland, the crime for which Jennifer would *most likely* be convicted based on the facts is:

   A. First-degree murder

   B. Second-degree murder

   C. Depraved heart murder

   D. Felony murder

8. Sam is standing on top of Baltimore's World Trade Center. Sam thinks it would be funny to push off of the top a piano, although Sam doesn't want anyone to get hurt and he honestly doesn't think anyone will be hurt. Sam just wants to see the panic in the streets. Much to Sam's surprise, seven people are crushed and killed when the piano hits the street below. The crime for which Sam would *most likely* be convicted is:

    A. First-degree murder

    B. Manslaughter

    C. Depraved heart murder

    D. Felony murder

9. Which of the following statements is accurate?

    A. Murder has malice while manslaughter does not

    B. Manslaughter has malice while murder does not

    C. Murder always has premeditation while manslaughter never does

    D. Manslaughter always has premeditation while murder never does

10. Tom, Dick, and Jane rob a liquor store. Jane waits in the car as the get-away driver, Dick waits immediately inside of the store as the look-out, and Tom robs the cashier. During the robbery, Tom accidentally shoots the cashier and kills him when Tom's gun discharges while Tom is trying to scare the cashier. Who is guilty of felony murder?

    A. Tom

    B. Tom and Dick

    C. Tom, Dick, and Jane

    D. None of them because the shooting was accidental

chapter four

Rape and Sexual Offenses

Introduction

This chapter covers rape and sexual offenses. This will include first and second degree rape, and first through fourth degree sexual offenses. Please keep in mind that in understanding the specifics of various criminal laws, it is necessary to discuss a suspect's actions in detail and analyze the applicable laws. Some of the actions may be shocking, but unfortunately, your readings and hypotheticals are based upon what happens in the real world. Sometimes, we will try to use some humor in our hypotheticals to inject some levity and prevent one from becoming overwhelmed by the gravity of these crimes.

Focus Crimes

1st Degree Rape—Md. Code Ann., Crim. Law § 3-303 (West 2002); MPJI-Cr. 4:29.1.

2nd Degree Rape—Md. Code Ann., Crim. Law § 3-304(a)(1) (West 2002); MPJI-Cr. 4:29.

1st Degree Sexual Offense—Md. Code Ann., Crim. Law § 3-305 (West 2002); MPJI-Cr. 4.29.5.

2nd Degree Sexual Offense—Md. Code Ann., Crim. Law § 3-306(a)(1) (West 2002); MPJI-Cr. 4.29.4.

3rd Degree Sexual Offense—Md. Code Ann., Crim. Law § 3-307(a)(1) (West 2002); MPJI-Cr. 4.29.7.

4th Degree Sexual Offense—Md. Code Ann., Crim. Law § 3-308(a)(1) (West 2002); MPJI-Cr. 4.29.9.

Objectives

Upon completing this chapter, you should be able to:

- ◌ Distinguish between rape, sexual acts, and sexual contact;
- ◌ Compare and contrast the use of an aggravator during the commission of a sexual offense and no use of aggravator; be able to identify what the potential aggravators are and the legal consequences of the use of an aggravator;
- ◌ Explain the concept that some sexual offenses, though consensual in nature, are still criminal;
- ◌ Explain the concept of marital rape; and
- ◌ Analyze hypotheticals, identifying crimes, identifying elements of such crimes, and applying the facts to each element.

Rape and Sexual Offense Chart

	FORCIBLE	AGE	INCAPACITATION

First Degree Rape	1. vaginal intercourse;
	2. by force or threat of force;
	3. without consent of victim; and
	4. one of the following aggravators exist:
	  a. employs or displays a dangerous or deadly weapon or an article that the defendant believes was a dangerous and deadly weapon;
	  b. inflicts suffocation, strangulation, disfigurement or serious physical injury upon the victim or anyone else in the course of the offense;
	  c. threatens or places the victim in fear that the victim or any person known to the victim will be imminently subjected to death, suffocation, strangulation, disfigurement, serious physical injury, or kidnapping;
	  d. the person commits the offense aided and abetted by one or more other persons; or
	  e. the person commits the offense in connection with a burglary in the first, second, or third degree		

Second Degree Rape	1. vaginal intercourse; 2. by force or threat of force; and 3. without consent of victim	1. vaginal intercourse; 2. with victim under 14 years of age; and 3. suspect at least 4 years older than victim	1. vaginal intercourse; 2. with victim who is mentally defective, mentally incapacitated, or physically helpless; and 3. suspect knows or should reasonably know that the other person is mentally defective, mentally incapacitated, or physically helpless

	FORCIBLE	AGE	INCAPACITATION	PENALTY

First Degree Sexual Offense	1. sexual act with victim;
	2. by force or threat of force;
	3. without consent of victim; and
	4. one of the following aggravators exist:
	  a. employs or displays a dangerous or deadly weapon or an article that the defendant believes was a dangerous and deadly weapon;
	  b. inflicts suffocation, strangulation, disfigurement or serious physical injury upon the victim or anyone else in the course of the offense;
	  c. threatens or places the victim in fear that the victim or any person known to the victim will be imminently subjected to death, suffocation, trangulation, disfigurement, serious physical injury, or kidnapping;
	  d. the person commits the offense aided and abetted by one or more other persons; or
	  e. the person commits the offense in connection with a burglary in the first, second, or third degree
				Generally imprisonment for no more than natural life, except if the victim was a child under 16 years of age and violation of other sections . . . the defendant may be sentenced to life without possibility of parole

Second Degree Sexual Offense	1. sexual act; 2. by force or threat of force; and 3. without consent of victim	1. sexual act; 2. with victim under 14 years of age; and 3. suspect at least 4 years older than victim	1. sexual act; 2. with victim who is mentally defective, mentally incapacitated, or physically helpless; and 3. suspect knows or should reasonably know that the other person is mentally defective, mentally incapacitated, or physically helpless	Not more than 20 years

Rape and Sexual Offense Chart (continued)

	FORCIBLE	AGE	INCAPACITATION	PENALTY

Third Degree Sexual Offense	1. sexual contact with victim;
	2. against the will and consent of the victim; and
	3. one of the following aggravators are present:
	  a. employs or displays a dangerous or deadly weapon or an article that the defendant believes was a dangerous and deadly weapon;
	  b. inflicts suffocation, strangulation, disfigurement or serious physical injury upon the victim or anyone else in the course of the offense;
	  c. threatens or places the victim in fear that the victim or any person known to the victim will be imminently subjected to death, suffocation, strangulation, disfigurement, serious physical injury, or kidnapping; or
	  d. the person commits the offense aided and abetted by one or more other persons
		3 Types
		A. Under 14
		1. sexual contact;
		2. with victim under 14 years of age; and
		3. suspect at least 4 years older than victim
		
		B. 14–15 Sexual Act
		1. sexual act;
		2. with victim age 14–15; and
		3. suspect at least 21 years of age
		
		C. 14–15 Intercourse
		1. vaginal intercourse;
		2. with victim age 14–15; and
		3. suspect at least 21 years of age
			1. sexual contact;
			2. with victim who is mentally defective, mentally incapacitated, or physically helpless; and
			3. suspect knows or should reasonably know that the other person is mentally defective, mentally incapacitated, or physically helpless
				Not more than 10 years

Fourth Degree Sexual Offense	1. sexual contact with victim; and 2. against the will and consent of the victim	**2 Types** *A. Sexual Act* 1. sexual act; 2. with victim 14–15 years of age; and 3. suspect at least 4 years older than victim but still under 21 *B. Intercourse* 1. vaginal intercourse; 2. with victim 14–15 years of age; and 3. suspect at least 4 years older than victim but still under 21		Misdemeanor Not more than 1 year imprisonment Fine of not more than $1000 or Both fine and imprisonment

CASE LAW

State v. Baby, 404 Md. 220, 946 A.2d 463 (2007)

. . . In December 2003, Appellee, Maouloud Baby, was indicted for first degree rape, first degree sexual offense, attempted first degree sexual offense, conspiracy to commit first degree rape, and third degree sexual offense. Baby was initially tried in the Circuit Court for Montgomery County in 2004, but a mistrial was declared because of a hung jury. Baby was retried on December 13–17 and 20–21, 2004 before a jury on two counts of first degree rape, one count of attempted first degree rape, one count of first degree sexual assault, one count of attempted first degree sexual offense, one count of conspiracy to commit first degree rape, and

two counts of third degree sexual offense. He was convicted of one count of first degree rape, one count of first degree sexual offense, and two counts of third degree sexual offense. . . .

At trial, the complaining witness ("J.L.") testified that on the night of December 13, 2003, she and her best friend, Lacey, went to Best Buy and purchased CDs and then drove in J.L.'s car to the McDonald's restaurant in Montgomery Village. Inside the McDonald's, they encountered some of Lacey's brother's friends, including Baby and Mike. J.L. recognized Baby from high school but did not otherwise know him.

J.L. further testified that she and Lacey left the Mc-Donald's, went outside, and entered J.L.'s car, at which time Mike asked J.L. if she could give him and Baby a ride to a party. J.L. agreed, and allowed Baby, Mike, and an unidentified "Hispanic boy," to ride in the back seat of the car. On the way to the party, Baby instructed J.L. to stop at a gas station, which she did, where Baby and the Hispanic boy got out of the car. Although Baby returned to the car approximately one minute later, the Hispanic boy did not return.

J.L. said that the remaining four continued to drive to the party, which took approximately ten to fifteen minutes. Baby and Mike decided not to attend the party. J.L. stated that she drove back to the McDonald's, planning to drop Baby and Mike off there. During the trip back to the restaurant, Baby told J.L. to turn into a residential development and directed her to a parking spot. All four alighted from the vehicle and walked towards a clearing between two end townhouses. Baby and Mike smoked marijuana and engaged J.L. and Lacey in conversation. Baby and Mike discussed getting a hotel room, noting that J.L. and Lacey were both 18 and old enough to do so. Neither J.L. nor Lacey expressed interest.

J.L. further testified that, after the four returned to the McDonald's, Lacey left the group, but Baby and Mike stated that they did not want to leave the car. Lacey gave J.L. her cell phone, which she placed on the passenger seat. J.L. agreed to drive Baby and Mike to a residential neighborhood. Upon their arrival, she parked her car, whereupon Baby and Mike asked J.L. to sit between them in the back seat so they could talk. J.L. climbed into the back seat and sat between the two. She removed her jacket because she was warm. Baby then put his hand between her legs and Mike tried to put J.L.'s hand down his pants. Baby told J.L. to "flash him" and Mike told her to "just lick it." When J.L. did not comply with their requests, Baby began to fondle her breast with his hand.

J.L. also testified that she told Baby and Mike that they had to return to the McDonald's, but they asked to stay ten more minutes. J.L. then "somehow ended up on [her] back," at which point Baby attempted to remove her pants and Mike tried to place his penis in her mouth. J.L. told them to stop, but Baby and Mike moved her around so that her body was against Baby. Baby then held her arms as Mike attempted to have intercourse, briefly inserting his penis mistakenly into her rectum. Mike again unsuccessfully attempted intercourse, and Baby inserted his fingers into J.L.'s vagina.

J.L. further testified that Baby then got out of the car. Mike inserted his fingers and then his penis into

J.L.'s vagina. Mike then left the automobile and Baby got into the car. J.L. testified that Baby told her "it's my turn now." According to J.L., the following then transpired:

Q. [ASSISTANT STATE'S ATTORNEY]: And what else did he say?

A. He, after that we sat there for a couple seconds and he was like so are you going to let me hit it and I didn't really say anything and he was like I don't want to rape you.

Q. And what did you say?

A. . . . [W]ell first of all they told me that . . . I wouldn't be able to leave until I was done . . .

Q. They had told you that?

A. Huh?

Q. They had told you that you would not be able to leave?

A. Yes, earlier. They were just, they were like you can leave as soon as we're done.

Q. And by that you assumed what or that you understood that to mean what?

A. That as soon as I finished whatever they told me to do, I could leave.

Q. So when [Baby] said I don't want to rape you, did you respond?

A. Yes. I said that as long as he stops when I tell him to, then

—

Q. Now, that he could?

A. Yes.

Q. Now, [J.L.], at the time that [Baby] got back in the car, how were you feeling?

A. I don't know.

Q. Did you feel like you had a choice?

A. Not really. I don't know. Something just clicked off and I just did whatever they said.

Q. Were you tired?

A. Yes.

Q. Did you want to go home?

A. I just wanted to go home.

Q. Now when you told [Baby] if I say stop, something like that, you have to stop. What did he do after you spoke those words?

A. Well he got on top of me and he tried to put it in and it hurt. So I said stop and that's when he kept pushing it in and I was pushing his knees to get off me.

Q. You were on your back and he was on top of you?

A. Yes.

Q. Did he stop pushing his penis into your vagina?

A. Not right away.

Q. About how long did he continue to push his penis into your vagina?

A. About five or so seconds.

Q. And then what happened?

A. And that's when he just got off me and that's when Mike got in the car and—

Q. Let me stop you for a minute. When he was, he put himself in you and you said, ow, it hurts, stop—

A. Yeah.

Q. —did he stop?

A. No.

Q. How many times did you tell him to stop?

A. I, well I yelled stop, that it hurt, and I was pushing him off me.

Q. And he didn't stop—

A. No.

Q. —until at some point he did?

A. Yes.

J.L. also stated that Mike, without her permission, then drove the car to a neighborhood across the street from the McDonald's. During the drive, Baby asked J.L. to "jack him off" and she declined. She did give Baby her phone number when he requested it. Baby returned Lacey's cell phone to J.L., which he or Mike had taken from her previously, and J.L. used it to call Lacey. The two women spoke briefly. Mike parked the car across from the McDonald's and hugged J.L. before he and Baby departed.

J.L. then drove to the McDonald's to pick up Lacey. They then drove to Shoppers Food Warehouse, where they met J.L.'s mother to shop for groceries. After the grocery shopping, J.L. and Lacey proceeded to Lacey's home where J.L. told Lacey's mother what had occurred. The police were called, whereupon J.L. went to the hospital to be examined.

Baby also testified at trial and his testimony was similar to that of J.L., except his recollection of the events that occurred in J.L.'s car after they had dropped off Lacey at the McDonald's:

Q. [BABY'S COUNSEL]: Before you got out of the car, did you touch [J.L.] in any way?

A. No, I didn't.

Q. Hold her?

A. No.

Q. Grab her?

A. No.

Q. Did you take your penis out before you got out of the car?

A. No, I didn't.

Q. Did you see [Mike's] penis before you got out of the car?

A. No, I didn't.

Q. Did you have any contact with [J.L.] prior to getting out of the car?

A. No contact prior to getting out of the car.

Q. What happened after you sat there for that amount of time?

A. After I sat, Mike got out of the car and, while I was walking towards the car, he told me that, he said in quote that he "just hit that," which means he just had sex with her. So, then I got in the car, and right when I sat down in the car, she was sitting on the driver's side of the car.

Q. What did that mean to you when Mike said he "just hit that"?

A. He just had sex with her.

Q. Which side did he get out?

A. He got out of the driver's side.

Q. And what side did you get in?

A. I was in the, I got in from the driver's side, too.

Q. When she was sitting there, was she dressed?

A. She didn't have nothing on but her shirt.

Q. How did she appear?

A. She appeared normal.

Q. Was she crying?

A. No, she wasn't.

Q. When you got in the car, what, if anything, did you say or do?

A. I asked her if she was going to let me have sex with her.

Q. What exactly did you say?

A. I said, "Are you going to let me hit that?"

Q. And what does that mean to you, "Can I hit that?"

A. Have sex.

Q. What, if anything, did she say?

A. She said yes, as long as I stop when she says to. And then I said, "I'm not going to rape you."

Q. Did you feel that was permission?

A. Yeah, I thought that that was permission.

Q. Why did you say "I don't want to rape you"?

A. Just to, because she said, "Stop when I say to," just to tell her that. It's kind of like to confirm the permission.

Q. So, after she said "Stop when I say stop," what did you do, if anything?

A. That's when I took off the condom, I mean, I took the condom out of my pocket and I ripped it open, I put on the condom, put the condom, threw the condom, like, on the floor, on her door, and she picked it up and told me to throw it out the window. …

A. She was, first she was sitting in the car when we was talking, and then she was still sitting when I put on the condom. But then after, when I was trying to go in there, she was like laying down in the car in the backseat.

Q. What did you do physically?

A. I placed myself in between her legs and then I tried to put it in….

Q. What did you do with your penis?

A. I tried to put it in.

Q. Do you know where it was touching or what happened to it?

A. No. After I tried to put it in once, it wouldn't go in, and I tried a couple more times and it wouldn't go in. I didn't feel nothing there.

Q. What happened? What did she say or do?

A. And then she sat up. She was like, "It's not going to go in," and that's when, after she sat up and said "It's not going to go in," that's when I took off the condom and I put it in my pocket and then knocked on the window for Michael to come in.

Q. Who said, "It's not going to go in?" You or her?

A. She did.

Q. When she sat up, what did that mean to you?

A. That meant stop.

Q. Did she say "Stop"?

A. No, she didn't. She just sat up.

Q. And you took that to mean stop?

A. Yeah.

Q. When she sat up, did you try to put it in again?

A. No, I didn't. . . .

The trial court instructed the jury on the elements of first degree rape, using language substantively similar to that in the pattern jury instructions. After the jurors began deliberation, they initially submitted two notes which related to the duration of their discussion. A short time later, the jury submitted a third note which was read into the record: "If a female consents to sex initially and, during the course of the sex act to which she consented, for whatever reason, she changes her mind and the man continues until climax, does the result constitute rape?" . . .

THE COURT: . . . All right. How is this: "I am unable to answer this question as posed. Please reread the instructions as to each element and apply the law to the facts as you find them"?

[BABY'S COUNSEL]: Judge, it seems to me the note indicates that the female in the note consented to penetration.

THE COURT: I hear you, but I don't think that is an absolute. I don't think you can necessarily know what they mean by that note. That is the problem. They have to decide the facts, apply the law to the facts.

The following morning, the jury submitted another note which read, "If at any time the woman says stop is that rape?" Baby's counsel requested that the court provide the jury with "the exact answer that you gave to the note last night." The court replied, "Right. This is the same question in simpler form or at least a variation of the same question." The court then instructed the jury, "This is a question that you as a jury must decide. I have given the legal definition of rape which includes the definition of consent."

On December 21, 2004, the jury found Baby guilty "[a]s to Count I, First Degree Rape (Being aided and abetted by [Mike] in the act of vaginal penetration)," guilty "[a]s to Count II, First Degree Sexual Assault (Aiding and abetting [Mike] in the act of anal penetration)," guilty "[a]s to Count V, Third Degree Sexual Offense (touched vagina)," and guilty "[a]s to Count VI, Third Degree Sexual Offense (touched breast)." The jury found Baby not guilty of one count of first degree rape, of one count of attempted first degree sexual offense, and of one count of conspiracy to commit first degree rape. On February 17, 2005, Baby was sentenced to fifteen years imprisonment, with all but five years suspended, and five years probation upon release. . . .

Thereafter, the State filed a Petition for Writ of Certiorari, raising the following two questions for our review:

1. If a woman initially consents to vaginal intercourse, withdraws consent after penetration, and then is forced to continue intercourse against her will, is she a victim of rape? . . .

I. The Rape Conviction and the Jury Instruction

In this case, the Court of Special Appeals held that if a woman "consents [to sexual intercourse] prior to penetration and withdraws the consent following penetration, there is no rape." *Baby,* 172 Md.App. at 617, 916 A.2d at 427. In so concluding, the intermediate appellate court relied on what it characterized as a holding in *Battle,* 287 Md. at 675, 414 A.2d at 1266, and determined that it was a correct statement of the common law of rape.

In *Battle,* the victim met John Battle when she parked her car at a service station near the Pimlico Race Track. When she returned to her car after visiting the Track, she discovered that Battle, who was in charge of parking, had washed her car. Upon learning that she did not have any money to pay him, Battle suggested that she "drive [him] past home" and told her where he lived. *Id.* at 677, 414 A.2d at 1267 (alteration in original). She informed him that she did not have enough gas to do so, and he provided her with a couple of dollars with which to purchase fuel. She testified that on the way to his home they discussed a radio that he wanted to sell, and she accepted his invitation to examine the radio and determine if she wanted to purchase it.

Upon reaching his home, she accompanied Battle upstairs to his room to look at the radio. She testified that once they were upstairs he struck her and ordered her to remove her clothing. She responded "You got to be kidding," but he pulled a screwdriver from his pocket and put it against her head and again ordered her take off her clothes. *Id.* She testified that "he said he would kill me because he killed one time and he said he would kill again." *Id.* In fear for her safety, she took off her clothes, got in bed with him, and had vaginal intercourse.

While she and Battle were having intercourse, a persistent knocking was heard at the downstairs door. The victim testified that when Battle went to answer the door, she went to a room across the hall from his bedroom and attempted to summon help. She stated that "I was getting ready to get out of the window on the roof and he came in and caught me and pulled me back in and hit me." *Id.* at 678, 414 A.2d at 1267. Battle then dragged her back into bed and disrobed himself and her. There was again the sound of someone at the door; when Battle answered the door, the victim was able to attract the attention of some nearby children who summoned the police to rescue her.

Conversely, Battle testified that the victim asked him to have sexual intercourse with her. He said that he found her disrobed in his bedroom but denied that any sexual contact occurred.

After a period of deliberation, the jury addressed a written question to the trial judge, asking: "When a *possible* sexual consensual relationship becomes non-consensual for some reason, during the course of the action—can the act then be considered rape?" *Id.* at 678, 414 A.2d at 1268 (emphasis in original). Because the trial judge was not certain that she understood the question, she inquired of the jury whether the question asked was "where the original act of sex is by consent whether is it then possible the circumstances could change because of the victim's lack of consent after the original situation began as a consensual one," and the jury replied that that was what was meant. *Id.* The trial judge then told them, "I will answer your question by saying, 'Yes, that it is possible for a situation to start out as consensual and then become a non-consensual one in the course of the event,'" *id.*, and continued with language taken from *Hazel v. State,* 221 Md. 464, 469, 157 A.2d 922, 925 (1960), in which this Court stated:

> With respect to the presence or absence of the element of consent, it is true, of course, that however reluctantly given, consent to the act at any time prior to penetration deprives the subsequent intercourse of its criminal character. There is, however, a wide difference between consent and submission to the act. Consent may involve submission, but submission does not necessarily imply consent. Furthermore, sub-

mission to a compelling force, or as a result of being put in fear, is not consent.

The trial judge then added, "It is not altogether clear as to what degree of resistance is necessary to establish the absence of consent; that is a question that you . . . would have to determine on the basis of the evidence that you have heard during the course of trial." *Battle,* 287 Md. at 679, 414 A.2d at 1268. She also provided additional instructions related to fear and resistance.

When counsel were asked whether they had any objection to the court's instructions, defense counsel stated that he thought that in the jury's question, "during the course of the action" referred specifically to intercourse and that once intercourse has commenced one cannot withdraw consent "and start screaming rape." *Id.* at 679-80, 414 A.2d at 1268. The State suggested that the term also could have referred to the "whole chain of events, from the time the victim got to the parking lot" or to a time after the parties "got in the bedroom or maybe after they had sex." *Id.* at 680, 414 A.2d at 1268.

In determining whether the trial court correctly responded to the jury's instruction, this Court began by stating that Maryland's statutory definition of rape was an outgrowth of the common law definition of rape interpreted in *Hazel.* We then engaged in a review of the history of rape in American common law. From our review, we concluded that "consent subsequent to the act of intercourse will not prevent its being rape." *Battle,* 287 Md. at 681, 414 A.2d at 1269.

We then turned to the question of "the effect of a withdrawal of consent prior to penetration," *id.* at 683, 414 A.2d at 1270 . . . We concluded that, "[g]iven the fact that consent must precede penetration, it follows in our view that although a woman may have consented to a sexual encounter, even to intercourse, if that consent is withdrawn prior to the act of penetration, then it cannot be said that she has consented to sexual intercourse." *Battle,* 287 Md. at 684, 414 A.2d at 1270. We then continued: "On the other hand, *ordinarily* if she consents prior to penetration and withdraws the consent following penetration, there is no rape." *Id.* (emphasis added).

We held that "the combination of the ambiguous [jury] question, ambiguously clarified by the trial judge, and the answer create sufficient confusion in this case to warrant reversal and a remand for a new trial." *Id.* at 685, A.2d at 1271 . . .

Our statement in *Battle,* 287 Md. at 684, 414 A.2d at 1270, that "ordinarily, if she consents prior to penetration and withdraws the consent following penetration, there is no rape," is properly characterized as *obiter dictum* and will not be afforded precedential weight. It was not made on a point that was argued by counsel and deliberately addressed by this Court, but rather was a collateral statement. Most important is the fact that our decision in *Battle* was not dependent upon this statement; the holding would indeed be unaffected were that language to be removed.

Additionally, the sentence in issue appears to be tacked on as an articulation of the converse of the Court's previous statement, although one should note, a converse which is predicated by the term "ordinarily." That the converse is not subjected to any analysis as to its application provides further support for the proposition that it is merely *obiter dictum,* and not part of our holding in *Battle.*

The sole issue before us in *Battle* was whether withdrawal of consent before penetration, followed by vaginal intercourse accomplished through force or threat of force, constituted rape. In addressing this issue, we relied upon 19th century commentaries and an analysis of the decisions of courts in our sister States to bulwark our conclusion. The Court of Special Appeals in this case, in turn, in addressing the issue of post-penetration withdrawal of consent, appropriately looked to the common law for guidance. The intermediate appellate court relied on the *Battle* analysis, and it is this reliance on our historical analysis in *Battle* as applicable to the present case, with which we disagree. It is proverbially mixing apples and oranges, because the analysis in *Battle* only addressed the withdrawal of consent before penetration and was not extensive enough to be applicable to the issue of post-penetration withdrawal of consent. . . .

. . . [W]e hold that a woman may withdraw consent for vaginal intercourse after penetration has occurred and that, after consent has been withdrawn, the continuation of vaginal intercourse by force or the threat of force may constitute rape. We iterate that force or the threat of force is, however, an essential element of the crime of rape as we first emphasized in *Hazel,* 221 Md. at 469, 157 A.2d at 925:

> Force is an essential element of the crime and to justify a conviction, the evidence must warrant a conclusion either that the victim resisted and her resistance was overcome by force or that she was prevented from resisting by threats to her safety. But no particular amount of force, either actual or constructive, is required to constitute rape. Necessarily that fact must depend on the prevailing circumstances. . . . [F]orce may exist without violence. If the acts and threats of the defendant were reasonably calculated to create in the mind of the victim—having regard to the circumstances in which she was placed—a real apprehension, due to fear, of imminent bodily harm, serious enough to impair or overcome her will to resist, then such acts and threats are the equivalent of force. . . .

We, nevertheless, agree with the Court of Special Appeals that, in responding to the jury's questions, the trial court should have directly addressed the jurors' confusion on the effect of withdrawal of consent during intercourse, rather than simply referring the jurors to previously provided instructions on the elements of rape. . . .

Conclusion

We conclude that post-penetration withdrawal of consent negates initial consent for the purposes of sexual offense crimes and, when coupled with the other elements, may constitute the crime of rape. We also hold, however, that the trial court erred in failing to sufficiently address the jury's questions on post-penetration withdrawal of consent, and such error was not harmless beyond a reasonable doubt.

CASE END

Case Questions

Baby v. State

1. What were the facts in *Battle v. State*?

2. How was the issue before the court in *Battle* different from the issue before it in *Baby*?

3. What practical problems do you foresee with the court's holding in terms of prosecuting rape cases where the timing of consent is at issue?

4. Do you agree with the court's holding? Why or why not?

Additional Crimes to Consult

In addition to force/violence based sex crimes, there are also sex crimes based upon some type of incapacity, including young age, mental incapacity, and physical incapacity, that prevents the victim from being able to knowingly and voluntarily consent to the intercourse, sexual act or sexual contact. These incapacity based crimes are briefly discussed in the Rape & Sexual Offense Chart in this chapter. Additionally, Maryland's legislature has codified attempt crimes as they relate to sexual conduct, *see*, Md. Code Ann., Crim. Law § 3-310–3-312; provided for enhanced penalties for repeat offenders, *see*, Md. Code Ann., Crim. Law § 3-313; and have also made special provisions and penalties for sex crimes against children, *see*, Md. Code Ann., Crim. Law § 3-314–3-315.

HYPOTHETICAL #1

Brandy frequented the Fells Point bars and had a reputation as a tramp. During happy hour, she started flirting with a handsome devil named Harley. As happy hour wound down, Harley asked Brandy if he could walk her to her car and Brandy agreed. Harley asked Brandy the direction in which she was driving and after she responded, Harley requested a ride to his apartment. Brandy agreed but cautioned Harley on the way to the car that she was just giving him a ride home as a friend and that Harley should expect nothing more.

On the way to Harley's apartment, they continued the general conversation that they had started in the bar. After a long drive, they arrived at Harley's apartment. Brandy was totally unfamiliar with the area. She pulled the car at the curb and left the engine running. Harley asked Brandy to come in but she refused. Harley then reached over and turned off the ignition to Brandy's car and took her car keys. He got out of the car, walked over to her side, opened the door and said, "Now, will you come up?"

Brandy was unsure of whether she should run or comply with Harley's request. Brandy feared that Harley would rape her. Brandy accompanied Harley across the street and up to his one room flat. Harley asked Brandy to sit down on the bed. They talked for awhile and then Harley went to get some drinks for them. When Harley returned with the drinks, Brandy asked if she could leave. Harley still had Brandy's keys and responded by sitting on the bed with her and hugging her. Harley then undressed Brandy. Brandy again asked to leave. However, Harley had a strange look in his eyes and did not respond. Brandy started to cry. Harley then put his hands on Brandy's throat, just lightly choking her. Brandy then said, "If I do what you want, will you let me go without killing me?" Harley said "You can go whenever you want." As he said this, he inserted his penis into her vagina.

Immediately after Harley ejaculated, Brandy asked if she could leave. Harley said, "Yes," and tossed her car keys on the bed. Brandy got dressed and asked for directions to the highway. Harley drew her a map and walked her to her car. He asked Brandy if he could see her again, and although she had no intention of seeing him again, she said "Yes." Brandy drove from Harley's flat to the police station and reported that she had been raped. The police took Brandy to the hospital and a rape examination was performed. The examination showed that Brandy had recently had sexual intercourse, but that there was no tearing or trauma to her genitals. Semen was present in Brandy's vagina. DNA testing revealed that it was Harley's semen. The police arrested Harley and charged him with several crimes, including second degree rape.

MAIN ISSUE

Did Harley Commit a Second Degree Rape Based Upon Use of Force?

ISSUE	THESIS	RULE	ANALYSIS	CONCLUSION
Did Harley have vaginal intercourse with Brandy WHEN he inserted his penis into her vagina?	Harley had vaginal intercourse with Brandy WHEN he inserted his penis into her vagina.	VAGINAL INTERCOURSE—Penile penetration of the vagina. Only slight penetration is necessary and emission of semen is not required.	There is evidence that Harley had vaginal intercourse with Brandy BECAUSE Brandy testified that Harley put his penis into her vagina. It is also corroborated by the medical examination which revealed that Brandy had recently had sexual intercourse and that Harley's semen was present in Brandy's vagina.	Harley had vaginal intercourse with Brandy.
Did Harley have vaginal intercourse with Brandy by force or threat of force WHEN he took her keys, preventing her from leaving, and lightly choked her?	Harley most likely had vaginal intercourse with Brandy by force or threat of force WHEN he took her keys, preventing her from leaving, and lightly choked her.	BY FORCE OR THREAT OF FORCE—The only force necessary is that which is sufficient to overcome the resistance of the victim. The victim must have resisted and her resistance was overcome by force or threat of force or that the perpetrator's force or threat of force prevented the victim from resisting. The victim's fear that prevented her from resisting must have been reasonable under the circumstance.	It is possible that the prosecution can prove that Harley used force BECAUSE he "put his hands on Brandy's throat, just lightly choking her." However, after he put his hand on her throat, he told Brandy she could leave whenever she wanted. There was no medical evidence of trauma to Brandy's genitals. However, the force does not have to be in the sex act itself. Rather, force or threat of force can be used to otherwise accomplish the sex act. Although Brandy did not resist and, in fact complied with Harley's requests throughout the evening, it is evident that Brandy was fearful because she asked "If I do what you want, will you let me go without killing me?" She also indicated that when he took her keys, she was afraid he would rape her. Such fear was most likely reasonable under the circumstances, since he had taken Brandy's keys and had lightly choked her.	Harley most likely used force or threat of force against Brandy.
Did Harley have vaginal intercourse with Brandy without Brandy's consent WHEN Brandy submitted to the act because Harley choked her and she was fearful of Harley?	Harley had vaginal intercourse with Brandy without Brandy's consent WHEN Brandy submitted to the act because Harley choked her and she was fearful of Harley.	WITHOUT CONSENT OF VICTIM—Submission as a result of force or threat of force is not consent. Consent must be knowingly and voluntarily given.	Brandy did not consent BECAUSE although Brandy did not leave Harley's flat at any point, even after he told her she could leave whenever she wanted, her fear of Harley killing her and Harley lightly choking her may have caused her to submit to vaginal intercourse rather than consent to it.	Brandy did not consent to vaginal intercourse with Harley.

CONCLUSION

Harley most likely committed a second degree rape of Brandy because he used force and threat of force to have sexual intercourse with Brandy.

HYPOTHETICAL #2

Dan and Stan Baker are 21-year-old twins. Because they are notorious throughout their community for getting into minor scuffles with the law, they have earned the nickname "the Trouble-Maker Bakers." Although they usually commit relatively minor pranks such as vandalism, on this particular occasion they got in over their heads. Next door to the Bakers lives a family with two beautiful young girls—Ashley, who is 19, and Amanda, who is 13. Both are extremely attractive and popular. Ashley is known to be somewhat on the "wild side," but Amanda is as pure as the driven snow.

One day, the Trouble-Maker Bakers decided that they were going to have some "fun" with the girls next door. Dan knocked on the door, and Ashley welcomed them both inside. It was immediately obvious to the men that Ashley was drunk—she wreaked of alcohol, she was slurring her words, and she could barely stand up. Dan began to kiss Ashley on the lips. Ashley reciprocated, and then Dan began to fondle her breasts. Ashley responded by pulling up her shirt. Then, Dan pushed Ashley onto the couch and began to have vaginal intercourse with her. Half way through the intercourse, Ashley passed out. Dan, somewhat embarrassed, was unable to have an orgasm. Stan, who was standing by watching, said "let me show you how a real man does it." Stan then engaged in vaginal intercourse with Ashley and ejaculated.

Afterward, Stan became very interested in Amanda. Stan found Amanda in her bedroom and ordered her to perform fellatio on him. Amanda, obviously scared, refused. Stan then whipped out a Swiss Army knife, exposed the blade of the knife, and said "Do it or you die." Amanda complied. Afterwards, Stan said to Amanda, "Now, do you want to have some *real* fun"? Amanda quietly replied "yeah, okay." Stan then engaged in both vaginal and anal intercourse with Amanda.

Dan, who had just walked into Amanda's bedroom, said to Stan "hey, how come you get to have all the fun?" Dan then kissed Amanda and fondled her breasts on top of her clothing. Dan and Stan then left Amanda's bedroom. As they made their way out of the girls' home they were greeted by two police officers with shiny badges who arrived in light of Ashley's 911 call once she regained consciousness.

➲ List the crimes with which each defendant may be charged.

DEFENDANT	VICTIM	CRIMES
Dan	Ashley	
Dan	Amanda	
Stan	Ashley	
Stan	Amanda	

➲ For EACH crime identified, complete an Analysis Chart assessing the possibility of conviction of each defendant.

DISCUSSION QUESTIONS

1. Compare and contrast first degree sexual offense and second degree sexual offense.

2. Maryland defines sodomy as "sexual intercourse by a human with an animal, anal intercourse by a man with another person, fellatio, cunnilingus, and analingus." No force or threat of force is required. Read the U.S. Supreme Court case of *Lawrence v. Texas*, 539 U.S. 558 (2003). Based upon *Lawrence v. Texas*, do you think that Maryland's sodomy law is constitutional?

3. Jordan C. Reep saw Shelleeta Manup walking down the street and believed Shelleeta was a prostitute. Jordan called Shelleeta over. When no one was looking, Jordan grabbed Shelleeta and pulled her into an alley way with the intention of raping Shelleeta. When Jordan ripped off Shelleeta's skirt, he found that Shelleeta had a penis. Can Jordan C. Reep be guilty of attempted rape of Shelleeta?

4. Paul and Susan decided to burglarize Harriett's house and steal money, art and diamonds. Upon entering the bedroom, Paul and Susan found Harriett hiding under the covers. Paul pulled the covers off Harriett and jumped on top of her. Susan asked Paul what he was doing and he said he was going to rape Harriett and that Susan should act as a lookout. Susan agreed to be the lookout and positioned herself at the door while Paul raped Harriett. She alerted Paul when a car pulled in the driveway. The two made their getaway only to be apprehended by the police a few blocks away. Based upon your understanding of accomplice liability from Chapter 1 and your understanding of rape and sexual offenses from this chapter, can Susan be guilty of the rape of Harriett? Explain.

5. Can a woman rape a man? Explain your reasoning.

6. Can one spouse ever have the other spouse prosecuted for rape or a sexual offense? If your answer is yes, under what circumstances could a conviction be secured? *See*, Md. Code Ann., Crim. Law § 3-318.

7. Is the loss of a woman's virginity sufficient to constitute "disfigurement or serious physical injury" in order to elevate an otherwise second degree rape to a first degree rape based upon the use of an aggravator? *See Scott v. State*, 61 Md.App. 599, 487 A.2d 1204 (1985).

8. Ron, a 30-year-old man, went to a local bar where he needed to present valid identification to enter. While sitting at the bar drinking a beer, he met Jane. During the conversation, Jane told him that she recently graduated from law school and was working in Baltimore. She told Ron that she was 26-years-old. Ron and Jane left the bar and went to Ron's apartment. Jane asked Ron to have sexual intercourse with her and he did so. The next day, the police showed up at Ron's apartment and arrested him for rape because Jane was only 14-years-old and had fake identification to get into the bar. Will Ron be convicted? Why or why not? *See Walker v. State*, 363 Md. 253, 768 A.2d 631 (2001).

TEST BANK

True/False

_____ 1. A man can rape his wife.

_____ 2. A man can rape another man.

_____ 3. Brandon forces anal sex upon Jenny. Based upon these facts alone, Brandon has committed a 1st degree sexual offense.

_____ 4. Brandon forces anal sex upon Jenny while Bart and Barry stand as lookouts. Based upon these facts alone, Brandon has committed a 1st degree sexual offense.

_____ 5. A gynecologist performs a gynecological examination that is medically unnecessary. The gynecologist has not committed any type of sex crime because of his status as a doctor.

MULTIPLE CHOICE

6. For a rape to have occurred,
   A. A penis must penetrate the vagina
   B. The penile penetration must be complete
   C. The man must ejaculate
   D. All of the above

7. John holds a knife to Mary's throat. He then inserts an object into Mary's vagina against her will and consent. John has most likely committed
   A. First degree rape
   B. First degree sexual offense
   C. Second degree rape
   D. Second degree sexual offense
   E. None of the above

8. Leonard performed oral sex on Emmet, while Emmet was physically restrained with rope. Leonard also struck Emmet. Emmet consented to being restrained and never told Leonard to stop. Leonard would most likely:
   A. Be guilty of a 1st degree sexual offense
   B. Be guilty of a 2nd degree sexual offense
   C. Be guilty of a 3rd degree sexual offense
   D. Be found not guilty because Emmet consented to the conduct

9. Which of the following acts, if done by force and without the consent of the victim, constitutes a rape?
   A. Vaginal intercourse
   B. Analingus
   C. Cunnilingus
   D. All of the above

10. All of the following are felonies except:
   A. 1st degree sexual offense
   B. 2nd degree sexual offense
   C. 3rd degree sexual offense
   D. 4th degree sexual offense
   E. Both c and d

chapter five

Other Crimes Against the Person

Introduction

The offenses included within this chapter deal with crimes against the person that are non-homicidal and, other than the sexual child abuse statute, non-sexual in nature. The below crimes are the more significant crimes against persons either in terms of seriousness of punishment or ones that have a significant common law background.

Focus Crimes

Assault, Md. Code Ann., Crim. Law §§ 3-201 through 3-203 (West 2002); MPJI-Cr. 4:01.

Battery, Md. Code Ann., Crim. Law §§ 3-201 through 3-203 (West 2002); MPJI-Cr. 4:01.

False Imprisonment (common law offense not codified by statute, *see Street v. State*, 307 Md. 262, 513 A.2d 870 (1986)); MPJI-Cr. 4:13.

Kidnapping, Md. Code Ann., Crim. Law § 3-502 (West 2002); MPJI-Cr. 4:19.

Child Abuse—Physical Abuse, Md. Code Ann., Crim. Law § 3-601 (West Supp. 2004); MPJI-Cr. 4:07.

Child Abuse—Sexual Abuse, Md. Code Ann., Crim. Law § 3-602 (West Supp. 2004); MPJI-Cr. 4:07.1.

Objectives

Upon completing this chapter you should be able to:

- ➲ Distinguish between assault and battery;
- ➲ Explain the alternative ways in which an assault may be committed;
- ➲ Distinguish between false imprisonment and kidnapping;
- ➲ Distinguish between physical and sexual child abuse;
- ➲ Explain the concepts of physical child abuse by inaction as opposed to physical child abuse through action; and
- ➲ Analyze hypotheticals, identifying crimes, identifying elements of such crimes, and applying the facts to each element.

CASE LAW   *State v. Fabritz*, 276 Md. 416, 348 A.2d 275 (1975)

Maryland Code (1971 Repl.Vol., 1975 Cum.Supp.), Art. 27, s 35A(a) provides that any parent or other person having custody of a child under eighteen years of age "who causes abuse to such minor child" shall be guilty of a felony. The statute defines the term "abuse" in subsection (b) 7 to mean:

"any physical injury or injuries sustained by a child as a result of cruel or inhumane treatment or as a result of malicious act or acts . . . ."

Virginia Lynnette Fabritz (Virginia) was charged with violating this statute by abusing her three-and-one-half-year-old daughter Windy. Evidence adduced at the trial before a jury in the Circuit Court for Calvert County showed that Windy was brought to the Calvert County Hospital at 10:35 p.m. on October 3, 1973 in a badly beaten condition with approximately seventy bruises or contusions covering her body, ranging in size from one inch to five inches. She was pronounced dead on arrival at the hospital, her death being attributed to peritonitis resulting from a perforated or ruptured duodenum. The evidence showed that Windy's injuries were the result of "blunt trauma" caused by an instrument, or a fist, or some kind of blow inflicted within eighteen to twenty-four hours prior to her death.

Virginia had left Windy in the custody of Thomas Crockett and his wife Ann, with whom she resided, on October 1. Virginia did not see Windy again until 1 p.m. on October 3, at which time she noticed that Windy was very listless. Crockett told her that Windy had driven with him on his motorcycle and had gotten sick as a result of a bumpy ride. At 2:30 p.m. Windy complained of cramps and was running a slight fever; Virginia attributed this to the flu. She then bathed Windy and, after observing her badly beaten body, put her to bed and spent the remainder of the afternoon watching Crockett work on his motorcycle. At 5 p.m. Virginia observed that Windy appeared to be in a semiconscious state, but she did not take her to the hospital because she "was too ashamed of the bruises on her daughter's body." There was evidence that Windy thereafter sat up and appeared normal for a brief period, but at 6 p.m. she vomited and again complained that she did not feel well. At 7 p.m. Virginia put Windy back to bed and called a friend, Connie Schaeffer, and asked that she look at Windy. Miss Schaeffer arrived at 9 p.m. Windy was lying on the floor of the den, covered by a wet diaper. She was limp and appeared unconscious. When Miss Schaeffer questioned Virginia about the bruises on Windy's body, Virginia responded, "Tommy (Crockett) hits hard." Windy's condition worsened and at 9:45 p.m. Ann Crockett contacted the hospital. She was advised to bring Windy to the hospital immediately. After Mrs. Crockett left for the hospital with Windy, Virginia told Miss Schaeffer, "It is my fault. I killed her." Shortly thereafter, Virginia went to the hospital and learned that Windy was dead.

Expert medical evidence was adduced to show that a child with peritonitis would vigorously complain once she sustained the injury and would continue to complain until the onset of a coma; that at the time the injuries were sustained, there would have been immediate pain and the child would have begun to feel poorly; that the pain would have gradually increased, followed by fever, vomiting, and lack of appetite; that

within six hours prior to death, the child would have become stuporous and comatose; that Windy would have lived had an operation been performed within at least twelve hours prior to death; and that she would have had a chance to survive if surgery had been performed up to an hour before death. A pathologist testified that it was his medical opinion, based upon the degree of injury, the multiplicity of wounds and his examination of Windy's body, that the injuries did not happen accidentally. There was no evidence indicating that Virginia struck the blows which caused the initial injuries to her child, nor was there any evidence to show that Virginia had knowledge that the person in whose custody she left Windy would abuse her.

The trial court instructed the jury that a parent is under an affirmative duty to provide reasonable medical necessities to his child and would be guilty of child abuse under the statute if the treatment afforded to the child was "cruel or inhumane and it results in physical injury"; that the "physical injury may be death itself"; and that "the unattended worsening of obvious serious medical condition if cruel or inhumane and if more serious consequences result, is in itself . . . a physical injury within the meaning of the terms as they are used in the Statute." The jury found Virginia guilty of the offense and she was sentenced to five years' imprisonment.

The Court of Special Appeals reversed the judgment of conviction, holding that "to be guilty under the statute, the accused must be shown to have caused the injury, not simply aggravated it by failure to seek assistance." *Fabritz v. State*, 24 Md.App. 708 at 714, 332 A.2d 324 at 327 (1975). In so concluding, the court said that there was nothing in the statute indicating that it was the legislative intent to encompass within its provisions parents who withhold the necessities of life, including medical care, from their children. We granted certiorari to consider whether the Court of Special Appeals properly interpreted the child abuse statute.

The State contends that Virginia's failure to provide medical care to Windy in the circumstances of this case amounted to child abuse within the meaning of the statute. More specifically, the State urges that the evidence showed that Windy was the victim of a medical condition known as the "battered child syndrome"; that the beating Windy suffered caused peritonitis which resulted "in a gradual and continuous general deterioration of the child's health and well-being culminating in her death"; that although there was no evidence that Virginia was the individual who beat Windy, she was "fully aware of her child's beaten condition . . .

(but) failed for a period of several hours to seek medical attention for her child and . . . her inaction amounted to child abuse"; and that while there was no evidence that Windy's injuries resulted from any "malicious act" perpetrated by Virginia, her failure to obtain medical attention for her daughter constituted, within the sense contemplated by the statute, "cruel or inhumane treatment" and was a contributing cause of the "physical injury" which the child sustained.

On Virginia's behalf it is argued that to be guilty of child abuse under s 35A, a person must have "caused" the child to suffer physical injury as a result of cruel or inhumane treatment. Virginia claims that s 35A "concerns injuries as a result of the treatment or acts of the accused" and that because Windy was injured and died as a consequence of blows inflicted by someone other than herself, her failure to obtain medical aid for Windy was not the cause of the child's injuries or death. Virginia maintains that the gist of the statutory offense of child abuse is not cruel or inhumane treatment but rather the infliction of physical injuries upon a child as a result of such treatment.

* * *

. . . Codified under the subtitle "Child Abuse," the statute's declared legislative purpose is "the protection of children who have been the subject of abuse . . . ." As heretofore indicated, the statute defines "abuse" to encompass any "physical injury or injuries sustained by a child as a result of cruel or inhumane treatment or as a result of malicious act or acts." Under the statute, any person having custody of a child under eighteen years of age who "causes" such abuse is guilty of a felony. The precursor to s 35A was chapter 743 of the Acts of 1963, which was originally codified as Code (1957) Article 27, s 11A and included under the subtitle "Assault on Children"; that statute, which was recodified as Article 27, s 35A by chapter 500 of the Acts of 1970, provided that any person having custody of a minor child under fourteen years of age "who maliciously beats, strikes or otherwise mistreats such minor child to such degree as to require medical treatment" would be guilty of a felony. It would appear from its terms that that enactment was not intended to reach acts of individuals not constituting, in one form or another, an assault on a child. It was not until s 35A was amended by chapter 835 of the Acts of 1973 that the Legislature repealed the "maliciously beats, strikes, or otherwise mistreats" test of child abuse, and substituted in its place a new and different measure of the offense—one defined by new subsection (b)7 in terms of physical injuries caused by "cruel or inhumane treatment or as a result of mali-

cious act or acts." According to its title, one of the purposes underlying the 1973 amendment of s 35A was "generally amend(ing) the laws of child abuse." Considering the particular use and association of words and definitions used in s 35A, we think a doubt or ambiguity exists as to the exact reach of the statute's provisions, justifying application of the principle that permits courts in such circumstances to ascertain and give effect to the real intention of the Legislature. *See Clerk v. Chesapeake Beach Park*, 251 Md. 657, 248 A.2d 479 (1968); *Domain v. Bosley*, 242 Md. 1, 217 A.2d 555 (1966).

We think it evident that the Legislature, by its 1973 amendment to s 35A, plainly intended to broaden the area of proscribed conduct punishable in child abuse cases. Its use in the amended version of s 35A of the comprehensive phraseology "who causes abuse to" a minor child, coupled with its broad two-pronged definition of the term "abuse," supports the view that the Legislature, by repealing the narrow measure of criminality in child abuse cases then provided in s 35A, and redefining the offense, undertook to effect a significant change of substance in the scope of the statute's prohibitions. In making it an offense for a person having custody of a minor child to "cause" the child to suffer "a physical injury," the Legislature did not require that the injury result from a physical assault upon the child or from any physical force initially applied by the accused individual; it provided instead, in a more encompassing manner, that the offense was committed if physical injury to the child resulted either from a course of conduct constituting "cruel or inhumane treatment" or by "malicious act or acts."

As defined in Black's Law Dictionary 966 (3rd ed. 1933), an injury is "(a)ny wrong or damage done to another . . ."; the term is defined in Webster's Third New International Dictionary 1164 (1961) as "an act that damages, harms, or hurts: an unjust or undeserved infliction of suffering or harm." Of course, the injury would be a physical one if it relates to or pertains to the body. To be a "cause" of physical injury to another, a person would in some manner have to be accountable for the "condition that brings about an effect or that produces or calls forth a resultant action or state." Webster's Third New International Dictionary 356. Affording the term "physical injury" the broad meaning that the context of s 35A would seem to mandate, we think a parent would be criminally responsible as having "caused" such a physical injury to his child in the sense contemplated by the statute if, as a result of the parent's "cruel or inhumane treatment," the child suffered bodily harm additional to that initially sustained as a consequence of the injury originally inflicted upon him. Cf. *Palmer v. State*, 223 Md. 341, 164 A.2d 467 (1960) where in affirming an involuntary manslaughter conviction of a mother who knowingly permitted her infant child to be subjected to prolonged beatings by her paramour, we concluded that although the direct and immediate cause of the child's death was attributable to blows struck by the mother's paramour, her failure to remove the child from the paramour's presence constituted criminal negligence and "was a contributing cause of . . . (the child's) unfortunate death." 223 Md. at 353, 164 A.2d at 474.

Whether, in view of the evidence adduced at the trial, Virginia's failure to obtain medical assistance for Windy constituted cruel or inhumane treatment resulting in physical injury to the child is, of course, the crux of this appeal. That a parent under Maryland law is legally obligated to provide necessary medical care to his child is clear. Code (1970 Repl.Vol.) Art. 72A, s 1; *Craig v. State*, 220 Md. 590, 155 A.2d 684 (1959); *Baltimore City v. Fire Insurance Salvage Corporation*, 219 Md. 75, 148 A.2d 444 (1959). That Virginia knew of Windy's severely beaten condition in manifest from the evidence; indeed, as the photographic exhibits in the case so painfully demonstrate, Windy bore the multiple bruises of a vicious assault, of which Virginia was aware at least as early as 2:30 p.m. on October 3, 1973. Between that hour, and 10:35 p.m. when Windy died, Virginia failed to seek or obtain any medical assistance although, as the evidence heretofore outlined so plainly indicates, the need therefor was obviously compelling and urgent. There was evidence that Virginia's failure to seek such assistance was based upon her realization that the bruises covering Windy's body would become known were the child examined or treated by a physician. Other evidence in the case all too graphically illustrated the suffering to which Windy was subjected by Virginia's failure to provide the treatment needed to save the child's life. We think the jury properly could have concluded from the evidence that, as a result of Virginia's conduct, Windy's condition was permitted to steadily deteriorate until the child's ordeal was ended by death; that Virginia's failure to act caused Windy to sustain bodily injury additional to and beyond that inflicted upon her by reason of the original assault and constituted a cause of the further progression and worsening of the injuries which led to Windy's death; and that in these circumstances Virginia's treatment of Windy was "cruel or inhumane" within the meaning of the statute and as those terms are commonly understood. Accordingly, we conclude that the Court of Special Appeals was in error in its interpretation of s 35A and in its reversal of Virginia's conviction.

JUDGMENT OF THE COURT OF SPECIAL APPEALS REVERSED; CONVICTIONS AFFIRMED.

_____**CASE END**

CASE LAW — *McGrier v. State*, 125 Md.App. 759, 726 A.2d 894 (1999)

Louis McGrier, appellant herein, was convicted by a jury in the Circuit Court for Baltimore City of two counts of first degree rape, two counts of kidnapping, robbery, and assault and battery. He was sentenced to consecutive terms of life imprisonment for the rapes, concurrent thirty-year terms for the kidnappings, ten years consecutive for the robbery, and ten years consecutive for the assault and battery. In his appeal, appellant raises the following issues . . . Whether the evidence was sufficient to establish kidnapping . . . .

The offenses occurred on August 8, 17, and 23, 1996, at 1645 N. Calhoun Street in Baltimore City. The victims were three young women who gave the following accounts of being assaulted. Kia Thomas, age fifteen, testified that she went to 1645 N. Calhoun Street at 8 a.m. to visit a friend in a first floor apartment. She entered the building, a man put his arm around her neck, dragged her down several steps, forced her against a wall, and had vaginal intercourse with her from behind. He struck her in the back of her head and threatened to cut her with a knife if she did not stop screaming. Seventeen days after the assault, the victim identified appellant from a photographic array shown to her by a police officer. At trial, she was asked if she could identify her attacker. Pointing to appellant, she said, "I think that's him right there." On the day of the assault, the witness described her attacker as a dark skinned black male in his 30's, wearing a blue shirt and blue jeans, with a bald head and some facial hair.

Crystal Harris, age 14, lived at the N. Calhoun Street address. On August 17 at 2 p.m., a man pulled her from the hall into the stairway leading to the cellar. He pulled her to a landing six or seven steps down the stairway, threatened her, and then removed her shorts and had sexual intercourse with her. Before leaving, her assailant took a necklace and some money from her. The victim described her assailant as being bald, dark skinned, having a mustache, and resembling a bulldog. He was wearing a white Nike T-shirt, blue jeans, and tennis shoes. Nine days after being assaulted, the witness selected appellant from an array of six photographs.

Latisha Nelson, age 19, also resided in the N. Calhoun Street complex. At approximately 2 p.m. on August 23, she entered the building en route to the third floor. A man she later identified as appellant grabbed her from behind and said, "You look good, I want you." A fight ensued on the steps; the witness escaped to her apartment and appellant fled. She described him to the police as bald, wearing black sweat pants, a white tank top, and jewelry around his neck. Two days after the assault, the police asked the witness to accompany them to the first floor where she saw and identified appellant as her assailant.

Officer Keith Simmons testified that he went to the apartment building on August 25 in response to a complaint about a stranger in the building. He observed appellant in the hallway. The officer noticed that appellant was wearing a tank top, sweat pants, several necklaces, a bracelet, and a watch. He asked appellant why he was in the building and received three different answers: First appellant said he was visiting a male friend, then he said he was taking a shortcut, and finally he claimed he was visiting a female friend. During the discussion, Officer Simmons was holding the identification cards that appellant had produced. Officer Simmons had requested assistance when he and appellant first saw each other in the building. When Latisha Nelson arrived at the first floor, she identified appellant as the person who had attacked her and he was placed under arrest. At trial, appellant did not offer any evidence. Additional facts will be supplied as relevant to appellant's contentions . . . .

> Appellant alleged that the evidence of asportation was incident to the rape and, therefore, insufficient to constitute the crime of kidnapping. Maryland Code Article 27, sec. 337, defines kidnapping as follows: Every person, his counsellors, aiders, or abettors, who shall be convicted of the crime of kidnapping and forcibly or fraudulently carrying or causing to be carried out of or within this State any person, except in the case of a person under eighteen years of age, by a parent thereof, with intent to have such person carried out of or within this State, or with the intent to have such person concealed within the State or without the State, shall be guilty of a felony and shall be sentenced to the penitentiary for not more than thirty years.

The legislative intent in enacting this section of Article 27 was to broaden the common law crime of kidnapping to include the forcible or fraudulent carrying, or intent to carry a person within as well as without the State. *Hunt v. State,* 12 Md.App. 286, 278 A.2d 637, *cert. denied,* 263 Md. 715 (1971).

Initially, we point out that a person convicted of a conventional kidnapping is subject to a severe penalty. The maximum sentence is thirty years incarceration. The Legislature, we conclude, did not intend that where the forcible carrying of a person was incidental to the commission of another felony, and not a true kidnapping, that **any** forcible movement of a person would nevertheless support a kidnapping charge.

If a kidnapping statute is construed too broadly, all types of lesser crimes, including assault, transporting persons for purposes of prostitution, petty street crimes, and minor sex offenses, could provide a basis for adding a charge of kidnapping and a possible thirty-year sentence. A true kidnapping is usually a prelude to some other crime such as extortion or hostage taking. Whether the "carrying" is incidental to the commission of another offense requires a case-by-case analysis of the factors set forth by the Court of Appeals in a thorough discussion by Judge Alan M. Wilner of the kidnapping statute. Aligning Maryland with the majority of states which have considered the dual sentencing issue, the Court, in *State v. Stouffer,* 352 Md. 97, 721 A.2d 207 (1998), stated the following:

> We align ourselves with the majority approach that examines the circumstances of each case and determine from them whether the kidnapping—the intentional asportation—was merely incidental to the commission of another offense. We do not adopt any specific formulation of standards for making that determination, but rather focus on those factors that seem to be central to most of the articulated guidelines.

The Court set forth for consideration the following five factors: 1) How far, and where, was the victim taken? 2) How long was the victim detained in relation to what was necessary to the commission of the other crime? 3) Was the movement either inherent as an element, or as a practical matter, necessary to the commission of the other crime? 4) Did it have some independent purpose? 5) Did the asportation subject the victim to any additional significant danger?

Other Cases

The kidnapping cases we have reviewed are factually distinguishable from the case before us, primarily on the factors of the time involved in the commission of the offense, and in the asportation. For example, in *Lester v. State,* 9 Md.App. 542, 266 A.2d 361, *cert. denied,* 259 Md. 733 (1970), the victim was seized on a parking lot, forced into a car and driven some distance to a wooded area and raped, after which she was returned to the parking lot. In *Rice v. State,* 9 Md.App. 552, 267 A.2d 261, *cert. denied,* 259 Md. 735 (1970), the victim was taken forcibly from her home to an apartment several blocks away and kept all night. She was sexually assaulted and released the next day. An eleven-year-old was accosted while riding her bicycle in *Moore v. State,* 23 Md.App. 540, 329 A.2d 48 (1974). She was forced into her abductor's car and driven to an abandoned farmhouse and raped. In *Isaacs v. State,* 31 Md.App. 604, 358 A.2d 273, *cert. denied,* 278 Md. 724 (1976), kidnapping was established. In that case, the victim had stopped along the highway to question the occupants of a disabled vehicle which the victim recognized as belonging to a friend. He was forced to accompany the occupants in his own car for approximately sixty to ninety minutes from Pennsylvania into Maryland where he was taken into a wooded area and executed. *Carey v. State,* 54 Md.App. 448, 458 A.2d 90, *aff'd,* 299 Md. 17, 472 A.2d 444 (1984), involved an assault in an upstairs bedroom after which the victim was taken to the basement and locked in a closet for longer than one day. In upholding a conviction for kidnapping, the Court of Appeals said that the distance the victim had been transported was not significant, but the confinement occurred after the sexual assault had ended. Finally, in *Stouffer, supra,* the victim was forced into a car in Hagerstown, driven to a remote area, stripped, beaten and stabbed. He was then transported to another area and thrown into a ditch near the Pennsylvania Turnpike. The kidnapping ended with the death of the victim.

This Case

Unlike all of the cases cited above, in the present case the asportation was limited to wrestling Kia Thomas from the first floor hallway to the third step on a stairway leading to the basement, and dragging Crystal Harris seven steps to a landing on the stairway. We shall address the factors as each relates to the undisputed facts.

1. How far and where was the victim taken?

The distance, which we agree is not necessarily controlling, was a matter of several feet from the hallway to the stairs leading to the basement. We can assume that that location was not beyond the hearing of anyone on the upper stairway, or the hallway, because appellant struck Kia Thomas and ordered her to stop yelling. We can reasonably conclude that appellant's purpose in taking the victims to the stairway was to avoid being seen by anyone entering or leaving the building, because both incidents occurred during the daytime. Apparently, appellant intended to keep an escape route open by remaining in close proximity to the hallway, otherwise he could have taken each victim down to the basement. The "carrying" herein would not differ from wrestling the victim around a corner, or away from an open window, or into an alley. Such activity would constitute false imprisonment, but not kidnapping.

2. Period of detention.

Kia Thomas testified that she wrestled with appellant to keep him from removing her pants. That effort lasted for approximately two minutes, followed by appellant penetrating her from the rear and then turning her around and ejaculating on her clothing. He then ran from the building. Crystal Thomas, the fourteen-year-old, could not estimate the amount of time she spent with appellant. She said he removed her underwear, had intercourse with her, and took her necklace and ran out of the building. We think it is reasonable to conclude that the 901 time involved was limited to the brief period necessary to complete the rape and flee from the premises. That conduct is inconsistent with an intent to kidnap.

3. Was the movement necessary as an element of the rape?

As a practical matter, movement from the open hallway was prudent if not necessary in order to carry out the sexual assault.

4. Independent purpose.

There is no evidence of any independent purpose beyond having forcible sexual intercourse with the victims in this case.

5. Additional significant danger.

The asportation was from the hallway to the steps leading to the basement. We perceive no significant danger by being on the stairs beyond that which was necessary to accomplish the assault. Additional significant danger usually relates to possible injury over and above those to which a victim of the underlying crime is exposed. *See State v. Logan,* 60 Ohio St.2d 126, 397 N.E.2d

1345 (1979). For example, leaving a victim of a rape or robbery in a remote area, or locking employees in a bank vault or in a freezer would suffice to support a kidnapping charge in addition to a charge of rape or robbery. The facts of the present case, however, present no separate animus to support a charge of kidnapping.

Summary

The issue herein is whether the restraint or movement of the victims was merely incidental to a separate crime, or whether it had a significance independent of the other offense. The answer requires careful scrutiny of the factors set forth in *Stouffer*. No single factor is dispositive of the issue. Appellant received two consecutive life sentences for the rapes, plus twenty years consecutive sentences for robbery and assault. The sentences were appropriate. The thirty-year concurrent sentences for kidnapping must be stricken. The carrying or concealing was clearly incidental to the rapes. The record is devoid of any evidence of an intent to kidnap, which the statute requires. The singular purpose was to rape, which occurred, and for which appellant has been sentenced. Article 27, sec. 337 is a substantive criminal statute designed to punish severely those who forcibly deprive others of their liberty. It is not a "catch all" or "add on" to be used for punishment of other criminal acts.

JUDGMENT REVERSED ON KIDNAPPING CHARGES.

CASE END

Case Questions

State v. Fabritz

1. What were the underlying facts of the case that led Fabritz to be charged with child abuse?

2. How did a change in the wording of the child abuse statute by the legislature affect the court's decision in this case?

3. What if Thomas Crockett had sexually abused Windy during the time in which he had custody of her; do you think the court would have found Fabritz guilty of sexual child abuse? Explain.

4. Do you agree with the court's conclusion in this case? Explain.

McGrier v. State

1. What were the facts of the case that led to McGrier being charged with two counts of kidnapping?

2. What factors did the court consider for determining whether a true kidnapping had occurred as opposed to movement that was merely incidental to the commission of another offense? How did the court apply those factors to McGrier's crimes?

3. What other cases did the court discuss and how did they compare to the facts in this case?

Additional Crimes to Consult

The crime titled Assault now encompasses "the crimes of assault, battery, and assault and battery." Md. Code Ann., Crim. Law § 3-201 (West 2002). Assault is divided into two degrees: First-degree assault, the aggravated form with a heightened penalty, prohibits an assault either causing or attempting to cause "serious physical injury" to the victim or using a firearm. Second-degree assault encompasses traditional assault. The additional offense of reckless endangerment, a misdemeanor, also encompasses less serious forms of assaultive conduct. Md. Code Ann., Crim. Law § 3-204 (West 2002).

In addition to the traditional kidnapping prohibitions, Maryland also has a separate criminal offense for Child Kidnapping (*see* Md. Code Ann., Crim. Law § 3-503). This offense prohibits two classifications of kidnapping. First, it is a felony to either forcibly take or entice a child under 12 years of age from that child's home or from the custody of the child's parent or legal guardian. Second, it is also a felony to kidnap any child under the age of 16. This statute was designed primarily to deal with non-custodial parental kidnappings, which has been a crime in Maryland since 1876. *See State v. Ghajari*, 346 Md. 101, 110, 695 A.2d 143 (1997).

In 2003 the General Assembly revised Maryland's child abuse statutes. The offense was divided into degrees: First-degree child abuse provides an aggravated form of physical abuse that either "results in the death of" the child or "causes severe physical injury" to the child. Second-degree child abuse encompasses physical abuse in which the child's "health or welfare is harmed or threatened." Additionally, the statute includes a provision for repeat offenders. Finally, the penalties for both physical child abuse and sexual child abuse were increased.

HYPOTHETICAL #1

One night, a group of close friends were all hanging out with nothing do to. "I know, let's have some fun," said Albert, and Barbara replied, "Okay, sounds good to me." Albert, Barbara, and Chuck all went down to the liquor store to buy some beer. As they were about to purchase their alcohol, Chuck, not the smartest one in the group of friends, had an idea. "Hey, let's scare the cashier," Chuck said. He put his arm in his shirt pocket and stuck his finger through as if he had a gun. "Don't move or I'll shoot!" Chuck exclaimed. The cashier obviously took Chuck seriously, because he dropped the change in his hands and said "Please don't hurt me, I'll do anything!" Chuck, still having fun playing his prank, ordered the cashier to walk into the back room. The cashier did, and Chuck locked the door behind the cashier. With the cashier out of the way, Barbara replied, "Hey, we can get a lot more beer now!" Barbara and Albert then proceeded to get as much beer as they could carry. The three then made their way out of the liquor store and over to the Campus Café, their favorite hangout . . . .

MAIN ISSUE

Did Chuck Commit a Kidnapping Based on Movement of the Victim with the Intent to Carry or Conceal?

ISSUE	THESIS	RULE	ANALYSIS	CONCLUSION
Did Chuck detain the cashier WHEN he told the cashier "Don't move or I'll shoot"?	Chuck detained the cashier WHEN he told the cashier "Don't move or I'll shoot."	For kidnapping, the victim must be CONFINED or DETAINED by the defendant, however brief in time.	Chuck detained the cashier BECAUSE he ordered the cashier not to move hence the cashier was forced to stay because of Chuck's command.	Chuck detained the cashier.
Did Chuck move the cashier from one place to another WHEN Chuck ordered the cashier to walk into the back room?	Chuck moved the cashier from one place to another WHEN Chuck ordered the cashier to walk into the back room.	Kidnapping is distinguished from the lesser included offense of false imprisonment because kidnapping requires MOVEMENT or asportation.	Chuck moved the cashier BECAUSE Chuck ordered the cashier to walk to the back room of the liquor store.	Chuck moved the cashier.
Did Chuck detain and move the cashier against his will WHEN the cashier was placed in fear by Chuck's actions?	Chuck detained and moved the cashier against his will WHEN the cashier was placed in fear by Chuck's actions.	For kidnapping the victim must be detained and moved AGAINST HIS WILL.	The cashier was detained against his will BECAUSE Chuck's actions placed the cashier in immediate fear (cashier dropped change in his hands and said "please don't hurt me I'll do anything.).	Chuck detained and moved the cashier against his will.
Did Chuck use force or threat of force to accomplish the confinement and detention of the cashier WHEN Chuck feigned having a weapon in order to scare the cashier?	Chuck used threat of force to accomplish the confinement and detention of the cashier WHEN Chuck feigned having a weapon in order to scare the cashier.	For kidnapping, FORCE OR THREAT OF FORCE must accompany the detention. From the victim's perspective it must be reasonable that the perpetrator has the ability to carry out the threatened force.	Chuck used threat of force BECAUSE his actions (putting finger in pocket and pointing it as if a gun), words ("Don't move or I'll shoot") and circumstances (in liquor store which robbery is not uncommon, Chuck there with friends) placed the cashier in fear for his safety.	Chuck detained and moved the cashier by threat of force.
Did Chuck move the cashier with the intent to conceal the cashier WHEN Chuck ordered the cashier into the back room of the store?	Chuck did not move the cashier into the back room with the intent to conceal the cashier WHEN Chuck ordered the cashier into the back room of the store.	The MOVEMENT needed for kidnapping must be for the purpose of concealing the victim and may not be incidental to the commission of another crime.	Chuck's actions did not satisfy the movement requirement for kidnapping BECAUSE (1) the distance taken was very short; (2) the movement added no additional danger to the crime; (3) the movement was merely incidental and not an objective of Chuck.	Chuck did not move the cashier with the intent to carry or conceal.

CONCLUSION

Chuck did not commit kidnapping because the victim was not moved with the purpose to carry or conceal. (Note: Chuck could successfully be charged with the lesser included offense of false imprisonment.)

HYPOTHETICAL #2

. . . On their way over to the Campus Café, an elderly woman was walking slowly in front of the three. Albert, annoyed that the old woman wouldn't speed up, pushed the woman aside. The old woman mumbled something under her breath, and Chuck shouted "Look lady, don't mess with my friend or we'll kill you right now and right here!" The little old lady was so upset that she immediately fainted and lay flat on the sidewalk.

Once at the Campus Café, the three friends met up with their other friend Denise. Denise explained how her evil twin sister Emily was in "big trouble." Apparently Emily, who was a well-known porn star, went to a playground in Central Park and picked up her niece Candy, who was 10-years-old, after school as Emily had done every day. Emily explained to Candy that if she came with Emily, she (Candy) could make big money. Candy went, and before she knew it she was on the set of an x-rated movie with lots of men with little clothes on. Emily encouraged Candy to take her clothes off and pose for the camera. Reluctantly, Candy did. When Candy got tired and said she wanted to stop, Emily slapped Candy. Candy cried, and Fred, one of the male "actors," beat Candy until she was unconscious. Emily just stood there and watched the entire time.

After Denise finished telling her friends the story, Barbara replied "You know, I just don't understand it anymore. Everyone breaks the law. Thank goodness we're such good friends and we'd never to anything like that." The six had some coffee and played cards for the rest of the night.

➲ List the crimes with which each defendant may be charged.

DEFENDANT	VICTIM	CRIMES
Albert	old woman	
Chuck	old woman	
Emily	Candy	
Fred	Candy	

➲ For EACH crime identified, complete an Analysis Chart assessing the possibility of conviction for each defendant.

DISCUSSION QUESTIONS

1. Alice and Bert are members of a very strict religion that forbids any and all medical intervention. One day Charlie, their 6-year-old son, is critically injured at school while playing at recess. Charlie is immediately transported to the hospital. When his parents arrive they are told that if he does not have an immediate operation, he will die. Alice and Bert refuse to consent to the operation and Charlie dies. Under *State v. Fabritz*, are Alice and Bert guilty of child abuse?

2. When does parental discipline rise to the level of child abuse? What if parents feel it is appropriate to spank their children using their bare hand as a means of punishment? Using a belt? An iron rod? What if a public school were to carry out the same method of punishment?

3. In Maryland, both physical child abuse and sexual child abuse carry the same maximum potential penalty: 25 years if the abuse results in the death of the child or causes severe physical injury to the child. Do you agree that both types of offenses carry the same penalty or do you think one should deserve a more severe penalty than the other? Why?

4. Debbie is a 14-year-old ninth grader in high school. Mr. Henderson is a math teacher at the same school. Debbie has never been in one of Mr. Henderson's classes, but she knows Mr. Henderson from occasions in which she would stay after school to tutor other students in math. On a few occasions Mr. Henderson drove Debbie home from school, and Debbie eventually developed a crush on Mr. Henderson. The two would discuss romantic relationships and Mr. Henderson told her that at some point in the future a relationship was possible although at that time she was too young. On the last day of school he again offered to drive Debbie home from school, but while en route he suggested they stop off at his house to play a game of pool. Debbie agreed, and once at his home the two engaged in consensual sexual activity. Is Mr. Henderson guilty of sexual child abuse? *See Anderson v. State*, 372 Md. 285, 812 A.2d 1016 (2002).

5. Research challenge: How did the kidnapping and eventual murder of famed pilot Charles Lindbergh's one-year-old son Charles Jr. in 1932 impact the kidnapping laws in this country?

6. Kathy has been longing for a child of her own, so one day she goes to a local hospital, and while no one is watching, she removes a two-week old infant from his crib and takes him home. Is Kathy guilty of kidnapping if she did not use any force or threat of force to accomplish the taking of the infant? Under the logic that an infant could not be taken by force or threat of force, then could an individual be guilty of kidnapping an unconscious individual? Why or why not? *See Stancil v. State*, 78 Md.App. 376, 553 A.2d 268, cert. denied, 315 Md. 692, 556 A.2d 674 (1989).

7. Martin takes his thirteen-year-old daughter to the set of a pornographic movie. His daughter watches the movie being filmed and Martin encourages her to actively participate in the movie. Is Martin guilty of sexual child abuse?

8. What other crimes discussed in Chapters 1 through 4 would also include an underlying battery?

TEST BANK

True/False

_____ 1. Some physical injury must occur to the victim in order to have a battery.

_____ 2. Jennifer has witnessed her husband Kurt physically abuse their three-year-old daughter, but she has done nothing about it because she is afraid of the potential consequences of reporting the abuse. Jennifer and Kurt are both guilty of physical child abuse.

_____ 3. Spanking your child as a means of parental discipline would likely qualify as physical child abuse.

_____ 4. You may never have the crime of sexual child abuse without some form of touching of the child.

_____ 5. False imprisonment may only be accomplished if the victim is aware she is being detained.

MULTIPLE CHOICE

6. For the crime of sexual child abuse in Maryland, which of the following is NOT an element of that offense:
   A. The child must sustain some injury to genitals or other intimate areas of the body
   B. The defendant must be an individual with legal care or custody of the child
   C. The child must be under 18 at the time of the offense
   D. The defendant must have either sexually molested or exploited the child

7. Which of the following statements is NOT true about assault in Maryland:
   A. Assault may be committed in alternative ways
   B. You may never have an assault without also having a battery
   C. A form of "aggravated assault" is recognized whereby the assault is committed with the use of a firearm
   D. The defendant must have intended either to harm the victim or to frighten the victim

8. Which of the following crimes would never constitute a battery:
   A. Slapping someone across the face without any significant injury
   B. Kissing someone on the mouth
   C. Engaging in forcible sexual intercourse
   D. All of the above could potentially qualify as a battery

9. Tom intentionally runs over his ex-wife Betty with his car while Betty isn't looking and Betty suffers life threatening injuries. Has Tom committed the offense of battery?
   A. No, because Tom did not actually touch Betty himself
   B. No, because Betty did not die as a result of her injuries
   C. Yes, because the car was an extension of Tom and hence Tom caused offensive physical contact to Betty
   D. Yes, because Tom did not warn Betty before he struck her and hence she had no opportunity to avoid the harm

10. A hostage situation is a classic example of what crime?
    A. Assault
    B. Battery
    C. False Imprisonment
    D. Kidnapping

Hybrid Crimes

Introduction

In substantive criminal law, three offenses exist which are not easily classified either as crimes against persons or crimes against property. In fact, various text books on the subject treat them differently. Therefore, we have chosen to address these three crimes separately in their own chapter entitled "Hybrid Crimes." The name comes from the fact that each of these three offenses possess elements of a crime against the person, namely some force or threat of force against the victim or fear instilled in the victim during the commission of the crime, and they also possess elements of a crime against property, namely the theft of or destruction of personal property. The hybrid nature of these crimes makes them unique and worthy of separate attention.

Focus Crimes

Robbery, Md. Code Ann., Crim. Law § 3-402 (West 2002); MPJI-Cr. 4:28.

Carjacking, Md. Code Ann., Crim. Law § 3-405 (West 2002); MPJI-Cr. 4:04.

Burglary, Md. Code Ann., Crim. Law § 6-202 (West 2002); MPJI-Cr. 4:06.

Objectives

Upon completing this chapter you should be able to:

- ➲ Define and explain the concept of a "hybrid crime";
- ➲ Define and explain the offenses of robbery, carjacking, and burglary; and
- ➲ Analyze hypotheticals, identifying crimes, identifying elements of such crimes, and applying the facts to each element.

CASE LAW   *Reed v. State*, 316 Md. 521, 560 A.2d 1104 (1987)

On a July night, at 4:00 a.m., the Petitioner Kevin Reed and his brother came to the locked door of the lobby of a Baltimore City apartment complex housing retired and disabled senior citizens. Among the residents of the complex was Ellis Reed, Kevin Reed's father. Under the rules of the apartment complex, only residents were admitted to the building between 1:00 a.m. and 7:00 a.m. When Kevin Reed and his brother reached the locked outside door of the apartment complex, the guard on duty in the lobby, Ms. Payne, saw them through the glass in the door and went up to the door.

Kevin Reed and his brother told Ms. Payne that they wished to visit their father, that their mother had died, and that they wanted to inform their father of her death. Ms. Payne unlocked and opened the door. She allowed them to enter the building and had them sign the registry book. She then escorted Kevin and his brother to their father's apartment, 13K, where they knocked on the door and were admitted. Ellis Reed testified that when his sons arrived he told them to mop his floor and that they did so.

Charles Keller was a resident of the same apartment complex, in apartment 13L. On the night Kevin Reed and his brother were visiting Ellis Reed, Mr. Keller was asleep with his apartment door open in order to increase ventilation. At 4:30 a.m. Mr. Keller awoke and saw Kevin Reed and his brother running from Mr. Keller's apartment. Mr. Keller then determined that a bank credit card, a food emergency identification card, and $130.00 in cash were missing from his apartment. Shortly afterwards, Kevin Reed and his brother returned to the lobby, signed out, and left the building. Mr. Keller called the police who later brought Kevin Reed and his brother to Mr. Keller's apartment where he identified them as the men fleeing his apartment earlier. The bank card, the emergency food identification card, and $118.00 in cash were found in Kevin Reed's home.

Kevin Reed was charged in the Circuit Court for Baltimore City with burglary, and he elected a nonjury trial. At the trial, Ellis Reed, the defendant's father, testified that the defendant's mother was alive. The trial judge found the defendant guilty of burglary and sentenced him to five years imprisonment. The Court of Special Appeals affirmed in an unreported opinion, and this Court granted the defendant's petition for a writ of certiorari.

The defendant Kevin Reed argues that his conviction should be overturned because the State failed to prove the requisite elements of burglary. Specifically, Reed claims (1) that there was no breaking, (2) that the lobby of the complex was not a dwelling, and (3) that even if there was a breaking into a dwelling, the defendant lacked the necessary intent at the time of the breaking.

In contending that there was no breaking of Mr. Keller's apartment, the defendant relies on the settled principle that entry through an open door is not a breaking. . . . The State argues that there was a constructive breaking by the defendant when he gained admittance to the building by lying about his mother's death.

At common law, a constructive breaking occurred "when entry was gained by fraud or threat of force." 2 Lafave and Scott, *Substantive Criminal Law,* § 8.13 (1986). The notion of constructive breaking was recognized by this Court in *Brooks v. State,* 277 Md. 155, 159-160, 353 A.2d 217, 220 (1976):

> "[T]he term 'breaking' may be satisfied where . . . the breaking occurred 'constructively,' through an entry gained by artifice, 'by fraud, [by] conspiracy (with those within) or [by] threats.'"

The defendant maintains that his entry was not a constructive breaking because he and his brother sought entry in order to visit their father, that Ms. Payne allowed them in for the purpose of seeing their father, and that they did in fact visit their father. The defendant asserts that the entry was not gained by fraud, even though the reason given for wanting to visit Ellis Reed was false. The defendant cites *Reagan v. State, supra,* 2 Md.App. at 267-268, 234 A.2d at 281, that "the breaking, actual or constructive, requires a break of the dwelling by trespass" and that an entry is not a breaking "if the one entering had authority to do so at that particular time." *See also Finke v. State,* 56 Md.App. 450, 467, 468 A.2d 353, 362 (1983), *cert. denied,* 299 Md. 425, 474 A.2d 218, *cert. denied,* 469 U.S. 1043, 105 S.Ct. 529, 83 L.Ed.2d 416 (1984); *Martin v. State,* 10 Md.App. 274, 279, 269 A.2d 182 (1970).

Generally, in constructive breaking cases where defendants have gained entry by claiming to have a lawful objective, upon gaining entry the defendants have turned out to have no such lawful objective. *See, e.g., Com. v. Hayes,* 314 Pa.Super. 112, 460 A.2d 791 (1983) (defendant gained entry by falsely claiming that he had come to read the meter in the basement, then burglarized house); *State v. Van Meveren,* 290 N.W.2d 631 (Minn.1980) (defendant gained entry claiming that he needed to use the bathroom and immediately, after gaining entry, commenced assault); *State v. Maxwell,* 234 Kan. 393, 672 P.2d 590 (1983) (after gaining entry into antiques dealer's home on the pretext of wanting to discuss a watch, the defendant robbed the occupants). In this case, while Kevin Reed was not truthful about the reason for wanting to visit his father, he did gain entry in order to visit his father, and, for some time after being admitted, he did in fact visit his father.

Alternatively, the defendant contends that even if there was a constructive breaking, a constructive breaking of the lobby of the apartment complex fails to satisfy the requirement that the breaking be of a dwelling house. The common law limitation of burglary to breaking into a dwelling house "found its theoretical basis in the protection of man's right of habitation." Lafave and Scott, *supra* § 8.13. . . .

The defendant's arguments that there was no constructive breaking and that the lobby was not a "dwelling" have much force. Nevertheless, we shall not resolve these difficult issues at this time. In our view, even if there were a breaking of a dwelling-house, there was in this case insufficient evidence that the defendant had the requisite intent at the time of the breaking.

To warrant a burglary conviction, the defendant must have had, at the time of the breaking, an intent to commit a felony or theft under $300. "[I]n burglary there must be a felonious intent at the time of the breaking and entering, and it is not burglary if the intent is formed after the breaking and entering are completed." Burdick, *Law of Crime*, § 710 (1st ed. 1946). A number of Maryland cases in similar contexts have held that the intent at the time of the breaking controls. . . .

This Court has stated that "[f]inding the requisite intent to steal is . . . never a precise process for intent is subjective, and it must therefore be inferred from the circumstances of the case if it is found at all." *Yopps v. State*, 234 Md. 216, 220-221, 198 A.2d 264, 266, *cert. denied*, 379 U.S. 922, 85 S.Ct. 279, 13 L.Ed.2d 336 (1963). We have also said that "[t]he most conclusive evidence that the breaking was with the intent to steal is the larceny itself." *Felkner v. State*, 218 Md. 300, 307, 146 A.2d 424, 429 (1958).

The circumstances of the instant case, however, do not permit the conclusion that because Kevin Reed stole Mr. Keller's goods his intent when entering the building was to commit a crime. Several factors militate against this conclusion. The breaking in this case was, at best, a constructive breaking. A surreptitious or forceful breaking would more strongly suggest criminal intent. Although the defendant lied at the time he gained entry, his statement was not completely misleading. It would be as reasonable to infer that he lied in order to see his father as to infer that he lied in order to commit a crime. The defendant's use of his real name when signing into the building suggests that he lacked criminal intent at that point. The thirty minute lapse of time between the defendant's entry into the lobby and the theft of Mr. Keller's possessions also suggests that the defendant had no criminal intent upon entry. Additionally, the way in which the defendant spent those thirty minutes—mopping his father's floor—indicates no criminal intent at the time of entry. The lapse of time between a breaking and a subsequent crime has been considered as significant evidence of no criminal intent upon breaking. *See, e.g., Garcia v. State*, 463 N.E.2d 1099, 1101 (Ind.1984); *Bonds v. State*, 436 N.E.2d 295, 297 (Ind.1982).

Perhaps most significant is the lack of any evidence that Kevin Reed, when entering the building, was aware that Mr. Keller's door would be open. This strongly suggests that the defendant's criminal intent was not present until inspired by the chance encounter with Mr. Keller's open door. These factors lead us to conclude that there was insufficient evidence for the trial judge to find that Kevin Reed entered the apartment building with the intent to commit a crime. . . .

We hold that the evidence was insufficient in this case for the trier of fact to find that the defendant Kevin Reed had a criminal intent at the time he entered the lobby of the apartment complex.

CASE END

CASE LAW	*Price v. State*, 111 Md.App. 487, 681 A.2d 1206 (1996)

This is an appeal from a jury trial held in the Circuit Court for Prince George's County (Sothoron, Jr., J.) on September 6, 1995, at the conclusion of which appellant, Tyrone Price, was found guilty of carjacking and of theft of property valued at more than $300. On December 8, 1995, the trial court sentenced appellant to fifteen years incarceration, five years suspended, for the carjacking conviction and to a one-year term, to be served concurrently, for the theft conviction. Appellant presents the following questions for our review . . . Is the evidence sufficient to support appellant's conviction for carjacking?

* * *

On February 13, 1995, after arranging to have a ministorage facility near the Landover Metro Station outside of Washington, D.C. remain open until 11:00 p.m., Valores Evans drove to the facility in her 1990 Ford Probe at approximately 10:50 p.m. When Evans arrived at the front gate of the storage facility, it was locked. Evans blew her vehicle's horn in an attempt to gain an employee's attention. When that did not work, Evans got out of her car, walked toward the fence, and shouted for either one of the two men who earlier in the day had agreed to meet her at the facility. Still, there was no response from inside the gates. Evans's shouts did, however, rouse some unwanted attention. Appellant approached Evans with his hand at his waist and said, "Shut up, bitch." Evans turned around, realized her situation, and said, "Oh, please don't shoot me" and ran away from the car, eventually falling to the ground. Appellant then took Evans's vehicle and drove away.

In the early morning hours on February 14, 1995, Officer Peter Woodburn of the Metropolitan Police observed Evans's 1990 Ford Probe driving on Stanton

Road in Southeast Washington, D.C. at a high rate of speed and running multiple red lights. Officer Woodburn pulled up behind the vehicle and turned on his lights and siren. The vehicle then increased its speed and attempted to evade capture. Less than five minutes later, the 1990 Ford Probe ran into a fence and came to a stop. The driver alighted from the vehicle and ran from the officer. Officer Woodburn chased the driver, but eventually lost sight of him for about ten to fifteen minutes, until another officer, Dennis Spalding, who responded to Officer Woodburn's call for help, found appellant lying face down behind a retaining wall surrounding a patio. Officer Woodburn identified appellant as the driver at that time and again in court.

Ten days later, on February 24, 1995, Evans was asked by Detective Darren Palmer to come to the police station. While there, Evans identified appellant's picture in approximately twenty seconds from six presented to her in a photo array. Evans also made an in-court identification of appellant as her attacker. At the conclusion of the trial, the jury convicted appellant of both counts. From that conviction, appellant now appeals.

Appellant contends that the trial court erred when it denied his motion for judgment of acquittal made at the end of his trial because the State failed to produce sufficient evidence to sustain his conviction. Appellant asserts that the State's case was fatally flawed in two ways: 1) the prosecution failed to produce evidence demonstrating that appellant used force or threat of force to effect the carjacking; and 2) the prosecution failed to show that the car was in Evans's "actual" possession at the time appellant allegedly carjacked it. Appellant argues that each of these facts must be proven beyond a reasonable doubt to sustain a conviction for carjacking pursuant to Md. Ann. Code art. 27, § 348A (1993).

Maryland Annotated Code art. 27, § 348A (1993), created the statutory crime of carjacking and established its elements as follows:

> An individual commits the offense of carjacking when the individual obtains unauthorized possession or control of a motor vehicle from another individual *in actual possession* by force or violence, *or by putting that individual in fear through intimidation or threat of force or violence.*

(Emphasis added). As appellant notes, no evidence was produced at trial to suggest that appellant used actual force to carjack Evans's automobile. Hence, in order to convict appellant, the jury necessarily found that he took the car by putting Evans in fear through intimidation or threat of force or violence. Appellant

asks that we reverse his conviction in part because he argues that there was insufficient evidence to support such a finding.

* * *

In the case *sub judice,* the State produced sufficient evidence from which a rational trier of fact could have found that Evans was in fear at the time appellant carjacked her automobile. As Evans was attempting to gain entry to the storage facility, appellant walked up behind her and stated, "Shut up, bitch." When he said this, according to Evans's testimony, one of appellant's hands was near his waist and, as a result, she believed he had a gun. In fact, Evans stated that appellant's order "frightened [her]" and that she believed appellant was going to shoot her. Because Evans was actually in fear at that time, she ran away and appellant was able to take her car. Appellant argues that it was unreasonable for Evans to have been in fear merely because he said, "Shut up, bitch," and had one arm by his waist. We disagree. Evans was by herself at approximately 10:50 p.m. and was accosted in a threatening manner. Appellant asserts that his statement, "Shut up, bitch," was no more than an admonition to Evans to stop yelling and implied nothing else. To the contrary, this comment, by itself, under these circumstances would be enough to cause the average person to be put in fear.

Actual Possession Under § 348A

Appellant chronicles the sordid events that spawned the legislation in the 1993 Session of the General Assembly involving the tragic death of Pamela Basu at the hands of Rodney Solomon and Bernard Miller. In his brief, appellant refers to the enactment of § 348A in the 1993 Session of the General Assembly "in response to the alarming escalation of armed hijacking of vehicles" and specifically as a result of the case of Pamela Basu who was dragged to her death when her arm became entangled in the vehicle's seatbelt after defendants Rodney Solomon and Bernard Miller forcibly took her car and drove away with her daughter in the back seat. Appellant observes in his brief that Steven B. Larsen of the Governor's Legislative Office testified to 445 carjacking incidents within the first nine months of 1992, in which twelve people were seriously injured or killed and that thirty-nine others received minor injuries. He also references the statement of Myron V. Wotring, Governmental Relations Officer of Anne Arundel County, in support of Senate Bill 339, referring to the terror of the victim "being ordered out of one's vehicle at gun point."

The testimony of Larsen, speaking for the Governor's Legislative Office, set forth in appellant's brief, included the observation that the "death of Pamela Basu in Howard County during a carjacking demonstrated the brutal dangers associated with the theft of an *occupied motor vehicle*." Larsen's testimony concluded that "the automobile can no longer be considered a safe haven." According to appellant, the amendment to the bill "indicates clearly that the legislature intended that the statute apply to thefts of *occupied* vehicles." At the outset, appellant's principal argument regarding actual possession is that the language of the statute was intended only to apply to a victim seated within the interior of the vehicle at the point when it is commandeered. This contention is based on the premise that the legislation was intended to apply only to "occupied vehicles." This argument is akin to, but slightly different from, the assertion that the victim was several feet from the vehicle at the time the car was driven away, a circumstance which resulted because the victim fled in fear of her assailant. Where the victim was when the assailant drove off with her car need not detain us long because whether the victim fled after being accosted while inside her car or, in the alternative, next to the hood, the result is the same. In either event, the vehicle would have been commandeered when the victim was initially accosted by appellant not at the point in time when she had fled some distance from the vehicle. Consequently, that appellant drove off at a point in time when there existed some distance between where the victim was and the point from which the car was driven away is of no moment. Her flight was the result of fear generated by the actions of appellant. Turning to the question of whether the legislature intended the statute only to apply to "occupied vehicles," appellant stresses the legislative history in an attempt to discern the intent of the legislature. The goal of statutory construction is to ascertain and effectuate the legislative intent. *Jones v. State,* 336 Md. 255, 260, 647 A.2d 1204 (1994); *Mustafa v. State,* 323 Md. 65, 73, 591 A.2d 481 (1991). To determine legislative intent, the reviewing court looks "first to the words of the statute, read in light of the full context in which they appear and in light of external manifestations of intent or general purpose available through other evidence." *Richmond v. State,* 326 Md. 257, 262, 604 A.2d 483 (1992), quoting *Cunningham v. State,* 318 Md. 182, 185, 567 A.2d 126 (1989). In so doing, the court gives the language of the statute its ordinary and common meaning. *Richmond,* 326 Md. at 262, 604 A.2d 483. Moreover, statutory language is analyzed from a "com-

monsensical" rather than a technical perspective, with the reviewing court seeking to avoid giving the statute a strained interpretation or one that reaches an absurd result. *Id.; Dickerson v. State,* 324 Md. 163, 171, 596 A.2d 648 (1991). It is axiomatic that the cardinal principle of statutory interpretation is that the words of the statute must be accorded their ordinary meaning. *Condon v. State,* 332 Md. 481, 491, 632 A.2d 753 (1993); *Reisch v. State,* 107 Md.App. 464, 480, 668 A.2d 970 (1995). In that regard, it is significant that the statute itself refers to an individual obtaining unauthorized possession or control "from another individual in actual possession by force or violence." Nowhere does the statute refer to an "*occupied* motor vehicle." In an attempt to equate Evans's possession of her vehicle as constructive, appellant cites *Nutt v. State,* 9 Md.App. 501, 508, 267 A.2d 280 (1970) (holding that a conviction for control of a narcotic drug is duplicitous with one for constructive possession) and *Cable v. State,* 65 Md.App. 493, 498, 501 A.2d 108 (1985) (holding that the possession of a ticket for a briefcase was tantamount to possession of the briefcase itself). Admittedly, the language of § 348A does not contemplate constructive possession nor must we consider such an interpretation. Appellant asserts "a victim who is not in the car is not in 'actual' possession of it; she possesses the car constructively." We disagree.

When accosted by appellant, Evans was positioned outside of her car along side of the hood. It matters not that, once Evans ran away from the car and fell in reacting to being accosted by appellant, as appellant indicates "at that time she was no longer near the car." The subjugation of Evans to intimidation or threat of force or violence occurred at the point in time when Evans was in the proximity of the hood of her car. In arguing an insufficiency of force, violence, threat, or intimidation, citing *West v. State,* 312 Md. 197, 202, 539 A.2d 231 (1988), appellant analogizes carjacking with robbery. Indeed, it may be argued that carjacking under § 348A is little more than the robbery of a motor vehicle without the requirement of proving the offender's specific intent permanently to deprive the owner of his or her property.

The intent of the legislature was to proscribe actions which although already crimes, *i.e.*, robbery, were deemed to be of such an aggravated nature as to require specific legislation and punishment. *See* Bill Analysis, Senate Bill 339, Senate Judicial Proceedings Committee, Testimony of Steven B. Larsen before Senate Judicial Proceedings Committee.

* * *

When one is charged with carjacking, we are not concerned with the victim's dominion and control over the vehicle except insofar as such possession is interrupted by an act of intimidation or violence on the part of an actor bent on wresting possession from the operator of the vehicle. In other words, the *actus reus* of carjacking has nothing to do with the possession by the victim of the vehicle. The only significance of the relationship between the victim and the vehicle at the time of the carjacking is in permitting a determination of whether the actor perpetrated a crime against person, *i.e.*, carjacking, or a crime against property, *i.e.*, theft. Such a distinction is no different from the distinction to be made between theft and robbery when, as an example of the former, a pickpocket simply removes a wallet without the victim's knowledge from his back pocket or, as in the latter, when a mugger forcibly wrestles a shoulderbag or pocketbook from the victim's grasp. Thus, we are concerned here not with imputing criminal responsibility, but rather with whether the defendant's actions constituted forcible taking of the vehicle or a simple theft thereof. Under the circumstance here extant, it is clear that pursuant to the language in *Foster v. State, supra,* citing *Commonwealth v. Homer, supra,* the vehicle was so within the victim's reach, inspection, observation and control, that she could have, "if not overcome by violence or prevented by fear, [have] retain[ed] [her] possession of it."

In *Hartley v. State,* 4 Md.App. 450, 243 A.2d 665 (1968), *cert. denied,* 395 U.S. 979, 89 S.Ct. 2136, 23 L.Ed.2d 768 (1969), we held that the office manager of a company was in actual possession of the money stolen when money for which he was responsible was taken from an office where he was present. *Id.* at 465, 243 A.2d 665. Nothing in the legislative history or language of § 348A suggests that "actual possession" means anything different here than it means in the robbery context. Consequently, Evans was in actual possession of her car when appellant caused her to flee by putting her in fear through the intimidating acts of accosting her at 10:50 in the evening, placing his hand at his waist indicating he had a gun, and ordering her to, "Shut up, bitch." As we observed in *Mobley v. State,* 111 Md.App. 446, 455-456, 681 A.2d 1186, slip op., pp. 9-10 (No. 1981, Sept. Term, 1995, filed September 3, 1996):

> Put another way, the victim need not actually be seated in, or operating the vehicle in order for a carjacking or attempted carjacking to be consummated. Rather, the victim need only be entering, alighting from, or otherwise in the immediate vicinity when an individual obtains unauthorized possession or control of the vehicle by intimidation, force, or violence, or by threat of force or violence. Finally, the victim's right to the vehicle need be only superior to that of the perpetrator in order for a carjacking or an attempted carjacking to have occurred.

(Footnote omitted.)

* * *

JUDGMENTS AFFIRMED.

CASE END

Case Questions

Reed v. State

1. Which element of burglary did Reed contest?

2. Which element of burglary did the court base its decision on? What facts from the alleged crime did the court use to support its decision?

3. Suppose that Bryan breaks into a home in order to use the bathroom. On his way out, he notices a diamond ring on the dresser, and he takes it. According to the court's opinion in *Reed,* has Bryan committed a burglary? Explain.

Price v. State

1. What two issues did Price raise on appeal? What did the court conclude with respect to each issue?

2. Why was the fact that the victim fled from Price irrelevant to the court's determination of whether the victim was in possession of the vehicle? Explain.

Additional Crimes to Consult

In addition to the traditional robbery offense, Maryland also has a separate offense for Robbery with a Dangerous Weapon (Md. Code Ann., Crim. Law § 3-403 (West 2002)), (commonly referred to as "armed robbery"), which carries a heightened penalty over traditional robbery. Carjacking may be committed either armed or unarmed, but both scenarios are addressed in § 3-405 of the Code and both have the same penalty. Burglary underwent a major revision in the Legislature in 1994. At that time, burglary was divided into four separate degrees depending upon a combination of 1) the premises burglarized and 2) the underlying purpose of the burglary. Different penalties accompanied the various burglary offenses (see generally Md. Code Ann., Crim. Law §§ 6-203 through 6-208 (West 2002)).

HYPOTHETICAL #1

Mary, Molly, and Megan were three beautiful young women who also happened to be three of Maryland's most elusive criminals. They were known throughout the state as "Maryland's Mysterious Mademoiselles," and this is why . . .

One day, Mary decided it was time to make some money. While walking along a busy street in Annapolis, Mary spotted a young woman walking along the street with a very large purse just barely hanging on her shoulder. Mary knew that this was an opportunity she couldn't pass up. Mary walked up quickly behind the young woman and yanked her purse off of her shoulder. Although the young woman felt a slight tug on her shoulder, she just thought it was from the weight of her purse. About two minutes later she realized her purse was gone, and she could barely make out Mary walking in the opposite direction with the same purse about two blocks up the street. Mary looked inside the purse and began counting the cash . . .

MAIN ISSUE

Did Mary Commit a Robbery by Taking Property from the Young Woman by Force or Threat of Force?

ISSUE	THESIS	RULE	ANALYSIS	CONCLUSION
Did Mary take property from the victim WHEN she removed the purse from the young woman's shoulder and left?	Mary took property from the victim WHEN she removed the purse from the young woman's shoulder and left.	To constitute a robbery PROPERTY of the victim must be taken, which is anything of value.	Mary took property BECAUSE the purse itself had value as well as the cash found inside of the purse.	Mary took property of the victim.
Did Mary take the property from the victim's presence or control WHEN she removed the purse from the young woman's shoulder?	Mary took the property from the victim's presence or control WHEN she removed the purse from the young woman's shoulder.	The property of the victim must be taken from her PRESENCE AND CONTROL.	Mary took the property from the victim's presence and control BECAUSE the purse was on the victim's shoulder hence giving the victim immediate physical possession and control of the purse and its contents.	Mary took property from the victim's presence and control.
Did Mary take the property by force or threat of force WHEN the victim was unaware her purse had been taken?	Mary did not take the property by force or threat of force WHEN the victim was unaware her purse had been taken.	The property must be taken by FORCE OR THREAT OF FORCE, hence the victim must be aware of the threatened harm and the taking of property.	Mary did not take the property by force or threat of force BECAUSE the victim only felt a slight tug and thought it was from the weight of her purse; hence, Mary did not use direct force and the victim was not placed in fear of harm or threatened by Mary.	Mary did not take the property by force or threat of force.
Did Mary intend to deprive the victim of the property WHEN she fled with the property?	Mary intended to deprive the victim of the property WHEN she fled with the property.	The perpetrator must intend to DEPRIVE the owner of their property (i.e., borrowing property with the intent to return it would not fulfill the requirement of deprivation).	Mary intended to deprive the victim of her purse BECAUSE Mary immediately fled with the purse and began looking through its contents, thus one can infer she intended to keep the purse and its contents.	Mary intended to deprive the victim of her property.

CONCLUSION

Mary did not commit a robbery because the property was not taken from the victim by force or threat of force. (Note: Based on the fact pattern Mary could be successfully charged with theft.)

HYPOTHETICAL #2

. . . Mary next approached an elderly woman on the street. Mary took out a gun and said, "Give me all your money or I'll kill you." The elderly woman, clearly panicked, replied "I don't have any money, but please don't kill me!" and handed Mary her bag. Mary took the bag and ran, but much to Mary's dismay, when she opened the bag all she found were numerous different types of make-up. Not a single dollar was in the bag!

Meanwhile, Molly was up to her own version of no-good. Molly was also known around town as "the beautiful bandit." Late one afternoon, Molly broke into one of the row homes on Duke of Gloucester Street by pushing open an unlocked window. She looked around and saw that the place wasn't even furnished, but she did manage to find a safe behind a mirror in a back bedroom. She pried open the safe and found jewels and savings bonds. Molly took everything inside and made her way out. Come to find out, Molly noticed a "For Sale" sign on the front lawn, and a lock box on the front door. It looked like no one was living there at the time, and the owners appeared to be in the process of moving out.

Megan had heard of what her companions in crime had been up to, and so she figured she needed to contribute as well. So, Megan spotted two teenage girls standing around a shiny red Corvette. The one teenager had the driver's side door opened and was leaning on the roof of the car with her foot propped inside the front seat. The second teenager was sitting on the curb directly in front of the car. Megan walked up to the girls and struck up a conversation. After talking to them for awhile, Megan said, "I just love your car, would you mind if I take it for a spin?" "Sure" said the girl seated on the curb, and she handed Megan the keys. Megan burned rubber out of there and never went back. As Megan was driving the Corvette, she spotted a Mercedes she liked much better. So, she got out of the car, walked over to a man seated in the Mercedes, and put a gun to his head. "Get out this minute or I'll blow your brains out!" she said. The man quickly got out. As it turned out, the "man" was only a 14-year-old boy (although he looked much older) who was sitting in the driver's side while his father ran into a 7-11 store to buy some cigarettes. Megan fled in the vehicle.

Unfortunately, Maryland's Mysterious Mademoiselles weren't quite as elusive as they thought. All three were apprehended by the police on the same day of their little crime spree. You are the prosecutor assigned to their cases.

➲ List the crimes with which each defendant may be charged.

DEFENDANT	VICTIM	CRIMES
Mary	elderly woman	
Molly	[home]	
Megan	teenage girls	
Megan	14-year-old boy	

➲ For EACH crime identified, complete an Analysis Chart assessing the possibility of conviction for each defendant.

DISCUSSION QUESTIONS

1. Alice walks into a department store, takes a sweater from a clothing display and puts it into her purse without paying for it. She then exits the store. Unbeknownst to her, a mall security officer watches Alice take the sweater and confronts her in the parking lot of the store. Alice then produces a gun, points it at the security officer, and says "You can't stop me from taking this sweater, now back away." Has the crime of robbery been committed? Why or why not? *See Ball v. State*, 347 Md. 156, 699 A.2d 1170, *cert. denied*, 522 U.S. 1082 (1998).

2. Ben walks up to Amanda, points a gun at her, and says "Give me all your money or I will kill you." Amanda hands over her wallet which contains $1,000, Ben takes it and runs. Ben then walks up to Bonnie, points a gun at her and says, "Give me all your money or I will kill you." Bonnie hands over her wallet which contains $1, Ben takes it and runs. Ben finally walks up to Cathy, points a gun at her, and says "Give me all your money or I will kill you." Cathy hands over her brand new wallet, Ben takes it and runs only to find that the wallet is completely empty. In which of the three scenarios has a robbery been committed? In which of the three scenarios, if any, has a felony robbery been committed?

3. Under Maryland law, could someone be charged with the crime of carjacking a moped? A scooter? A bicycle? *See* Md. Code Ann., Transp. § 11-135 (West 2002).

4. Suppose Diane is in her upstairs bedroom looking out the window at her driveway. She sees a man forcing her car door open and attempting to start her car. She yells out the window, "Hey, that's my car, you can't do that!" The man then produces a gun, points it at her, and yells back "How are you going to stop me?" Would that constitute the crime of carjacking? What if at the time Diane had in her hand a remote access to her vehicle which would allow her to unlock the vehicle and start it, would your answer change? Why or why not?

5. Eddie walks up to a convenience store and notices what he believes to be an unoccupied vehicle with the keys in the ignition and the engine running. Eddie gets into the vehicle and flees. Unbeknownst to Eddie, a two-month-old infant is in a car seat in the back of the vehicle. The infant's mother is inside the store and is unaware of Eddie's presence. Has Eddie committed a carjacking? What if instead of an infant there was a seven-year-old boy sleeping across the back seats who never woke the entire time. Would your answer change?

6. One cold December night, Frank sees a house in which it appears that no one is home. Frank decides he will break into the house in order to warm up and maybe even take a nap. He smashes a window, enters the house, and lies down on a couch. Before he falls asleep, Frank notices a large amount of cash sitting on the coffee table next to him. He puts it in his pocket and leaves the house. Has Frank just committed the crime of burglary of a dwelling? Why or why not?

7. Gary doesn't like his neighbor Henry. Gary therefore decides he wants to kill Henry. Late one night Gary picks the lock on the front door of Henry's home, walks through the house until he gets to Henry's bedroom, where Henry is sound asleep. Gary fatally shoots Henry. Has Gary committed a burglary of a dwelling?

8. Ian's house has a full basement which he rents to John as a separate apartment. John's apartment may be accessed either by a sliding glass door leading directly from the basement to the back yard, or by a door leading from the main hallway of the house to the basement steps. Both doors are kept locked and John is the only one who possesses the keys to those locks. One evening, Ian picks the lock on the door in the hallway, proceeds down the stairs into John's apartment, where Ian steals $1,000 worth of John's valuables. Has Ian committed the burglary of a dwelling?

9. Karl loathes his boss Lenny. After work one day, Karl stabs Lenny to death. Following the murder, the idea comes to Karl to check Lenny's wallet for any cash. Karl finds $300 in cash and three credit cards, all of which he takes. Is Karl guilty of robbery? *See Metheny v. State*, 359 Md. 576, 755 A.2d 1088 (2000).

TEST BANK

True/False

_____ 1. An individual may be the victim of a carjacking when she is in possession of the vehicle even if she is not the rightful owner of the vehicle.

_____ 2. A robbery will also by definition always include a felony theft.

_____ 3. Pushing open an unlocked window and then entering another's dwelling would not satisfy the "breaking" requirement for a burglary.

_____ 4. A summer vacation home could not be the subject of burglary of a dwelling if no one was staying at the home when the crime was committed.

_____ 5. A person must flee in a vehicle in order to be guilty of a carjacking.

MULTIPLE CHOICE

6. Regarding the crime of burglary in Maryland, which of the following would NOT satisfy the element that the breaking and entry must be of "someone else's dwelling":

A. Breaking and entering a summer home in the middle of February

B. Breaking and entering a hotel room where the occupant is there only for an overnight stay

C. Breaking and entering a motor home that is used primarily as a residence and is placed on concrete blocks on the ground

D. Breaking and entering a newly built home in which the residents are scheduled to move in later that month

7. Which of the following situations would NOT constitute the crime of robbery in Maryland:

A. Bob pushed Tom to the ground, reached into Tom's pocket, took Tom's wallet, and ran. The wallet was empty.

B. Bob pushed Tom to the ground, reached into Tom's pocket, pulled out a Swiss Army knife, and ran.

C. Tom was sitting in a chair in a restaurant when Bob walked up to Tom holding a baseball bat and said "give me your money or I'll beat you senseless." Tom replied "don't hurt me, I have nothing." Frustrated, Bob hit Tom in the chest with the bat and ran away.

D. Tom was sitting in a chair in a restaurant with his coat hanging on the back of his chair. Bob walked up to Tom holding a baseball bat, said "give me your money or I'll beat you senseless," and Tom reached into his coat pocket and handed Bob his wallet full of money.

8. The elements of carjacking in Maryland are:

A. The defendant obtained unauthorized possession of a vehicle; the vehicle was in actual possession of another at the time; and the defendant used force or violence against the person or put the person in fear of violence.

B. The defendant obtained unauthorized possession of a vehicle; the vehicle was in actual possession of another at the time; the defendant used force or violence against the person or put the person in fear of violence; and the defendant fled in the vehicle.

C. The defendant obtained unauthorized possession of a vehicle; the vehicle was being driven by another person at the time; and the defendant used force or violence against the person or put the person in fear of violence.

D. The defendant obtained unauthorized possession of a vehicle; the vehicle was in actual possession of another at the time; and the defendant used force or violence.

9. Abby knocks on the door of Wilma's home. When Wilma answers, Abby explains that she is selling encyclopedias. Wilma invites her inside. While Wilma goes into the kitchen to fix the two women some iced tea, Abby puts all of Wilma's good silverware into a brief case she was carrying ostensibly with the encyclopedias. Abby then flees. Has Amy committed a burglary?

   A.   No, because Wilma willingly let Abby into her home
   B.   No, because Wilma assumed the risk when she let Abby into her home
   C.   Yes, because Abby gained entry by means of deception
   D.   Yes, because Abby waited until Wilma had left the room to steal the silverware

10. Based on the scenario in question #9, why is Abby not guilty of the crime of robbery?

   A.   Because the silverware was not taken by force or threat of force
   B.   Because the silverware was not taken from Wilma's presence and control
   C.   Both A and B
   D.   Neither A nor B

Crimes Against Property

chapter seven

Introduction

This chapter covers crimes against property. This will include arson, forgery, uttering, and theft offenses. These crimes have a significant common law background that focused on tangible personal property. More recently, the Legislature has expanded these crimes to cover harm to intangible property, such as theft of cable television service or unauthorized intrusion into a computer network.

Focus Crimes

Arson, Md. Code Ann., Crim. Law §§ 6-101 through 6-109 (West 2006); MPJI-Cr. 4:00.

Forgery, Md. Code Ann., Crim. Law § 8-601 (West 2006); MPJI-Cr. 4:14 & 4:14.1.

Uttering, Md. Code Ann., Crim. Law § 8-602 (West 2006); MPJI-Cr. 4:14.2.

Theft, Md. Code Ann., Crim. Law § 7-104 (West 2006); MPJI-Cr. 4:31 & 4:32.

Objectives

Upon completing this chapter, you should be able to:

- Identify the crimes of forgery and uttering, and distinguish those crimes from writing checks on insufficient funds;
- Identify the common law theft offenses and how they have been consolidated into the modern-day theft laws;
- Identify the requirement to elevate theft from a misdemeanor offense to a felony offense, and understand the concept of aggravating values of a series of thefts;
- Identify the crime of arson and the various establishments that can be the subject of said arson; and
- Analyze and apply the elements of each of these crimes.

 CASE LAW

Kelley v. State, 402 Md. 745, 939 A.2d 149 (2008)

Petitioner, Robert Kelley, was convicted by a jury in the Circuit Court for Washington County on three counts of felony theft—theft of property having a value of $500 or more. *See* Maryland Code, § 7-104(g) of the Criminal Law Article (CL). The maximum penalty prescribed for felony theft is imprisonment for fifteen years and a fine of $25,000. Upon each of the three convictions in this case, the court imposed a six-year prison sentence, the sentences to run consecutively for an aggregate of eighteen years.

The thefts, which petitioner no longer contests, involved multiple items of property taken from three different owners, over differing periods of time, from three separate locations a mile or more apart from one another. Count 5 charged the theft of two items of property from Mary Trumpower between December 4

97

and December 18, 2003. During that period, an antique sleigh was stolen from her barn and an antique wheelbarrow was taken from her garage. Count 11 involved the theft of several items from Donald Spickler. During the period November 27 to 29, 2003, an antique sleigh was taken from Mr. Spickler's barn and miscellaneous glassware and a toy tank were taken from his house. Count 16 dealt with various items taken from Eliza Spickler, Donald Spickler's mother. During the period November 1 to December 18, 2003, certain items were taken from her vacant house and others were taken from her store. The house was vacant because Ms. Spickler was in a nursing home.

In each of the theft counts, the State relied on CL § 7-103(f) to aggregate the value of each item taken in order to reach the $500 threshold for felony theft. Section 7-103(f), which is part of the section dealing with the determination of value for purposes of the theft law, provides:

"When theft is committed in violation of this part under one scheme or continuing course of conduct, whether from the same or several sources:

(1) The conduct may be considered as one crime; and

(2) the value of the property or services may be aggregated in determining whether the theft is a felony or a misdemeanor."

Kelley believes that it is impermissible for the State to aggregate the value of the property taken with respect to the three individual counts, so as to make the separate takings one felony theft in each case, but then to consider the three series of thefts separate for sentencing purposes. The necessary underpinning of his argument is that he had but one scheme to steal from all three victims, not three separate schemes, and that all of the thefts were therefore committed pursuant to that one scheme as one continuing course of conduct. Accordingly, he urges, there was only one crime of felony theft, for which only one sentence could lawfully be imposed. . . .

At issue is what is known as the "single larceny doctrine," the substance of which this Court first recognized in *State v. Warren,* 77 Md. 121, 26 A. 500 (1893) and discussed most recently in *State v. White,* 348 Md. 179, 702 A.2d 1263 (1997). . . .

In 1978, the General Assembly, following the lead of the Model Penal Code, enacted a new, consolidated theft statute that encompassed seven pre-existing larceny offenses. *See* 1978 Md. Laws, ch. 849. The new statute was the product of a joint subcommittee of the Legislature. *See* REVISION OF MARYLAND THEFT

LAWS AND BAD CHECK LAWS, Joint Subcommittee on Theft Related Offenses, Maryland General Assembly (1978). As part of the statute, the Legislature codified the common law single larceny doctrine as it had been applied in *Warren, Delcher,* and *Horsey* and extended it to cover the previously unaddressed circumstance. That statute, now codified as CL § 7-103(f), makes clear that, when theft is committed "under one scheme or continuing course of conduct, whether from the same or several sources: (1) the conduct may be considered as one crime; and (2) the value of the property or services may be aggregated in determining whether the theft is a felony or a misdemeanor."

In its Report, the joint subcommittee noted:

"The paragraph on aggregation was inserted on the basis that a person who steals property at different times from several persons and places as part of a continuing scheme has engaged in activity which is just as reprehensible as a person who steals an equal amount from a single person and place at one time. It is a marked departure from the common law which requires that the property be stolen from a single person at a single time and place."

In that last sentence, the joint subcommittee apparently overlooked this Court's pronouncements in *Warren, Delcher,* and *Horsey,* which were not mentioned but where, as noted, the Court had applied at least the substance of the single larceny doctrine where property was stolen from several persons at the same time or, if as part of a continuing scheme, from one person at different times. In those settings, the statute merely codified the then-existing Maryland common law. What the statute clearly added to the law, however, was that the doctrine could also apply in the setting not reached in *Warren, Delcher,* or *Horsey*—where, as part of one continuing scheme or course of conduct, several items are stolen from *different* persons at *different* times.

The Court of Special Appeals considered this statutory expansion in *State v. Hunt,* 49 Md.App. 355, 432 A.2d 479 (1981). In that case, the defendant was charged in two counts with stealing goods from seven different stores on a single day. The two counts were identical, except that one charged felony theft and the other misdemeanor theft. Although all of the thefts were alleged to have occurred on the same day, it appeared that all of the stores were in one shopping mall, so the court treated the thefts as having occurred at different times, as Hunt went from one store to another. Hunt contended that the counts were duplicitous, because they charged separate offenses, and both the circuit court and the Court of Special Appeals agreed with him.

Citing the Maryland statute and the joint subcommittee's comment, the intermediate appellate court observed that "before a series of thefts from different owners at different times and places can be considered as one offense, charged in a single count of the charging document, and the value of the stolen property aggregated, the thefts must be committed pursuant to one scheme or continuing course of conduct." *Id.* at 361, 432 A.2d at 482. The court then added:

> "The charging documents in question allege a series of thefts but fail to allege that they were committed pursuant to one scheme or continuing course of conduct. Therein lies the problem. Absent such an allegation, the charging documents merely allege separate and distinct crimes in a single count which makes them duplicitous." *Id.*

Although in *Hunt* the single larceny doctrine was not applied because the indictment failed to allege a single scheme and continuing course of conduct, the clear implication is that, had the indictment contained such an allegation and had the State been able to prove that allegation, a conviction for felony theft would have been sustained.

White involved the theft of two items of property—a canvas bag and a small television set—from a schoolhouse office shared by two or more teachers. The evidence indicated that White entered the office and stole the two items at the same time. It was not clear who owned the television set, but the case proceeded on the assumption that it was not owned by the teacher whose canvas bag was stolen, so the case presented the situation of the theft of two items owned by different persons at the same time. Instead of aggregating the value of the items, however, the State charged White with two counts of misdemeanor theft, of which he was convicted and for which he received consecutive sentences of eighteen months. On appeal, the Court of Special Appeals applied the single larceny doctrine, regarded the two takings as one offense, and merged the convictions, thereby striking one of the sentences. We affirmed.

In *White*, the Court addressed two basic issues raised by the State: first, whether Maryland had ever, in fact, adopted the common law single larceny rule, and second, whether what is now CL § 7-03(f) precluded application of that rule. As to the first, we "ma[d]e explicit what might otherwise have been implicit from *Warren*—that, although application of the [single larceny] doctrine may depend on the factual circumstances presented, the single larceny doctrine was part of Maryland common law" and that, under that common law "the stealing of several articles of property at the same time, belonging to several owners (or the same owner) *ordinarily* constituted one offense." 348 Md. at 192, 702 A.2d at 1269. (Emphasis in original.) In a footnote to that statement, we observed that we stressed the word "ordinarily" so as not "to foreclose the prospect of a different result where the facts clearly would have indicated that separate and distinct thefts were intended and accomplished" and that, "[i]n such a circumstance, the different result would not arise from rejection of the single larceny doctrine but rather from a conclusion that it did not apply." *Id.,* n. 5. . . .

Two things are clear from *White*, and most particularly from our footnote 5 in the *White* Opinion, *see ante*. First, when considering whether the theft of multiple items of property, at the same time or at different times, from the same owner or from different owners, constitutes one offense or separate offenses (and with that, whether the value of the different items can be aggregated or not aggregated), the ultimate criterion is whether the separate takings were part of a single scheme or continuing course of conduct. If so, one offense must be charged and the values may be aggregated to determine whether the offense is a felony. To the extent that is not the case, the takings constitute separate offenses and aggregation of values is permissible only with respect to the takings included in each of the respective separate offenses.

The second lesson from *White* is that the determination of whether multiple takings were part of a single scheme or course of conduct, for any purpose other than resolving the sufficiency of the charging document, is a factual matter that must be based on evidence. We observed there that the single larceny doctrine "rests on the notion that the separate takings are all part of a single larcenous scheme and a continuous larcenous act, and, *when the evidence suffices to establish that fact, directly or by inference,* most courts have had no problem applying the doctrine." *White*, 348 Md. at 188-89, 702 A.2d at 1268. (Emphasis added.) The question, then, is whether the State has sufficiently established beyond a reasonable doubt that there was, or, in this case, was *not*, a single larcenous scheme or course of conduct. . . .

Our case law, supplemented by CL § 7-103(f) and the gloss put on that statute by the Comment of the legislative subcommittee that drafted it, makes it much easier to find the requisite single scheme or continuing course of conduct and apply the single larceny doctrine to the taking of property from one or several owners at the same time or multiple takings from a single owner, even if carried out over a period of time. That seems to be consistent with the law nationally. . . .

Although the same principles apply where there are multiple takings from different owners at different times and at different locations, the courts have been very reluctant to find a single scheme or continuing impulse or course of conduct in that situation. *See State v. Rowell,* 121 N.M. 111, 908 P.2d 1379 (1995); *People v. Perlstein,* 97 A.D.2d 482, 467 N.Y.S.2d 682 (1983); *State v. Maggard,* 61 S.W. 184 (Mo.1901); *State v. Cabbell,* 252 N.W.2d 451 (Iowa 1977). Indeed, the general rule outside of Maryland seems to be that the takings in that situation may not be consolidated and regarded as a single offense, but must be treated as separate offenses. Professors Torcia and LaFave are in agreement on that principle. Torcia notes:

> "When several articles are stolen by the defendant from different owners on different occasions, multiple larcenies are committed. It matters not that the takings occur on the same expedition, and are committed in rapid succession or in pursuance of a larcenous scheme or plan."

3 Charles E. Torcia, WHARTON'S CRIMINAL LAW, § 347 (1995). LaFave states, just as succinctly, "A thief may steal different articles from different victims at different times and places, and such takings cannot be aggregated for the purpose of making one grand larceny out of several petit larcenies." 3 Wayne R. La-Fave, SUBSTANTIVE CRIMINAL LAW, § 19.4(b) at 82 (2nd ed.2003).

CL § 7-103(f) is not so rigid. It would allow a court, upon evidence establishing the fact beyond a reasonable doubt, to find that takings from different owners at different times and locations were pursuant to a single scheme and constituted a continuing course of conduct. Such a single scheme conceivably may be found where multiple takings from different owners at different locations are in quick and unbroken succession and from a limited area. As noted, *State v. Hunt, supra,* 49 Md.App. 355, 432 A.2d 479, left that implication. Where there is a more significant time lapse between the takings, however, or they occur from locations that are not in very close proximity, the general rule that the takings are not part of a single scheme or a continuing course of conduct should be applied, for it is far more difficult to infer a single scheme or continuing impulse or course of conduct in that situation.

This is not a case in which the takings from the three owners occurred in quick and unbroken succession *or* from a limited area *or* from locations that were in close proximity. They occurred during different time periods, at least two of which (Mary Trumpower and Donald Spickler) did not even overlap; there was no evidence that any of the takings from one owner occurred in quick or unbroken succession of those from another; and, as noted the locations were separated from each other by at least a mile. For these reasons, we agree that the State proved three separate felony thefts and that separate sentences were appropriately imposed on each of them. The fact that Donald Spickler exercised some general dominion and control over the property of his mother, Eliza, while she was in a nursing home, is irrelevant. There were still separate thefts.

CASE END

CASE LAW

Richmond v. State, 326 Md. 257, 604 A.2d 483 (1992)

. . . On February 5, 1987, a fire broke out in a two story apartment building located at Dallas Place in Temple Hills. The building contained approximately ten units. The fire originated in the ground floor apartment of Martha Gobert and quickly spread to the apartment located across a common hallway, occupied by Wanda Pfeiffer, and to the apartment located above the Gobert unit, occupied by Evelyn Saunders. All three apartment units were substantially damaged before the fire could be extinguished.

An official investigation of the fire disclosed that Guy L. Richmond, Jr., the appellant, had arranged for three of his confederates to set fire to Gobert's apartment. Richmond and Gobert worked for the same employer, and Richmond recently had been suspended from his job because of a work place grievance filed against him by Gobert.

On October 19, 1987, after a bench trial before the Circuit Court for Prince George's County, Richmond was convicted of three separate counts of an indictment, charging violation of Maryland Code (1957, 1982 Repl.Vol.) Article 27, § 6 for procuring the burning of the "dwelling houses" of Gobert, Pfeiffer, and Saunders. Thereafter, he was sentenced to 15 years imprisonment on each count with the terms to run consecutively. The Court of Special Appeals affirmed his convictions and sentences in an unreported opinion filed on December 22, 1988. . . .

Richmond contends that the burning of three apartments was the result of one criminal act, that it is but one offense proscribed by Art. 27, § 6, and that the imposition of multiple sentences for this one offense violates double jeopardy principles. The Double Jeopardy Clause of the Fifth Amendment protects against a second prosecution for the same offense after acquittal, a second prosecution for the same offense after conviction, and multiple punishments for the same offense. . . . Because Richmond was subjected to only one prosecution, his contention deals with the prohibition against multiple punishments for the same offense. Multiple punishment challenges generally arise in two different sets of circumstances: those involving two separate statutes embracing the same criminal conduct, and those involving a single statute creating multiple units of prosecution for conduct occurring as a part of the same criminal transaction. *Gore v. United States*, 357 U.S. 386, 393-94, 78 S.Ct. 1280, 1285, 2 L.Ed.2d 1405, 1411 (1958) (Warren, C.J., dissenting); *Randall Book Corp.*, 316 Md. at 324, 558 A.2d at 720; *Brown*, 311 Md. at 431, 535 A.2d at 487. Richmond's contention in the instant case is of the second type. . . .

It is manifest from the language employed in Art. 27, § 6 that the General Assembly intended the unit of prosecution to be "any dwelling house" burned. The issue before us is not thereby resolved, however, because the term "dwelling house" is not defined in the statute; we must determine whether each individual apartment unit burned constitutes a separate dwelling house.

By Ch. 138 of the Acts of 1809 the Legislature prescribed punishments for various common law crimes. Section 5 of that Act dealt with the crime of arson, which at common law is the willful and malicious burning of the dwelling house of another, either by night or by day. R. Perkins and R. Boyce, *Criminal Law*, 273-74 (3d ed. 1982); 3 C. Torcia, *Wharton's Criminal Law*, § 345 (14th ed. 1980). It merely referred to the common law crime and provided for the punishment of death or, alternatively, a maximum of 20 years in the penitentiary. Ch. 138, § 5 of the Acts of 1809. *See Cochrane v. State*, 6 Md. 400, 405 (1854) (The Act of 1809, ch. 138, only provides for the punishment of the crime of arson without defining it; the crime is therefore left as it stood at common law). In 1904, the General Assembly slightly expanded upon the common law definition of arson by making illegal the burning of one's own dwelling house if the intent in burning it was to injure or defraud. Ch. 267, § 6 of the Acts of 1904.

The first substantive attempt to codify the elements of the crime of arson occurred in 1929. Ch. 255, § 6 of the Acts of 1929. The wording of the statute in force today, Art. 27, § 6, remains unchanged since that time. While retaining the common law definition of arson in Art. 27, § 6, other sections of Art. 27 have been added by the Legislature to cover burning of buildings not specified in § 6, burning of personal property of another, burning goods with the intent to defraud an insurer, attempted arson, and other criminal burnings. Art. 27, §§ 7-10. The language of Art. 27, § 6 prohibiting the burning of a "dwelling house," however, which was adopted from the common law, has not been varied.

Thus, Maryland has retained the common law definition of arson in Art. 27, § 6. *Hannah v. State*, 3 Md.App. 325, 329-30 n. 1, 239 A.2d 124, 127 n. 1, *cert. denied*, 251 Md. 749 (1968). Sir William Blackstone explained the reasons why arson is considered such a serious crime:

"ARSON, *ab ardendo*, is the malicious and wilful burning of the house or outhouses of another man. This is an offence of very great malignity, and much more pernicious to the public than simple theft: because, first, it is an offence against that right, of habitation, which is acquired by the law of nature as well as by the laws of society; next, because of the terror and confusion that necessarily attends it; and, lastly, because in simple theft the thing stolen only changes it's [sic] master, but still remains *in esse* for the benefit of the public, whereas by burning the very substance is absolutely destroyed."

4 W. Blackstone, Commentaries. Thus, at common law, arson is an offense against the security of habitation or occupancy, rather than against ownership or property. 3 C. Torcia, *Wharton's Criminal Law* § 345 (14th ed. 1980). Expounding on what constitutes a "dwelling house," Blackstone stated that "if a landlord or reversioner sets fire to his own house, of which another is in possession under a lease from himself or from those whose estate he hath, it shall be accounted arson; for, during the lease, the house is the property of the tenant." 4 W. Blackstone, Commentaries *221-22 (footnote omitted). Thus, since each leased apartment is the property of a separate tenant, and a burning of that property, whether by the landlord or some other individual, constitutes arson, each separate apartment burned constitutes a separate unit of prosecution.

The language of Art. 27, § 6 further confirms the conclusion that each individual apartment burned constitutes a separate dwelling house and a separate offense of arson. Section 6 states that "[a]ny person who wilfully and maliciously sets fire to or burns or causes to be burned or who aids, counsels, or procures the burning of *any* dwelling house" shall be guilty of arson (emphasis added). We have previously construed the use of the word "any" in a criminal statute to mean "every" and to support a legislative intent authorizing multiple convictions. . . .

Generally, a structure which qualifies as a dwelling house for the purpose of burglary also qualifies as a dwelling house for the purpose of arson. 3 C. Torcia, *Wharton's Criminal Law*, § 350 (14th ed. 1980). In describing what places could be subjects of a burglary, Blackstone observed, "[a] chamber in a college or an inn of court, where each inhabitant hath a distinct property, is, to all other purposes as well as this, the mansion-house of the owner." 4 W. Blackstone, Commentaries *225.

Several cases dealing with convictions for breaking and entering a dwelling house indicate that one separate portion of a building can independently be a dwelling house subject to being invaded by the offender. In *Jones v. State*, 2 Md.App. 356, 234 A.2d 625 (1967), Jones broke into a building where two floors were occupied by a club and one floor was used as an apartment by an individual. The Court of Special Appeals held that the part of the building used as an apartment was a dwelling house and the part used as a club was a storehouse. *See id.* at 360 n. 1, 234 A.2d at 627 n. 1. In *Herbert v. State*, 31 Md.App. 48, 354 A.2d 449 (1976), the defendant walked down a row of motel rooms, entered Room 66 for several minutes, and then attempted to enter Room 76. He was convicted of burglary of Room 66 and attempted storehouse breaking of Room 76. The court upheld his conviction for burglary of Room 66 because the State had proven that one room of the motel to be a dwelling house. *Id.* at 52, 354 A.2d at 451-52. Thus, for the purposes of satisfying a necessary element of the crime of burglary, a separate unit of a building may be a separate dwelling house. These cases support the conclusion that each separate apartment is a dwelling house under Art. 27, § 6. *See also* R. Perkins and R. Boyce, *Criminal Law* 257 (3d ed. 1982) ("There may be more than one dwelling under the same roof and this applies not only to apartment houses . . . each apartment in a tenement house is 'the dwelling house of the particular occupant'" (footnote omitted)). . . .

Providing for multiple punishment when there are multiple victims also comports with the notion that the punishment for criminal conduct should be commensurate with responsibility. *Brown*, 311 Md. at 436, 535 A.2d at 490. It makes sense that the Legislature would provide for a greater penalty for setting fire to an apartment building, containing many separate residences, than for setting fire to a single home. The language of the statute clearly reflects the legislative intention that the unit of prosecution be each dwelling house burned. Each of the separate apartments in the building, occupied by separate tenants, constituted a separate dwelling house. Thus, each apartment burning was a separate offense of arson.

For all of the foregoing reasons, Richmond's convictions and sentences for procuring the burning of three separate apartments within one apartment building do not offend the Double Jeopardy Clause.

CASE END

Case Questions

Kelley v. State

1. How did this case deal with two distinct types of aggregation? Explain.

2. What is the "single larceny doctrine"?

3. Why would it have benefitted Kelley to have the thefts from Mary Trumpower, Donald Spickler, and Eliza Spickler charged as one common scheme?

4. Based on the court's decision which of the following thefts, if committed pursuant to "a single scheme or course of conduct," could be aggregated? (a) Multiple thefts from a single owner at different times; (b) thefts from multiple owners at the same time; and (c) thefts from multiple owners and different times.

Richmond v. State

1. How did the law with respect to burglary aid the court in deciding this case?

2. Why was the Double Jeopardy Clause of the 5th Amendment at issue in this case?

3. Suppose that Bill successfully burns down a high rise apartment complex in Baltimore. The complex contains 500 separate apartments that are all inhabited. Would Bill be guilty of 500 counts of arson with each count subject to a separate penalty? Explain.

Additional Crimes to Consult

In addition to the crimes discussed through this chapter, Maryland's Legislature criminalizes the more traditional offenses of malicious destruction of property (Md. Code Ann., Crim. Law § 8-103), and trespass (Md. Code Ann., Crim. Law § 6-402). Furthermore, the Legislature has prohibited the offenses of issuing and passing checks either with knowledge of insufficient funds or with the intent to stop payment on the check. (Md. Code Ann., Crim. Law § 6-301 et. seq.)

In our modern world, harm to property can occur even when property is not tangible. Therefore, Maryland's Legislature has made it a crime to access a computer or digital material without authorization. It can be a crime merely to access the computer, to destroy or alter data or to steal data or information. *See* Md. Code Ann., Crim. Law § 7-301 et. seq. Additionally, the offenses of credit card theft (Md. Code Ann., Crim. Law § 8-204) and identity theft (Md. Code Ann., Crim. Law § 8-301) have been prohibited.

HYPOTHETICAL #1

Gary had stolen a brand new BMW from a car dealership. He wanted to sell the car to Bernie who did not know that the car was stolen. Bernie had promised to pay Gary $50,000 for the vehicle. So, Gary used his computer to create a Maryland Certificate of Title representing that Gary was the true owner. Gary signed the document and intended to provide it to Bernie for Bernie to submit to the MVA. Gary did not submit it to the MVA himself.

MAIN ISSUE

Did Gary Forge the Certificate of Title to the Vehicle?

ISSUE	THESIS	RULE	ANALYSIS	CONCLUSION
Did Gary make a false writing WHEN he created a Certificate of Title on his computer and signed it?	Gary made a false writing WHEN he created a Certificate of Title on his computer and signed it.	Forgery requires the MAKING OF A FALSE WRITING.	The Certificate of Title was a writing BECAUSE it was a document that identified the owner to the vehicle. It was a document because it was printed on paper. It was a false document because the certificate represented that Gary was the true and lawful owner, when, in fact, he was not.	Gary made a false writing.
Did the Certificate of Title appear to be a valid legal document WHEN it was generated on a computer and signed?	The Certificate of Title most likely appeared to be a valid legal document WHEN it was generated on a computer and signed.	Forgery requires that the false writing APPEAR TO BE A VALID LEGAL DOCUMENT.	The Certificate of Title most likely appeared to be a valid legal document BECAUSE, by using a computer, Gary was most likely able to create a Certificate of Title that looked genuine to a common person. A careful study of the exact document will be necessary to fully ascertain if it appeared valid. The Certificate of Title was a legal document because it was used to establish the true ownership of the vehicle for the purposes of MVA records.	Gary most likely made a false writing that appeared to be a valid legal document.
Did Gary make the Certificate of Title with the intent to cheat or defraud WHEN he was using it to facilitate Bernie's purchase of a stolen vehicle?	Gary made the Certificate of Title with the intent to cheat or defraud WHEN he was using it to facilitate Bernie's purchase of a stolen vehicle.	The false writing must be DONE WITH THE INTENT TO CHEAT OR DEFRAUD.	Gary intended to defraud Bernie BECAUSE Gary intended to use the title to prove to Bernie that Gary was the true and lawful owner of the vehicle so that Bernie would purchase the vehicle. Gary knew that a title was necessary to complete the sale of the vehicle and wanted Bernie to believe that he was taking full possession and title to the vehicle in exchange for $50,000.	Gary intended to cheat or defraud Bernie.

CONCLUSION

Gary most likely forged the certificate of title to the vehicle.

HYPOTHETICAL #2

Only a few short years ago Ben and Jerry were sitting on a goldmine when they opened their own business selling delicious and delectable ice cream. But soon the economy took a down-turn and Americans decided to be health conscious so ice cream wasn't very high on anyone's list of things to buy. Before they knew it, Ben and Jerry were flat broke! They decided they couldn't live a life of poverty, and *something* was going to have to change!

Ben decided that since he wasn't making any money the legal way that he would literally make money of his own. With a little bit of planning he was soon printing crisp $20 bills in the basement of his home. He also came up with what he thought was a brilliant idea. Since he was already such an expert in the ice cream world, he created his very own identification card establishing him as a health inspector for the state's Health Department. The ID was flawless—he had copied the state seal, had his photo on it and signed it at the bottom. The next weekend Ben visited five different Baskin Robbins' stores. He flashed the store manager his ID and explained that he was there for a surprise inspection. After each store visit, he found $100 worth of bogus health code violations, and he collected the $500 in cash on the spot.

Meanwhile, that same weekend Jerry visited the Annapolis Mall. He first visited the food court where he bought a few slices of pizza and a soda from Sbarro's, paying the $11 bill with one of the $20s that Ben had printed in his basement just the day before. While eating his lunch, Jerry devised a little scheme. He supposedly went shopping in the mall, but he "accidentally" spilled soda in some of the stores. When the clerk went to clean up the mess, Jerry quickly pried open the cash register and took as much money as he could. In less than 30 minutes, Jerry pulled the same stunt four times, taking $75 from The Gap; $125 from Victoria Secret; and $100 each from Old Navy and Coach. Jerry was just about to leave the mall when he spotted a pet shop with the cutest kittens for sale in the window. The sign read "Purebred Siamese kittens, $350 each." Jerry just couldn't resist! He waited until the store manager was distracted by a Beagle puppy that had peed all over the floor, and he quickly grabbed one of the kittens and shoved it under his coat. Jerry bolted for the mall exit. Just as he was about to enter the parking lot, his unwilling stow-away gave *him* away—the kitten's meows alerted Ashe, the mall security guard, who quickly apprehended Jerry and returned the kitten safely to the pet store.

When Ben heard that his brother had been arrested he was furious! He immediately wanted to know who was responsible for this awful turn of events, and when he found out it was Ashe he decided to get his revenge. Late one night after the mall closed, Ben followed Ashe home. Ben watched as Ashe entered his residence, and when all the lights went out a short time later Ben poured gasoline around the entire structure and lit a match. Within seconds the home ignited. But much to Ben's dismay, Ashe lived right across the street from the fire station and firefighters were able to put the blaze out almost immediately. When the smoke cleared Ben learned that Ashe shared a duplex with Amber. Amber's residence suffered considerable damage by the fire, but other than being a little soggy from the fire hoses, Ashe's home had absolutely no damage. Ben was foiled!

As it turns out, the two brothers, who hadn't lived together since they were kids, got to be roomies once again—this time in a prison cell!

⊃ List the crimes with which each defendant may be charged.

DEFENDANT	VICTIM	CRIMES
Ben	—	
Jerry	—	

⊃ For EACH crime identified, complete an Analysis Chart assessing the possibility of conviction for each defendant.

DISCUSSION QUESTIONS

1. At common law it was impossible to commit a theft of services. Under the current law, theft of services is included. Do you agree with the current state of the law? Why or why not?

2. Is "phising" for personal information, such as credit card numbers and social security numbers, theft?

3. Do you think it is a crime or should be a crime to use someone's wireless computer network without their authorization when the network was unsecured?

4. Is it a crime to hack into a computer network without taking, altering or destroying any information located inside?

5. Is it or should it be a crime to steal computer passwords?

6. Beth created a computer virus that would deposit a keystroke monitor in to the computers of anyone who opened it. The keystroke monitors reported back to Beth everything that the user typed. Beth sent an email to Elizabeth with an attachment containing cute pictures of puppies and kittens. Hidden within the attachment was the virus. As soon as the attachment was opened the virus would be launched. Elizabeth did not have any virus protection software and did not know there was a virus in the email. She forwarded the email to Michael and his computer was infected when he opened the attachment. Can Beth be liable for unauthorized access into Elizabeth's computer? Can Beth be liable for unauthorized access into Michael's computer when she was not the person who sent Michael the infected email?

7. Is entering false amounts into an accounting ledger considered forgery?

8. What is the difference between forgery and uttering?

9. Is uttering essential to a forgery conviction? Is forgery essential to an uttering conviction?

10. Tina and Tom just went through a very bad break-up, and Tina wants revenge. One evening she goes over to the apartment complex where Tom lives, pours gasoline all around the base of the building, and lights a match. Poof! The entire apartment complex burns to the ground. Fortunately no one is home at the time, but six separate apartments are destroyed and six families are now homeless, including Tom. How many counts of arson should Tina be charged with? What if the complex was a high rise in the middle of the city and had 500 separate apartments within the building? *See Richmond v. State*, 326 Md. 257, 604 A.2d 483 (1992).

11. Other than forging a check or counterfeiting money, what are some examples you could think of that could be the subject of a forgery either by a false making or an alteration?

12. Mike is desperately in need of some cash, but he has also taken a few criminal justice classes and he knows that felony theft can land him in jail for a long time. The last thing he needs is to spend years behind bars. So, Mike decides he will outsmart the system: On January 1 he breaks into his neighbor's house when no one is home by pushing open a window, and he takes $200 in cash. It was all so easy that Mike does the exact same thing on January 2 to his other neighbor's house—he again takes $200. On January 3 he picks yet another neighbor's house and takes $200, but the police are tipped off and Mike is arrested. He is charged with one count of felony theft. Mike argues he is at most guilty of three misdemeanor thefts. Based on the court's opinion in *Kelley v. State*, 402 Md. 745, 939 A.2d 149 (2008) will Mike's argument succeed?

TEST BANK

True/False

_____ 1. Someone actually has to be living in a house, with 2 bedrooms, a bathroom and a kitchen, for such house to be considered a dwelling house for the purposes of arson.

_____ 2. Bill pours gasoline on the laminate floors in Beth's living room. The gasoline burns, but the floor and the rest of the house remains intact. Bill has committed the necessary burning for arson to have taken place.

_____ 3. Bill is Beth's enemy. Bill turns on the natural gas on Beth's stove without igniting the burner. Knowing Beth is a smoker, he is sure when she comes home and lights her cigarette the house will explode and burn to the ground. Bill was right in part. The house did explode when Beth lit her cigarette. However, it was not engulfed in flames as he expected. Instead there was just rubble and no fire. Bill has committed the necessary burning for arson to have taken place.

_____ 4. Benny found out that his partner Mitch has been cheating on him. Benny took all of Mitch's clothes, put them in a pile in the back yard, and started a bon fire with the clothes. Mitch came home to find Benny roasting hot dogs over the fire. Benny has not committed arson because a structure has not been burned.

_____ 5. Michaela signs William's name to a document entitled "Last Will and Testament of William" leaving all of William's belongings to Michaela. Michaela then arranges William's untimely death. Michaela can only be guilty of forgery after William is dead but not before his death.

MULTIPLE CHOICE

6. Michael grabbed what he believed was his jacket off a coat rack at a bar. When he got outside the bar and put it on he walked to the next bar about a mile down the road. When he reached in the jacket pocket to get money for the cover charge for the next bar, he pulled out someone else's wallet and realized he had picked up an identical jacket that had belonged to someone else. Michael is guilty of

   A. Robbery

   B. Theft

   C. Both A and B

   D. Neither A or B

7. Which of the following is the strongest proof that a defendant may have committed theft?

   A. Possession of recently stolen goods

   B. Knew of goods that were recently stolen

   C. Saw a stranger steal goods but did nothing about it

8. Jeff paid Susan, a dairy farmer, $500 for a shipment of 500 gallons of milk. Susan delayed delivery of a shipment of milk by four days past the delivery date on the contract. When the milk arrived it was spoiled. Susan is

   A. Not guilty of theft because she delivered the quantity of milk promised

   B. Is guilty of theft because the milk was spoiled and had no value to Jeff

   C. Is guilty of uttering

9. For the purposes of theft, deprivation means
    A.   To deprive for any portion of time
    B.   To deprive permanently
    C.   To make someone suffer personal injury as a result of the loss
    D.   None of the above

10. John received a check from Mary made payable to him in the amount of $50. John added another zero to the amount, making the check $500. John indorsed the check and gave it to a bank teller seeking to cash the check.
    A.   John uttered a forged instrument when he received the check from Mary
    B.   John uttered a forged instrument when he added the extra zero to the amount
    C.   John uttered a forged instrument when he indorsed the back of the check
    D.   John uttered a forged instrument when he gave the check to the teller

chapter eight

Drugs and Alcohol Offenses

Introduction

This chapter deals with drug and alcohol offenses, an area of law that has received significant attention from the Legislature in the last several years due in large part to the concerns of drug and alcohol abuse in our society. With regard to drug offenses, Maryland's laws classify hundreds of substances known as Controlled Dangerous Substances ("CDS") into five schedules depending upon a combination of each substance's 1) potential for abuse; 2) accepted medical use; and 3) potential for dependence. Md. Code Ann., Crim. Law §§ 5-402 through 5-406. These CDS include both what is commonly referred to as "street drugs" (drugs that have no legitimate uses, such as heroin or crack cocaine) and also drugs that are legal to possess assuming one has a valid prescription (such as Oxy-Contin or Xanax). With regard to alcohol offenses, in 2001 the Legislature lowered the legal limit and changed terminology with regard to operating a motor vehicle while under the influence of alcohol.

Focus Crimes

Possession, Md. Code Ann., Crim. Law § 5-601 (West 2006); MPJI-Cr. 4:24.

Possession with Intent to Distribute, Md. Code Ann., Crim. Law § 5-602(2) (West 2006); MPJI-Cr. 4:24.1.

Distribution, Md. Code Ann., Crim. Law § 5-602(1) (West 2006); MPJI-Cr. 4:24.2.

Manufacture, Md. Code Ann., Crim. Law § 5-602(1) (West 2006); MPJI-Cr. 4:24.3.

Maintaining a Common Nuisance, Md. Code Ann., Crim. Law § 5-605 (West 2006); MPJI-Cr. 4:24.8.

DUI/DWI, Md. Code Ann., Transp. II §21-902 (West 2002); MPJI-Cr. 4:10.

Objectives

Upon completing this chapter you should be able to:

- ➲ Analyze possessory-based drug offenses;
- ➲ Distinguish between actual and constructive possession of a CDS;
- ➲ Recognize the impact that 1) the drug; 2) the nature of the offense; and 3) the repetitive nature of the crime will have on potential penalties;
- ➲ Recognize collateral consequences of CDS possession; and
- ➲ Analyze the requirements for driving while impaired or under the influence of alcohol.

| CASE LAW | *Taylor v. State*, 346 Md. 452, 697 A.2d 462 (1997) |

Petitioner, Richard Jamison Taylor, was convicted of possession of marijuana in violation of Maryland Code (1957, 1996 Repl.Vol.) Art. 27, § 287. He argues that the evidence was insufficient to sustain his conviction. We agree and therefore shall reverse.

We shall set forth the evidence in some detail as our holding is based on the insufficiency of the evidence to sustain the conviction. Petitioner was charged with possession of marijuana. A co-defendant, Kristopher Klein, was charged with possession of marijuana and possession of paraphernalia. They were jointly tried in the Circuit Court for Worcester County in a bench trial. Klein was acquitted.

The charges arose from the following incident. On the morning of June 10, 1995, Petitioner, along with four friends, rented a room at the Days Inn Motel in Ocean City, Maryland. On that morning, Ocean City Police Officer Bernal and another officer went to the motel in response to a complaint about a possible controlled dangerous substance violation. The manager told the officers that the problem was in Room 306, the room occupied by Petitioner and four other people. The two officers and the manager went to the room, where they smelled marijuana coming from the room. While the officers were standing outside of the door, two of the occupants of Room 306 arrived, Kristopher Klein and a juvenile named Brandy. At Officer Bernal's direction, Klein knocked on the door to the room and Chris Myers, one of the occupants, admitted them. Officer Bernal asked if marijuana was being smoked in the room and Myers said no. The officer then requested permission to search for "dope"; Myers told him that he could search, but he would not find anything. When they entered the room, Taylor was lying on the floor with his head turned away from the door. Officer Bernal testified that he could not tell whether Taylor was asleep or awake. In addition to Taylor and Myers, the officers also found Jessica, another juvenile female, in the room. There were clouds of smoke in the room that smelled like marijuana.

Officer Bernal told Myers that he intended to search the room thoroughly, and again asked if there was any marijuana in the room. Myers walked over to a carrying bag, pulled out a baggie of marijuana, and told the officer that it was his marijuana. Officer Bernal asked Myers if that was all the marijuana in the room, and Myers told him yes. Myers was then arrested. Officer Bernal then began to search the room. Contrary to his prior statement that there was no more marijuana in the room, Myers told Officer Bernal that there was also marijuana located in a multi-colored bag, and Officer Bernal found another baggie of marijuana in the multi-colored bag. Inside Klein's wallet, which was secreted in another bag that did not belong to Petitioner, the officers also found rolling papers.

Officer Bernal then asked everyone in the room if they were smoking marijuana. He testified that Petitioner and the other occupants told him that friends who were not staying in the room had come by earlier and had smoked marijuana in their presence. Although Officer Bernal smelled a strong odor of marijuana in the room, he did not see anyone smoking marijuana, the ashtrays were clean, and no marijuana was visible.

Petitioner was charged with possession of marijuana in violation of § 287. The trial court found that Petitioner was in close proximity to the marijuana; that, because people were smoking marijuana in Petitioner's presence, Petitioner "knew" there was marijuana in the room; that, because he was on the premises asleep or pretending to be asleep, he had some possessory right in the premises; and that the circumstances were sufficient to draw a reasonable inference that Petitioner was participating with others in the mutual enjoyment of the contraband. Accordingly, the trial court found Petitioner guilty and sentenced him to fifteen days in the Worcester County jail, all suspended, with two years probation and a fine.

Petitioner appealed to the Court of Special Appeals, contending that the evidence was insufficient to sustain his conviction. The Court of Special Appeals affirmed in an unreported opinion. That court held that Petitioner not only knew of both the presence and illicit nature of the marijuana, but that "the discovery of marijuana in Myers's bags allowed for the inference that appellant knew of and had shared that supply when he was sharing the room with . . . Myers." The court further concluded that "appellant's presence in a room where marijuana had recently been smoked leads to the inference that appellant had himself smoked marijuana." We granted Taylor's petition for writ of certiorari challenging the sufficiency of the evidence.

* * *

Petitioner was convicted of possession of marijuana in violation of § 287. Possession is defined in § 277 as "the exercise of actual or constructive dominion or control over a thing by one or more persons." "Control" of a controlled dangerous substance has been defined as the exercise of a "restraining or directing influence over" the thing allegedly possessed. *See Garrison v. State,* 272 Md. 123, 142, 321 A.2d 767, 777 (1974); BLACK'S LAW DICTIONARY 329 (6th ed. 1990) ("To exercise restraining or directing influence over"). Possession may be constructive or actual, exclusive or joint. *See State v. Leach,* 296 Md. 591, 595, 463 A.2d 872, 874 (1983). Whether the possession is actual or constructive, exclusive or joint, the "evidence must show directly or support a rational inference that the accused did in fact exercise some dominion or control over the prohibited . . . drug in the sense contemplated by the statute, *i.e.,* that [the accused] exercised some restraining or directing influence over it." *Garrison,* 272 Md. at 142, 321 A.2d at 777.

The State's case against Petitioner for possession of a controlled dangerous substance rested on circumstantial evidence of joint and constructive possession. A conviction can rest on circumstantial evidence alone. A conviction resting on circumstantial evidence alone, however, cannot be sustained on proof amounting only to strong suspicion or mere probability. *See Wilson v. State,* 319 Md. 530, 535-36, 573 A.2d 831, 834 (1990). . . .

We agree with Taylor that, under the facts of this case, any finding that he was in possession of the marijuana could be based on no more than speculation or conjecture. The State conceded at trial that no marijuana or paraphernalia was found on Petitioner or in his personal belongings, nor did the officers observe Petitioner or any of the other occupants of the hotel room smoking marijuana. Viewing the evidence in the light most favorable to the State, Officer Bernal's testimony established only that Taylor was present in a room where marijuana had been smoked recently, that he was aware that it had been smoked, and that Taylor was in proximity to contraband that was concealed in a container belonging to another.

The record is clear that Petitioner was not in exclusive possession of the premises, and that the contraband was secreted in a hidden place not otherwise shown to be within Petitioner's control. Accordingly, a rational inference cannot be drawn that he possessed the controlled dangerous substance. *See Livingston v. State,* 317 Md. 408, 415, 564 A.2d 414, 418 (1989); *Leach,* 296 Md. at 596, 463 A.2d at 874; *Garrison,* 272 Md. at 142, 321 A.2d at 777; Annot., *Conviction of Possession of Illicit Drugs Found in Premises of Which Defendant Was in Nonexclusive Possession,* 56 A.L.R.3d 948, 957 (1974). Possession requires more than being in the presence of other persons having possession; it requires the exercise of dominion or control over the thing allegedly possessed. *See Livingston,* 317 Md. at 415-16, 564 A.2d at 418. Without more, Petitioner's presence in the room where marijuana had recently been smoked does not support a rational inference that Petitioner had possessed the marijuana. Furthermore, the existence of smoke in a room occupied by five people does not alone justify the inference that Petitioner was engaged in the mutual use or enjoyment of the contraband. *Cf. Wilson,* 319 Md. at 537-38, 573 A.2d at 835 ("[I]t is elementary that mere presence is not, *of itself,* sufficient to establish that that person was either a principal or an accessory to the crime.").

Knowledge is an essential ingredient of the crime of possession of marijuana. Writing for the Court, Judge Eldridge discussed the knowledge requirement of § 287 in *Dawkins v. State,* 313 Md. 638, 649, 547 A.2d 1041, 1046 (1988):

> [A]n individual ordinarily would not be deemed to exercise "dominion or control" over an object about which he is unaware. Knowledge of the presence of an object is normally a prerequisite to exercising dominion and control. The evidence in this case does not establish that Taylor had knowledge of the presence of the marijuana concealed in Myers's carrying bags.

As clearly indicated by *Dawkins,* without knowledge of the presence of marijuana in the room, it is not possible for Petitioner to have exercised dominion or control over the marijuana, another required ingredient of the crime of possession. The facts and circumstances, considered in the light most favorable to the State, do not justify any reasonable inference that Petitioner had the ability to exercise, or in fact did exercise dominion or control over the contraband found in the room. Although the evidence in this case might form the basis for a strong suspicion of Petitioner's guilt, suspicion is insufficient to support a conviction. "[M]ere proximity to the drug, mere presence on the property where it is located, or mere association, without more, with the person who does control the drug or property on which it is found, is insufficient to support a finding of possession." *Murray v. United States,* 403 F.2d 694, 696 (9th Cir. 1969) (internal quotation marks and citations omitted). In other words, there must be additional proof of knowledge and control to sustain a conviction for possession.

Although control of marijuana may be established by evidence that a person smoked marijuana, the smoke in the hotel room does not provide the additional proof necessary to sustain Petitioner's conviction. As discussed above, the record in this case supports merely an inference that *someone* smoked marijuana in the room, not that Petitioner, one of five occupants of the room, smoked marijuana.

In *Garrison*, 272 Md. 123, 321 A.2d 767, Judge O'Donnell, writing for the Court, extensively reviewed decisions of this Court and the Court of Special Appeals dealing with the sufficiency of evidence to support a conviction for possession. In *Garrison*, police officers executed a search warrant at the home of Shirley Garrison and her husband Ernest Garrison based on probable cause that heroin was being sold from the Garrison home. Upon entering a rear bedroom, the officers saw Mr. Garrison flushing a plastic bag down the toilet. Mrs. Garrison was found in the front bedroom, where no contraband was discovered. *Garrison*, 272 Md. at 126-27, 321 A.2d at 769. The Court held that there was insufficient evidence to support Mrs. Garrison's conviction for possession with intent to distribute heroin because there was no evidence that she was engaged in selling narcotics, she had made no inculpatory remarks, there were no "fresh needle marks" on her body, and there was no "juxtaposition between her (in the front bedroom) and contraband being jettisoned by her husband in the bathroom." *Id.* at 130-31, 321 A.2d at 771.

Judge O'Donnell then surveyed numerous cases of the Court of Special Appeals, some of them factually similar to the instant case, in which convictions for possession of contraband were reversed for insufficient evidence. The recurrent theme of these cases is that convictions for possession cannot stand when the evidence does not establish, nor provides any reasonable inference to establish, that the accused exercised dominion or control over the contraband. *See Tucker v. State*, 19 Md.App. 39, 45, 308 A.2d 696, 699 (1973) (holding evidence insufficient to establish defendant had physical or constructive possession of heroin when no drugs were found on his person and the only drugs discovered on the premises, which he shared with the co-defendant, were secreted out of plain view); *Barksdale v. State*, 15 Md.App. 469, 475, 291 A.2d 495, 498 (1972) (holding evidence insufficient to support conviction for possession when defendant merely present in an apartment in which a woman's purse and a cigarette case containing heroin were found); *Puckett v. State*, 13 Md.App. 584, 587-88, 284 A.2d 252, 254 (1971) (holding evidence of presence of marijuana plants on property Puckett jointly owned with his wife was not sufficient to create rational inference that Puckett was in possession of the marijuana); *Davis v. State*, 9 Md.App. 48, 55, 262 A.2d 578, 582-83 (1970) (holding conviction for possession that rests only on defendant's co-occupancy of apartment where marijuana was sold and on defendant's intimate relationship with a co-occupant who sold marijuana is not supported by sufficient evidence); *Wimberly v. State*, 7 Md.App. 302, 308, 254 A.2d 711, 714 (1969) (holding evidence insufficient for conviction of possession of marijuana, amphetamines and barbiturates when those drugs were not found on the person of or in the same room as the defendant, but were only found on other people on the premises); *Haley v. State*, 7 Md.App. 18, 33, 253 A.2d 424, 433 (1969) (holding evidence insufficient to support conviction for possession when none of the defendants had any proprietary interest nor previous association with the premises and there was no evidence of how long the defendants had been on the premises prior to the arrival of the police).

We have had the opportunity to address the sufficiency of evidence in drug possession cases since *Garrison*. In *Leach*, 296 Md. 591, 463 A.2d 872, PCP was found in a closed container in the bedroom of a residence. There was only one bed on the premises and the trial court found that the defendant's brother lived at the residence. *Id.* at 595, 463 A.2d at 874. Although the defendant gave the address at which the PCP was found as his own when he was booked by the police, the Department of Motor Vehicles records showed that he lived at that address, and he had ready access to the premises, "the fact finding that [the defendant's brother] was the occupant of the premises preclude[d] inferring that [the defendant] had joint dominion or control . . . over everything contained anywhere in it." *Id.* at 596, 463 A.2d at 874. Thus, even though he had ready access to the apartment, it could not be reasonably inferred that he exercised restraining or directing influence over PCP in a closed container in the bedroom. *Id.*, 463 A.2d at 874.

In *Livingston*, 317 Md. 408, 564 A.2d 414, this Court reversed the conviction of a passenger in the backseat of a car when two marijuana seeds were recovered from the floor in the front of the car. *Id.* at 416, 564 A.2d at 418. The Court held:

> Merely sitting in the backseat of the vehicle, [the defendant] did not demonstrate to the officer that he possessed any knowledge of, and hence, any restraining or directing influence over two marijuana seeds located on the floor in the front of the car.

Id. at 415-16, 564 A.2d at 418.

In sum, the evidence presented in this case was insufficient to establish that Taylor was in possession of the marijuana seized from Myers's carrying bags. Taylor's presence in a room in which marijuana had been smoked, and his awareness that marijuana had been smoked, cannot permit a rational trier of fact to infer that Taylor exercised a restraining or directing influence over marijuana that was concealed in personal carrying bags of another occupant of the room. Because Petitioner was in joint rather than exclusive possession of the hotel room, his mere proximity to the contraband found concealed in a travel bag and his presence in a room containing marijuana smoke were

insufficient to convict him. As this Court stated in *Johnson v. State,* 227 Md. 159, 165, 175 A.2d 580, 583 (1961), "[t]he conjectures of the trial judge might be entirely correct. . . . Nevertheless, a conviction without proof cannot be sustained."

JUDGMENT OF THE COURT OF SPECIAL APPEALS REVERSED. . . .

_____**CASE END**

CASE LAW
Dukes v. State, 180 Md. App. 38, 940 A.2d 211, *cert. denied,*
405 Md. 64, 949 A.2d 652 (2008)

. . . The underlying incident occurred on October 3, 2006. At trial, the court was informed that the parties disputed whether appellant was "driving" at that time, within the meaning of the relevant statutes. Appellant waived a jury trial and proceeded on an agreed statement of facts. The court read into the record the arresting officer's report, as follows:

> "On 10/3/06, at approximately 04:47 hours["]—so that is 4:47 in the morning—["]I located an '86 Cadillac" something. "A two-door, grey," with a Maryland registration that is identified here. I won't read it. "On Baydale Drive north and College Parkway. The vehicle was stopped in a right turn lane with its headlights on, but they were dim."

> "I had passed the vehicle approximately half an hour before in route to a B & E in progress. It had not moved from that position. I contacted the operator, who was asleep in the driver's seat, and the vehicle keys were on the floor mat below the steering wheel. I woke him and detected a strong odor of an alcoholic beverage emanating from his breath, and his speech was slurred."

> "He had trouble locating identif[ication] and handed me his wallet with a Maryland I.D. only. He couldn't find a vehicle registration card. His movements were slow and not fluid. He exited his vehicle to attempt several field tests at the rear. . . ."

According to the officer's report, appellant failed the field sobriety tests and was arrested. He "refused the chemical test . . .". . .

Discussion

Appellant does not challenge the sufficiency of the evidence to establish that he was intoxicated, nor does he dispute that, at the time in question, his license had been revoked. His sole claim on appeal is that the evidence set forth in the agreed statement of facts was insufficient to support the finding that he was "driving,"

because, argues appellant, he was not in "actual physical control" of an operable vehicle. We disagree. . . .

Transp. § 11-114 defines "drive" as follows: "to drive, operate, move, or be in *actual physical control* of a vehicle. . . ." (emphasis added). In *Atkinson v. State,* 331 Md. 199, 627 A.2d 1019 (1993), upon which appellant relies, the Court examined the meaning of the phrase "actual physical control." There, a sheriff's deputy found the defendant inebriated and asleep in his vehicle, which was parked on the shoulder of a road. The keys were in the ignition and the engine was off. *Id.* at 203-204, 627 A.2d 1019. In reasoning equally applicable to the case at bar, the *Atkinson* Court analyzed the definition of "drive" in § 11-114 and made the following observation, *id.* at 206, 627 A.2d 1019 (internal citations omitted):

> "[D]rive" (as a definition), "operate" and "move" are not at issue here, for each of these terms clearly connotes either some motion of the vehicle or some physical movement or manipulation of the vehicle's controls. To "move" a vehicle plainly requires that the vehicle be placed in motion. . . . "[T]he term 'driving' . . . mean[s] . . . steering and controlling a vehicle while in motion; the term 'operating,' on the other hand, is generally given a broader meaning to include starting the engine or manipulating the mechanical or electrical devices of a standing vehicle."

The Court considered the meaning of "actual physical control" of a vehicle. It declined to adopt the majority view, which is that "'[a]s long as a person is physically or bodily able to assert dominion in the sense of movement by starting the car and driving away, then he has substantially as much control over the vehicle as he would if he were actually driving it.'" *Atkinson,* 331 Md. at 212, 627 A.2d 1019 (quoting *Adams v. State,* 697 P.2d 622, 625 (Wyo.1985)). The Court characterized this view as "excessively rigid," reasoning that "intoxicated persons sitting in their vehicles while in possession of their ignition keys would, regardless of other circumstances, always be subject to criminal penalty. . . ." *Atkinson,* 331 Md. at 212, 627 A.2d 1019. In its view, "this construction effectively creates a new crime, 'Parked While Intoxicated.'" *Id.* (citing, with approval, *Petersen v. Dept. of Public Safety,* 373 N.W.2d 38, 40 (S.D.1985) (Henderson, J., dissenting)).

Instead, the *Atkinson* Court determined that the Legislature did not intend to punish criminally an intoxicated person who uses his vehicle merely to "sleep it off." *Atkinson,* 331 Md. at 214, 627 A.2d 1019. Rather, it concluded that the General Assembly "intended to differentiate between those inebriated people who represent no threat to the public because they are only entering their vehicles as shelters until they are sober enough to drive and those people who represent an imminent threat to the public by reason of their control of a vehicle." *Id.* at 216, 627 A.2d 1019.

In this regard, the Court identified six non-exhaustive factors relevant in determining whether an individual in a vehicle has "actual physical control" over the vehicle, or is merely using it as shelter:

1. whether or not the vehicle's engine is running, or the ignition on;
2. where and in what position the person is found in the vehicle;
3. whether the person is awake or asleep;
4. where the vehicle's ignition key is located;
5. whether the vehicle's headlights are on;
6. whether the vehicle is located in the roadway or is legally parked.

Id.

The Court cautioned that the inquiry "will inevitably depend on the facts of the individual case," and that "[n]o one factor alone will necessarily be dispositive. . . ." *Id.* Rather, "[c]ourts must in each case examine what the evidence showed the defendant was doing or had done, and whether these actions posed an imminent threat to the public." *Id.* at 216-17, 627 A.2d 1019. The *Atkinson* Court seemed to suggest that the factors are not all of equal weight, stating: "Perhaps the strongest factor . . . is whether there is evidence that the defendant started or attempted to start the vehicle's engine." *Id.* at 217, 627 A.2d 1019. Further, it explained that, "once an individual has started the vehicle, he or she has come as close as possible to actually driving without doing so. . . ." *Id.* Of import here, the Court also said that "the location of the vehicle can be a determinative factor in the inquiry because a person whose vehicle is parked illegally or stopped in the roadway is obligated by law to move the vehicle. . . ." *Id.*

Applying the factors to the case before it, the *Atkinson* Court observed that, although the defendant was in the driver's seat and the keys were in the ignition, the vehicle was legally parked, the ignition was off, and the defendant was fast asleep. *Id.* On balance, the Court concluded that there was reasonable doubt that the defendant was in "actual physical control" of his vehicle. *Id.* . . .

. . . Under the current statute, a person commits the crime of "driving" while intoxicated when he is intoxicated while in "actual physical control" of his vehicle, even if it is "left to conjecture" that he actually "drove" the vehicle, in the narrower sense, at some earlier time. As the State correctly points out, under *Atkinson* the fact that appellant's vehicle was stopped in the roadway was properly a "determinative factor" in the "actual physical control" analysis. The trial court recognized this when it said: "Quite candidly, the public is at risk just by the mere fact that he is sitting there and perhaps somebody might [hit] him."

In any event, the *Atkinson* Court opined that, even if a defendant was not in "actual physical control" of a vehicle at the time of his arrest, he could still be convicted of driving while intoxicated if circumstantial evidence proved beyond a reasonable doubt that he had driven the vehicle while intoxicated at an earlier time. The Court explained, *id.* at 218-19, 627 A.2d 1019 (internal citations omitted):

> It is important to bear in mind that a defendant who is not in "actual physical control" of the vehicle at the time of apprehension will not necessarily escape arrest and prosecution for a drunk driving offense. A person may also be convicted under § 21-902 if it can be determined beyond a reasonable doubt that before being apprehended he or she has actually driven, operated, or moved the vehicle while under the influence. . . . Those were the facts in . . . *Gore v. State* . . . discussed *supra,* where the court concluded that evidence of the ignition key in the "on" position, the glowing alternator/battery light, the gear selector in "drive," and the warm engine, sufficiently supported a finding that the defendant had actually driven his car shortly before the officer's arrival. Thus, our construction of "actual physical control" as permitting motorists to "sleep it off" should not be misconstrued as encouraging motorists to try their luck on the roadways, knowing they can escape arrest by subsequently placing their vehicles "away from the road pavement, outside regular traffic lanes, and . . . turn[ing] off the ignition so that the vehicle's engine is not running."
> . . .

In the instant case, had there been evidence to establish that Atkinson had driven prior to his apprehension, he might properly have been convicted—not because of what he was doing when the officer arrived on the scene, but because of what the factfinder could have inferred he had done previously, *i.e.,* actually drive, operate, or move his vehicle while intoxicated. While many forms of circumstantial evidence potentially could have lead [sic] to this conclusion, no such evidence was adduced in Atkinson's case. There is no evidence that Atkinson did anything but climb into his vehicle, put the key in the ignition, and go to sleep.

Here, the fact that appellant was intoxicated and asleep in the driver's seat of a vehicle that was stopped *in the roadway,* with its lights on, is powerful circumstantial evidence that appellant drove the vehicle to that location while intoxicated. . . .

CASE END

Case Questions

Taylor v. State

1. What were the facts that led to Taylor being charged with possession of marijuana?

2. What four types of possession are there? What two types of possession did the state contend that Taylor exhibited?

3. What is the key factor for determining whether a person is in possession of a CDS? Was that factor present in this case? Explain.

Dukes v. State

1. How did the court rely on its previous decision in *Atkinson v. State* when reaching a decision in this case?

2. What if Dukes had parked his vehicle in the parking lot of a bar, do you think the court's conclusion would have been different? Explain.

Additional Crimes to Consult

In addition to the crimes discussed herein, the Legislature has enacted several other laws that, although less frequently charged and prosecuted, evidence a growing concern over drug abuse and the ramifications of that abuse. Such crimes, all found in Title 5 of the Criminal Law Article of the Code, include drug kingpin (§ 5-613); distributing faked CDS (§ 5-617); use of a weapon or firearm in relation to a drug trafficking crime (§ 5-621 and 5-622); possession of CDS paraphernalia (§ 5-619) and possession of CDS near a school zone (§ 5-627). Maryland also provides for progressively harsher penalties for repeat offenders, potentially including increased fines, increased sentences, and mandatory minimum sentences, depending upon the number of violations and the particular CDS involved. (§§ 5-607 through 5-609). Furthermore, property used in connection with any of the drug offenses may be subjected to separate civil forfeiture proceedings in accordance with Title 12 ("Forfeiture—CDS Violations") of the Criminal Procedure Article of the Code.

With regard to the offense of driving while impaired or under the influence of alcohol, see the Maryland Legislature's definition of the term "drive" at Md. Code Ann., Transp. II § 11-1114 (West 2006).

HYPOTHETICAL #1

Larry and Harry were two of Baltimore's premier crime scene analysts. In fact, they were so popular that they made all the local headlines when television scouts from the hit show "CSI" visited their office to get ideas for the show. One day, however, Larry and Harry made the news for a quite different reason. You see, Patrick the police officer had been conducting an undercover drug operation for months, and much to his surprise Larry and Harry appeared to be at the center of the entire drug ring! So, Patrick went over to the office that Larry and Harry shared armed with a search warrant. When Patrick entered he was stunned at what he found . . .

Both desks sat in a wide opened office with numerous file cabinets, none of which was locked. In one very large file cabinet in particular that was only labeled as "CASE FILES," Patrick found almost twenty pounds of a green leafy substance that appeared to be marijuana, wrapped in several plastic bags! The cabinet was off by itself in the corner of the room, close to Larry's desk. The drugs were found in the third drawer down under some past case files that had all belonged to Larry. When Patrick pulled the bag out from the drawer and held it up for Larry and Harry to see, Harry exclaimed with surprise, "What on earth is that? I've never seen that before in my life!" Patrick continued by searching the office, and when he came to Harry's desk he found some breath mints, room freshener aerosol, a lighter, and small papers that looked as though they could be used to roll cigarettes. Harry claimed they were all used to conduct tests on various types of evidence recovered from crime scenes. Harry was arrested for possession of marijuana with intent to distribute, but Harry staunchly maintained he had no knowledge of the drugs in the file cabinet. And that the drugs belonged to Larry. Subsequent laboratory tests revealed that the green leafy substance was, in fact, marijuana.

MAIN ISSUE

Was Harry Guilty of Possession of Marijuana with the Intent to Distribute?

ISSUE	THESIS	RULE	ANALYSIS	CONCLUSION
Did Harry knowingly possess marijuana WHEN the drugs were found in the file cabinet drawer?	Harry possibly knowingly possessed marijuana WHEN the drugs were found in the file cabinet drawer.	The defendant must have KNOWINGLY POSSESSED THE CDS.	Harry possibly knowingly possessed the marijuana BECAUSE it was in an office that he shared with Larry, it was in an unlocked file cabinet that both had access to, and Harry had paraphernalia in his desk that would indicate knowledge of marijuana in the office. However, he could argue in his defense that the cabinet was near Larry's desk; and the drawer in which it was recovered had Larry's case files in it.	Harry possibly knowingly possessed marijuana.
Did Harry know of the general character or illicit nature of the substance WHEN Patrick pulled the bag out of the file cabinet drawer and held it up?	Harry most likely knew the general character or illicit nature of the substance WHEN Patrick pulled the bag out of the file cabinet drawer and held it up.	The defendant must KNOW OF THE GENERAL CHARACTER OR ILLICIT NATURE OF THE SUBSTANCE.	Harry most likely knew of the illicit nature of the substance BECAUSE the substance had the appearance of marijuana, Harry was a crime scene analyst who likely had experience in recognizing drugs, and he had paraphernalia in his desk drawer indicating use or distribution of marijuana.	Harry most likely knew the general character or illicit nature of the substance.

(continued)

MAIN ISSUE

Was Harry Guilty of Possession of Marijuana with the Intent to Distribute? (continued)

ISSUE	THESIS	RULE	ANALYSIS	CONCLUSION
Was the substance recovered a CDS WHEN it was subsequently tested and determined to be marijuana?	The substance recovered was a CDS WHEN it was subsequently tested and determined to be marijuana.	THE SUBSTANCE POSSESSED MUST HAVE BEEN A CONTROLLED DANGEROUS SUBSTANCE.	The substance possessed was a CDS BECAUSE subsequent laboratory tests concluded the substance was, in fact, marijuana.	The substance possessed was a controlled dangerous substance.
Did Harry possess the marijuana with the intent to distribute it WHEN the search yielded a high quantity of drugs and other evidence suggested an intent to distribute?	Harry possibly possessed the marijuana with the intent to distribute it WHEN the search yielded a high quantity of drugs and other evidence suggested an intent to distribute.	The defendant must have possessed the substance WITH THE INTENT TO SELL, EXCHANGE, OR TRANSFER POSSESSION OF THE SUBSTANCE OR GIVE IT AWAY.	Harry possibly possessed the marijuana with the intent to distribute it BECAUSE the quantity of drugs alone indicated an intent to distribute, and Harry had in his desk drawer paraphernalia that indicated an intent to distribute (rolling papers). However, Harry could argue in his defense lack of knowledge of the marijuana and the fact that the items in his desk drawer were for testing evidence recovered from crime scenes.	Harry possibly possessed the marijuana with an intent to distribute the CDS.

CONCLUSION

Harry is possibly guilty of possession of marijuana with the intent to distribute because he was in constructive possession of the CDS and other evidence indicated the intent to distribute. Enough evidence may be presented to prosecute Harry, but it may be a close question for a jury to determine guilty beyond a reasonable case given the facts in this case.

HYPOTHETICAL #2

Brian and Gina were old friends who shared a posh apartment together in downtown Annapolis. Neither of them had a job, but somehow they managed to have all of the finer things in life—fancy sports cars, lots of gold and diamond jewelry, and lots of cash on hand! The Annapolis police never could figure out how Brian and Gina could afford to live the high life when neither one ever worked an honest day in their lives! But one day, the cops figured everything out.

One evening, Oliver the officer got a call over his police cruiser radio that an unruly party was going on at Brian and Gina's apartment. Oliver radioed back that he would check it out. Oliver arrived at the apartment and knocked on the door. Jonathan, one of Brian and Gina's dear friends, opened wide the front door so that Oliver could see everyone in the living room. The guests of the party all froze as they saw Oliver in uniform, standing in the room. This is what Oliver saw. . . .

Jonathan stood frozen in the doorway with a joint of marijuana in his hand. Brian, Gina, and Willie were all seated around the living room coffee table on two couches. In the center of the table was a mirror, three razor blades, and little white rocks of something in a clear plastic bag. Gina had some white stuff on her nose, and Brian sniffled and got a slight nose bleed. Willie clutched a Corona in his hand and looked absolutely shocked. Willie later explained to Oliver that he had just arrived at the party, and he had no idea there would be drugs there. Willie said he never did drugs. Oliver arrested Jonathan, Willie, Gina and Brian and conducted a thorough search of the apartment.

In a kitchen drawer Oliver found seventy bags of white rocks along with three wads of twenty dollar bills wrapped with rubber bands, and a package of razor blades. In one of the bedrooms (which later turned out to be Gina's) he found three pots of dirt sitting in a window sill. He took the pots, dug up the dirt, and found tiny marijuana plants that had not yet broken through the soil. In another bedroom (which turned out to be Brian's) he found a hypodermic needle hidden under the mattress and a small bottle of what he figured to be heroin. In the coat closet off of the family room he found in a coat, which he could not tell if it was a man's or woman's coat, the remains of a joint with an odor of marijuana but no detectable marijuana inside. On the way out Oliver decided he'd check in Brian and Gina's car—inside the trunk he found nine briefcases full of hundred dollar bills, a notebook with "appointments" written in it and dollar amounts next to those appointments, two scales, two economy size boxes of razor blades, and a list of names of individuals under the heading "customers." Oliver the officer had struck gold! He would now finally get that promotion he'd always tried for!

The only person who missed all of the action that fateful night was Karen, a known alcoholic. After the drug bust was over, Oliver got back into his patrol car and headed towards the station to tell all of his buddy officers that he finally solved the mystery of Brian and Gina. While on the way, he noticed a car on the shoulder of the highway. In the passenger side of the car slumped Karen, passed out cold. The motor of the car was off but the key was in the ignition, the gear selector was in the "neutral" position, and when Oliver felt the hood of the car he noticed that the engine was warm. Oliver arrested Karen too. When Karen finally regained consciousness in her jail cell, hours later, her blood alcohol content was .20.

That was the last that anyone ever heard of Brian and Gina. Karen spent the next five years in an alcohol rehab facility, and Jonathan became the author of the best-selling book "Brian and Gina Get a Slap in the Face." Oliver was promoted to captain and appeared on the Oprah show.

➲ List the crimes with which each defendant may be charged.

DEFENDANT	CRIME(S)
Brian	
Gina	
Jonathan	
Willie	
Karen	

➲ For EACH crime identified, complete an Analysis Chart assessing the possibility of conviction for each defendant.

123

DISCUSSION QUESTIONS

1. Research challenge: Revisit Hypothetical #2, was Oliver's search of Brian and Gina's vehicle constitutional? Explain your answer in detail, citing to relevant constitutional provisions.

2. Other than the quantity of a drug or witnessing a hand-to-hand transaction, what other circumstances may result in the inference that a suspect had an intent to distribute a CDS?

3. Ronald is arrested and searched. In one pocket he has a joint, and in the other pocket he has a vial of heroin. How many counts of possession should Ronald be charged with? Jay is arrested and searched. In his pocket police find marijuana dipped or "laced" with PCP. How many counts of possession should Jay be charged with? *See State v. Owens*, 320 Md. 682, 579 A.2d 766 (1990).

4. Jenny buys what she thinks is a bag of pot from Kelly. Kelly, however, decided she'd pull a fast one and instead of pot, it is merely a bag of oregano. Has Jenny committed a crime? Has Kelly? *See* Md. Code Ann., Crim Law. § 5-617 (West 2006).

5. When you think of the term "manufacture" what comes to mind? In your opinion, is it possible to manufacture marijuana? *See Graybeal v. State*, 13 Md. App. 557, 284 A.2d 37 (1971).

6. Revisit the crime of conspiracy discussed in detail in Chapter 2. How might that offense enable law enforcement to arrest individuals for drug violations when the traditional drug offenses discussed in this chapter might not enable such an arrest?

7. In your opinion, should marijuana be legalized? What are the benefits to doing so? The detriments?

8. Joshua is found in possession of two small flakes of marijuana. He admits that the substance is marijuana but maintains he has committed no crime for two reasons: First he argues that the amount of which he is in possession is too small to permit its use. Second he argues that his friend had just handed him the marijuana flakes seconds before law enforcement confiscated it and therefore he was not in possession of the CDS for a long enough time. Will either of his arguments succeed? *See Cook v. State*, 84 Md. App. 122, 578 A.2d 283 (1990), *cert. denied*, 321 Md. 502, 583 A.2d 276 (1991).

9. In Maryland there is no such crime for the "use" of a CDS; the crime is merely for the possession of a CDS. Why do you think that is the case?

10. Sixteen-year-old Brittany is arrested and police officers suspect that she is high on cocaine. Brittany admits to having used cocaine recently, but during a search of her person no drugs or drug-related evidence is found. Assuming a blood test is done which yields positive results for cocaine in her system, can Brittany then be charged with possession of cocaine based on evidence of cocaine use in her bloodstream? Why or why not? What if it had been alcohol instead of cocaine, could the results from a portable breath test be used against her as evidence she consumed alcohol even if she did not have alcohol in her possession at the time?

11. Kathleen has a brand new Mercedes that for the past six months she has continually been using to store and distribute various drugs from. One day the police finally catch up with Kathleen and she is arrested for maintaining a common nuisance and other related offenses. What will likely happen to her vehicle?

12. Can more than one person be in possession of a CDS at the same time? Explain.

13. A car is pulled over with four passengers inside: the driver, the front-seat passenger, and two passengers in the back. Assuming cocaine is found in the vehicle in the following places, which of the four occupants would you charge with possession and why? Marijuana is found: 1) in the locked glove compartment; 2) under the front passenger's seat; 3) in the trunk; 4) in the driver's lap; 5) on the dashboard; 6) under the back seat.

14. Revisit the above question: What if the vehicle had been a rental car, would your answer to any of the above questions change? It is not uncommon for drug dealers to use rental cars frequently while engaging in drug transactions. Why do you think that is the case?

15. What are some examples of drug paraphernalia?

16. Frank is an undercover narcotics detective who has been working on infiltrating the Eastern Shore's largest drug distribution ring in decades. Dwayne, a dealer in the operation, sells heroin to Frank. Frank does not arrest him but instead takes the heroin and logs it as evidence. Why do you think Frank failed to arrest Dwayne? How common do you think this occurrence is? Explain.

TEST BANK

True/False

_____ 1. The key to maintaining a common nuisance is the continual nature of the crime.

_____ 2. A person cannot be found guilty of possession of a CDS unless that person is in actual possession of the CDS.

_____ 3. A person cannot be found guilty of distribution of a CDS if the person merely gave away the CDS.

_____ 4. Quantity possessed of a CDS along, without more, may be sufficient to indicate an intent to distribute.

_____ 5. The strongest factor in determining whether an individual attempted to drive a motor vehicle while intoxicated or under the influence of alcohol is if the person started or attempted to start the vehicle's engine.

MULTIPLE CHOICE

6. Candy has one little marijuana plant in her bedroom window sill that she grows and uses to smoke when she's having a "bad day." Is Candy guilty of manufacture of marijuana?
   A. No, because "growing" is not the same thing as "manufacturing"
   B. No, because Candy had no intent to distribute it to anyone and she only intended to use it herself
   C. Yes, because "growing" includes "manufacturing"
   D. Yes, because consumption for one's own use is included in the definition of manufacture

7. Which of the following locations could not be the subject of the offense maintaining a common nuisance?
   A. A house
   B. A car
   C. A boat
   D. Any of the above places could be the site of maintaining a common nuisance

8. Which of the following is not a knowledge element with respect to the possession of a CDS:
   A. Knowledge by the suspect that he possesses the CDS
   B. Knowledge by the suspect that the substance he possesses is the CDS
   C. Knowledge by the suspect of the circumstances under which he came to be in possession of the CDS
   D. All of the above are elements of possession of a CDS

9. Which of the following is not a factor when determining if someone is driving under the influence or while impaired by alcohol?

    A. Whether the person is awake or asleep

    B. Whether the headlights are on

    C. Where the vehicle is found

    D. All of the above are factors to be considered

10. Shane handed his friend Jim a joint and said "Here, this is a present for you since you're such a great friend." "Thanks," replied Jim, "But I don't do drugs. I'll keep it though and maybe give it to my sister." Jim put the joint in his pocket and walked away. Who is guilty of what?

    A. Shane—nothing; Jim—nothing

    B. Shane—distribution of CDS; Jim—nothing

    C. Shane—distribution of CDS; Jim—possession of CDS

    D. Shane—manufacture of CDS; Jim—possession of CDS

Crimes Against Morality

chapter nine

Introduction

This chapter generally covers crimes against morality, acts that are made criminal due to society's overall disapproval of the underlying action. We will specifically focus on weapons offenses, obscenity, and gambling. As you will see, weapons offenses may be crimes in and of themselves and also enhance penalties for other violent crimes in which a weapon is used. Weapons offenses are mostly derived from legislation. As such, the cases you read will interpret the language of such statutes.

Focus Crimes

Weapons, Md. Code Ann., Crim. Law §§ 4-101, 4-203, 4-204 (West 2002); MPJI-Cr. 4:35 through 4:35.4.

Gambling, Md. Code Ann., Crim. Law § 12-101 through 12-104 (West 2002); MPJI-Cr. 4:16.

Obscenity, Md. Code Ann., Crim. Law §§ 11-201, 11-202 (West 2002).

Obscenity—Child Pornography, Md. Code Ann., Crim. Law § 11-207 (West 2002).

Objectives

Upon completing this chapter, you should be able to:

- ⊃ Analyze the components of gambling, weapons offenses, and obscenity;
- ⊃ Identify other crimes against morality and understand the rationale for the prohibition behind the conduct; and
- ⊃ Analyze and apply the elements of each of these crimes and defenses.

CASE LAW   *Moore v. State,* 388 Md. 446, 879 A.2d 1111 (2005)

The question we must decide in this case is whether a person who downloads onto a computer visual representations of a minor engaged in obscene acts or sexual conduct violates Md.Code (2002, 2004 Cum.Supp.), § 11-207(a)(3) of the Criminal Law Article proscribing the "use [of] a computer to depict or describe a minor engaging in an obscene act, sadomasochistic abuse, or sexual conduct." We shall answer that question in the negative and reverse.

I.

Moore was indicted by the Grand Jury for St. Mary's County in a two count indictment, alleging violations of § 11-207(a)(3) and § 11-208(a) respectively. Count I alleged that Moore had "us[ed] a computer to depict and describe a minor engaging in an obscene act, sadomasochistic abuse, and sexual conduct" in violation of § 11-207(a)(3). Count II alleged that Moore "knowing[ly] possess[ed] a film, videotape, photograph, and other visual representation depicting an individual under the age of 16 years . . . engaged in sexual conduct" in violation of § 11-208(a).

Before the Circuit Court on June 21, 2004, Moore entered a plea of not guilty and proceeded on an agreed statement of facts. The State read the following agreed statement of facts into the record:

"[O]n or about October 7, 2003 a search and seizure warrant was served on the defendant's residence located at apartment 1012 Valley Court, Lexington Park, Saint Mary's County. The defendant, Jonathan G. Moore, was present when the warrant was served. He would be identified as the gentleman on my left. Upon entering the home, Detective Hall read Mr. Moore his Miranda rights. Mr. Moore acknowledged that he understood his rights and voluntarily waived those rights. The detective located a computer in the residence, which the defendant identified as being his computer. The defendant then voluntarily assisted the detectives in examining the computer. The defendant opened a file under My Documents named 'Cuts', quote unquote. The detective observed numerous photographic images in this file which included females who appeared to be under the age of 16. One file showed a female who appeared to be approximately three to five years old being penetrated in her vagina by a penis from an adult male. The defendant then opened the Windows Media Player on his computer, which listed numerous video files. He stated he knowingly down loaded from a web site named Kazza, K-A-Z-Z-A, dot com. Detectives then viewed the video file, and I will describe one of them, I think [defense counsel] and I agreed there are several others of this ilk, rather than go through them all. I will describe one of them. It was titled 'Four Year Old Refusal Come Shot.' The three second video shows an adult male ejaculating on the face and mouth of a nude white female who appears to be three to four years old.

"A further search of the residence revealed computer printouts near the defendant's bed. Many of the images on the printouts were females who appeared to be under the age of 16 and engaged in sexual intercourse and various sex acts.

"The defendant stated he printed those pictures from various web sites. A green, unlabeled floppy disc was also recovered from the home. The disc contained a file named 'cuts.' Inside the file were 11 photographs, some of which showed females who appeared to be under age of 16 years old engaged in sexual intercourse and various sex acts.

"The computer and other described items were seized by the detective. The computer case sent to the Computer Crimes Unit of the Maryland State Police Crime Lab where it was examined by a computer technician. An examination of the defendant's computer revealed it had two hard drives. An examination of the first hard drive revealed the following, 47 images of individuals who appeared to be under the age of 16 engaged in sexual intercourse and various sex acts, 32 images of individuals who appeared to be under the age of 16 in various stages of undress.

"Examination of the second hard drive revealed the following, 28 images of individuals who appeared to be under the age of 16 engaged in sexual intercourse and various sex acts, 13 images of individuals who appeared to be under the age of 16 and in various stages of undress, 11 video clips showing individuals who appeared to be under the age of 16 and engaged in intercourse and various sex acts.

"The defendant was interviewed at his house himself and gave a voluntary statement to the detectives. He stated that he downloaded the material from a web site named Kazza dot com, he stated he had not distributed the material to anyone nor has he engaged in making any pictures from the videos himself. He stated he began down loading the child pornography from late August of 2003 and that he used it for his own sexual gratification. The parties agreed to stipulate that the-a finder of fact would determine the age of all of the individuals on the pictures and videos and were engaged in sexual intercourse and sexual acts would be under 16 years old.

"The State is not alleging the defendant was involved in the taking-in the taking of the pictures or videos recovered. The State is not alleging the defendant distributed any of the recovered images or videos or that the defendant did possess them with the intent to distribute them.

"The computer which contained the aforementioned images or photos and images were recovered from the defendant's residence which was located in Saint Mary's County."

Moore moved for a judgment of acquittal as to Count I, arguing that his conduct was not prohibited by § 11-207(a)(3). The court denied the motion and found Moore guilty of both counts in the indictment. The court reasoned that the ordinary, plain meaning of the statutory language proscribed the conduct at issue and that Moore's acts fell within the intended scope of the statute. The court merged the two counts for sentencing purposes and sentenced Moore to a term of three years incarceration on Count I, with all but nine months suspended.

Moore noted a timely appeal to the Court of Special Appeals. Before that court considered the case, we granted certiorari on our own initiative to consider the following question:

"Does a person who downloads visual representations of a minor engaged in obscene acts or sexual conduct from a computer violate Md. Crim Law, § 11-207(a)(3)'s proscription against 'us[ing] a computer to depict or describe a minor engaging in an obscene act, sadomasochistic abuse or sexual conduct?' "

II.

Under § 11-207(a)(3), a person may not "use a computer to depict or describe a minor engaging in an obscene act, sadomasochistic abuse, or sexual conduct. . . ." To resolve the issue before us, we must interpret the phrase "to use a computer to depict or describe."

Interpretation of a statute is a question of law, and, therefore, we review *de novo* the decision of the Circuit Court. *See Collins v. State,* 383 Md. 684, 688, 861 A.2d 727, 730 (2004). The cardinal rule of statutory construction is to ascertain and effectuate the intent of the Legislature. *Piper Rudnick v. Hartz,* 386 Md. 201, 218, 872 A.2d 58, 68 (2005). In ascertaining legislative intent, we first examine the plain language of the statute, and if the plain language of the statute is unambiguous and consistent with the apparent purpose of the statute, we give effect to the statute as it is written. *Id.*

When there is more than one reasonable interpretation of a statute, the statute is ambiguous. *Comptroller v. Phillips,* 384 Md. 583, 591, 865 A.2d 590, 594 (2005). If the statutory language is ambiguous, we resolve that ambiguity in light of the legislative intent, considering the legislative history, case law, and statutory purpose. *See id.* We consider not only the ordinary meaning of the words, but also how that language relates to the overall meaning, setting, and purpose of the act. *See Deville v. State,* 383 Md. 217, 223, 858 A.2d 484, 487 (2004). We take into account the history of the statute, the evils or mischief the Legislature sought to remedy, and the "prevailing mood of the legislative body with respect to the type of criminal conduct involved." *Gargliano v. State,* 334 Md. 428, 436, 639 A.2d 675, 678 (1994) (quoting *Randall Book Corp. v. State,* 316 Md. 315, 327, 558 A.2d 715, 721 (1989)). We seek to avoid construction of a statute that is unreasonable, illogical, or inconsistent with common sense. *See Gwin v. MVA,* 385 Md. 440, 462, 869 A.2d 822, 835 (2005). We construe a statute as a whole so that no word, clause, sentence, or phrase is rendered surplusage, superfluous, meaningless, or nugatory. *Phillips,* 384 Md. at 591, 865 A.2d at 594.

III.

The federal government and almost every state in the country have enacted laws related to child pornography. *See New York v. Ferber,* 458 U.S. 747, 758, 102 S.Ct. 3348, 3355, 73 L.Ed.2d 1113 (1982) (stating that "virtually all of the States and the United States have passed legislation proscribing the production of or otherwise combating 'child pornography' "); *Outmezguine v. State,* 97 Md.App. 151, 162, 627 A.2d 541, 546 (1993), *aff'd* 335 Md. 20, 641 A.2d 870 (1994) (noting that by 1982, the federal government and forty-seven states had enacted statutes specifically addressing child pornography). The Supreme Court has recognized that "[t]he prevention of sexual exploitation and abuse of children constitutes a government objective of surpassing importance." *Ferber,* 458 U.S. at 757, 102 S.Ct. at 3355. In *Ferber,* the Court discussed extensively the danger of child pornography and the detrimental effect it has on children. The Court stated as follows:

> "The distribution of photographs and films depicting sexual activity by juveniles is intrinsically related to the sexual abuse of children in at least two ways. First, the materials produced are a permanent record of the children's participation and the harm to the child is exacerbated by their circulation. Second, the distribution network for child pornography must be closed if the production of material which requires the sexual exploitation of children is to be effectively controlled. Indeed, there is no serious contention that the legislature was unjustified in believing that it is difficult, if not impossible, to halt the exploitation of children by pursuing only those who produce the photographs and movies. While the production of pornographic materials is a low-profile, clandestine industry, the need to market the resulting products requires a visible apparatus of distribution. The most expeditious if not the only practical method of law enforcement may be to dry up the market for this material by imposing severe criminal penalties on persons selling, advertising, or otherwise promoting the product. Thirty-five States and Congress have concluded that restraints on the distribution of pornographic materials are required in order to effectively combat the problem, and there is a body of literature and testimony to support these legislative conclusions."

> *Id.* at 759-60, 102 S.Ct. at 3355-56
> (footnotes omitted).

In Maryland, two statutes target child pornography specifically. Section 11-207(a), provides as follows:

> "(a) *Prohibited.*—A person may not:

> "(1) cause, induce, solicit, or knowingly allow a minor to engage as a subject in the production of ob-

scene matter or a visual representation or performance that depicts a minor engaged as a subject in sadomasochistic abuse or sexual conduct;

"(2) photograph or film a minor engaging in an obscene act, sadomasochistic abuse, or sexual conduct;

"(3) use a computer to depict or describe a minor engaging in an obscene act, sadomasochistic abuse, or sexual conduct;

"(4) knowingly promote, distribute, or possess with the intent to distribute any matter, visual representation, or performance that depicts a minor engaged as a subject in sadomasochistic abuse or sexual conduct; or

"(5) use a computer to knowingly compile, enter, transmit, make, print, publish, reproduce, cause, allow, buy, sell, receive, exchange, or disseminate any notice, statement, advertisement, or minor's name, telephone number, place of residence, physical characteristics, or other descriptive or identifying information for the purpose of engaging in, facilitating, encouraging, offering, or soliciting unlawful sadomasochistic abuse or sexual conduct of or with a minor."

A violation of this section is a felony, and, upon conviction, the defendant is subject to imprisonment not exceeding ten years and a fine for the first offense, and imprisonment not exceeding twenty years and a fine for each subsequent violation. § 11-207(b).

Possession of child pornography is prohibited by § 11-208(a), which provides as follows:

"(a) *Prohibited.*—A person may not knowingly possess a film, videotape, photograph, or other visual representation depicting an individual under the age of 16 years:

"(1) engaged as a subject of sadomasochistic abuse;

"(2) engaged in sexual conduct; or

"(3) in a state of sexual excitement."...

IV.

A.

Section 11-207 does not define the phrase "use a computer to depict or describe." As with all legislation in this sensitive area that lies outside the protection of the First Amendment of the United States Constitution, the conduct to be prohibited must be defined adequately by the statute, as written or authoritatively construed. *See Ferber,* 458 U.S. at 764, 102 S.Ct. at 3358.

Moore's interpretation of the statutory phrase "use a computer to depict or describe" as "use a computer to

create" is consistent with the ordinary usage of "depict" and "describe." "Depict" is defined as either "to form a likeness of by drawing or painting" or "to represent, portray, or delineate in other ways than in drawing or painting." Webster's Third New International Dictionary 605 (1961) [hereinafter "Webster's"]; *see also Kelly v. William Morrow & Co.,* 186 Cal.App.3d 1625, 231 Cal.Rptr. 497, 500 (1986) (quoting Webster's); Funk & Wagnalls New Standard Dictionary of the English Language 683 (1952) [hereinafter "Funk & Wagnalls"] (defining "depict" as "[t]o portray or picture, as in words; describe or represent vividly" and "to portray or paint in colors"). "Describe" means "to represent by words written or spoken for the knowledge or understanding of others." Webster's, *supra,* at 610; *see also* Funk & Wagnalls, *supra,* at 687 (defining "describe" as "[t]o give the characteristics of, as in words or by signs, so that another may form a mental image or idea").

The definitions indicate that the terms denote creative acts. Artists and artisans form a likeness by drawing or painting—they depict. Poets, narrators, and orators represent, portray, or delineate—they depict—and represent by words—they describe. A person who photographs or films pornographic images of a child, who captures such images directly into a computer by means of a digital camera or who first translates a motion picture or photograph of such images into a computer file is engaged in a creative act even though the perverse, heinous, and cruel nature of this creative act differentiates it from the creative acts that society values and tolerates. . . .

The grammatical form of "depict or describe" further evidences that the meaning of the statute is to use a computer to create, not to use a computer to download. Section 11-207(a)(3) states "to use a computer to depict or describe," employing the verb forms of "depict" and "describe." Moore's interpretation of "depict or describe" as "to create" conforms with the verb forms of the terms. The State's interpretation conforms with the use of depict or describe either in the passive form, such as "that depict" or "that describe," or in the nominalized form (*i.e.* as abstract nouns), such as "depiction" or "description." *See* Joseph M. Williams, *Style: Ten Lessons in Clarity & Grace* 43-44 (4th ed.1994) (discussing nominalizations). The person who downloads a picture transfers and copies a depiction or a file that depicts—the image already has been depicted when the person downloads it. The act of downloading is covered by § 11-208, which prohibits a person from knowingly possessing a "visual representation *depicting* an individual under the age of 16 years" (emphasis added). Section 11-208 prohibits the possession of an image that already has been depicted, or created. Thus, the possession statute employs the nominalized, gerund form of the verb depict. *See id.*

Similarly, § 11-207(a) uses the passive form of depict in two other provisions. A person may not "cause, induce, solicit, or knowingly allow a minor to engage as a subject in the production of obscene matter or a visual representation or performance *that depicts* a minor. . . ." § 11-207(a)(1) (emphasis added). A person may not "knowingly promote, distribute, or possess with the intent to distribute any matter, visual representation, or performance *that depicts* a minor. . . ." § 11-207(a)(4) (emphasis added). These two provisions do not concern the creation of child pornography, but rather proscribe the recruitment of children for such offensive material or the distribution of child pornography that has been created. As such, the statute employs the passive voice to describe that which results from the recruitment and that which is distributed. In contrast, § 11-207(a)(3) governs the creation of child pornography by computer and thus uses the active forms of depict and describe. . . .

We conclude that the plain language of the statutory terms "to depict or describe" is unambiguous. The plain meaning of "use a computer to depict or describe" is to use a computer to create, not to use a computer to download. We hold that a person who downloads visual representations of a minor engaged in obscene acts or sexual conduct does not violate the proscription of § 11-207(a)(3) against "us[ing] a computer to depict or describe a minor engaging in an obscene act, sadomasochistic abuse, or sexual conduct." Accordingly, the Circuit Court erred in finding that Moore violated § 11-207(a)(3).

B.

Our conclusion is bolstered by the legislative history of § 11-207(a)(3). In 1978, Congress passed Pub.L. No. 95-225, the Protection of Children Against Sexual Exploitation Act, 18 U.S.C. §§ 2251-2253. The federal law punished the inducement or employment of minors to engage in sexually explicit conduct "for the purpose of producing any visual or print medium depicting such conduct" if the visual or print medium was intended for interstate or foreign commerce. *Id.; see also Outmezguine,* 97 Md.App. at 159-60, 627 A.2d at 545. The federal act represented a recognition of the interstate nature of the traffic in child pornography and the failure of most states to target child pornography. *See Outmezguine,* 97 Md.App. at 160, 627 A.2d at 545.

Three months after Congress passed the federal act, the Maryland General Assembly enacted the first Maryland statute to address child pornography. *See* 1978 Md. Laws, Chap. 573. The Maryland statute was codified as Md.Code (1957, 1976 Repl.Vol., 1978 Cum. Supp.), Art. 27, § 419A, and is found currently at § 11-207 of the Criminal Law Article. The statutory language and the legislative history of the initial Maryland child pornography statute suggest that the Legislature was targeting the child pornography industry, *i.e.,* the creators and distributors of the material. The statute made it a felony to solicit, cause, induce, or knowingly permit a person under sixteen to engage as a subject in the production of obscene matter, or to photograph or film a person under sixteen engaged in an obscene act. *See* 1978 Md. Laws, Chap. 573. The bill file contains a letter from an Assistant Attorney General describing the bill as "legislation which is designed to prohibit the production and distribution of [child pornography] within the boundaries of this State . . . complement[ing] the federal bill." Additionally, a member of the National Conference of State Legislatures testified before a subcommittee of the House Judiciary Committee detailing the steps being taken by states across the country to criminalize and "to prosecute those responsible for using children in obscene materials and selling them for profit."

In *New York v. Ferber,* 458 U.S. 747, 102 S.Ct. 3348, 73 L.Ed.2d 1113 (1982), the United States Supreme Court reviewed a New York child pornography statute that prohibited material depicting sexual conduct by a child under sixteen, rather than merely "obscene" material. *See id.* at 750-51, 102 S.Ct. at 3351. The Court upheld the statute, holding that the First Amendment permits a state to proscribe the distribution of sexual materials involving minors without regard to an obscenity standard. *See id.* at 760-61, 102 S.Ct. at 3356-57.

Congress responded to *Ferber* by enacting Pub.L. 98-292, the Child Protection Act of 1984, 18 U.S.C. §§ 2251 to 2254. *See Outmezguine,* 97 Md.App. at 164, 627 A.2d at 547. That law amended the 1977 law, *inter alia,* to include depictions of "sexually explicit conduct" that need not be legally obscene and to redefine "minor" to include children ages sixteen and seventeen. *See id.*

The Maryland Legislature responded to *Ferber* with a series of amendments to Art. 27, § 419A. *See Outmezguine,* 97 Md.App. at 164, 627 A.2d at 547. In 1985, the General Assembly increased the fine under the statute from $15,000 to $25,000 and expanded the reach of the statute beyond obscene matters to include the knowing promotion, distribution, or possession with the intent to distribute of "any matter or other visual representation, which depicts a child engaged as a subject in sexual conduct." *See* 1985 Md. Laws, Chap. 494; *Outmezguine*, 97 Md.App. at 164-65, 627 A.2d at 547-48. As it had done with the promotion and distribution provisions in 1985, the Legislature subsequently expanded the reach of the provision outlawing the photographing or filming of children beyond "obscene" matter to specifically include children engaged in "sexual conduct." *See* 1986 Md. Laws, Chap. 112; *Outmezguine*, 97 Md.App. at 165, 627 A.2d at 548. In 1989, the Legislature expanded each provision of the child pornography statute to include children ages sixteen and seventeen. *See* 1989 Md. Laws, Chap. 398; *Outmezguine*, 97 Md.App. at 165, 627 A.2d at 548.

Simple possession of child pornography was not a crime in Maryland until 1992. In 1992, the Legislature enacted Md.Code (1957, 1992 Rep. Vol., 1992 Cum. Supp.), Art 27 § 419B, making it a misdemeanor to "knowingly possess any film, videotape, photograph, or other visual representation depicting [a minor] engaged as a subject of sadomasochistic abuse or in sexual conduct, or in a state of sexual excitement." *See* 1992 Md. Laws, Chap. 443. The crime was punishable by a fine or not more than one year imprisonment, or both, for a first offense, and a fine or not more than two years imprisonment, or both, for a second or subsequent offense. *Id.* This section became § 11-208 of the Criminal Law Article.

Until 1996, the proscriptions against child pornography in Maryland made no reference to the use of computers. The Legislature amended § 419A(c) to read as follows: "Every person who photographs, films, *or by means of computer depicts or describes* a minor engaging in an obscene act or engaging in sexual conduct or sadomasochistic abuse" is guilty of a felony. 1996 Md. Laws, Chap. 443 (emphasis added)—207(a)(5).

The Legislature did not need to specify computers in the provision prohibiting the distribution of child pornography, because Md.Code (1957, 1996 Repl.Vol.), Art. 27 § 419A(d), now § 11-207(a)(4), proscribed the promotion, distribution, or possession with intent to distribute of "any matter or other visual representation or performance." That provision includes computers.

The Legislature included the words "or describe" in the 1996 amendment to ensure that the provision included pornographic texts. During the 1995 legislative session, the session before the Legislature passed the amendment adding computers, the Senate passed Senate Bill 22. Senate Bill 22 added nearly identical language as was added in the 1996 session, except that Senate Bill 22 added "depict," not "depict or describe." *See* "Bill Analysis" in the bill file for Senate Bill 133.

Senate Bill 22 received an unfavorable report from the House Judiciary Committee. *Id.*

The bill passed in the 1996 session originally did not include the words "or describe." The bill file contains a September 4, 2005 draft of Senate Bill 133, which indicates that the bill originally was identical to Senate Bill 22. The drafter added by hand the words "or describe." This addition apparently stemmed from comments made by a reviewer written on the "Session of 1996 L[egislative] R[eference] Request Form." On September 6, the reviewer noted as follows: "Does (c) apply only to visual depiction (*i.e.* picture) or could it also be text that is pornographic (*i.e.* a story). I think you may want to clarify it." The Request Form indicates that the drafter noted this suggestion on September 25. The September 28 draft of the bill included this new language. The Senate adopted the bill in its revised form, and the House adopted the change following the Conference Committee. *See* "Conference Committee Report."

In 2002, as a result of the Code Revision, Art. 27, § 419A(b) through (g) was repealed and reenacted as § 11-207 of the Criminal Law Article and Art. 27, § 419B was repealed and reenacted as § 11-208. The relevant provision of § 11-207 contained two changes from § 419A. First, § 419A(c) was divided into two sections— "photograph and film" and "use a computer to depict or describe" were separated into § 11-207(a)(2) and (3) respectively. Second, the term "by means of a computer" was replaced with the term "use a computer." *See* 2002 Md. Laws, Chap. 26. As pointed out by the Revisor's Note, § 11-207 was derived from Art 27, § 419A without substantive change. *Id.*

Our review of the legislative history of § 11-207 supports our conclusion that "use a computer to depict or describe" means to use a computer to create. First, the inclusion of "or describes" in § 11-207(a)(3) indicates that the Legislature did not intend for the provision to include the downloading of files. It is clear that the recipient of a text file does not "describe" the subject matter of the text when the recipient downloads the file. Instead, the author describes the subject matter by writing the text, and the recipient copies and transfers the description onto the computer screen or drive. For example, a person who downloads a poem has not described a rose—the poet described the rose when writing the poem. The act of downloading a picture is more confusing because it involves an image within an image—the picture itself and the projection of the image onto the computer screen. The photographer depicts a subject by creating an image—the photograph. The recipient does not depict the subject of the picture, but rather copies or transfers the photograph onto the computer screen or drive. A person who downloads a picture of a rose does not depict the rose—the photographer depicts the rose when taking the picture. The inclusion of "or describe" thus elucidates the meaning of "depict" and further indicates that § 11-207(a)(3) does not proscribe the act of downloading files.

Second, as we have noted, the Legislature did not intend to change the substance of the statute when it bifurcated the following provision from the 1996 amended statute: "Every person who *photographs, films, or by means of computer depicts or describes* a minor engaging in an obscene act or engaging in sexual conduct or sadomasochistic abuse . . . is subject to [a penalty]." Md.Code (1957, 1996 Repl.Vol.), Art. 27, § 419A(c) (emphasis added). The terms "photographs" and "films" are verbs describing creative acts—a person takes a photograph or makes a film. Unfortunately, there is no equivalent verb for the creative act of depicting or describing by computer—a person cannot computer a computer. For that reason, the Legislature was compelled to add the long phrase "or by means of computer depicts or describes," despite the fact that the wording does not parallel the structure of "who photographs, films."

The original placement of the phrase "by means of computers depicts or describes" at the end of a list that included the creative verbs "photographs" and "films" indicates that the Legislature intended the phrase to mean "to create by means of computers." A summary of the proposed amendment contained in the bill file supports this conclusion. A "Bill Analysis" to Senate Bill 133 described the amendment as an expansion of the provision relating to photography and film making. The "Bill Analysis" summarized the bill as follows:

> "The bill *expands* a current child pornography law relating to certain types of photographs and film *to make it applicable to computer generated images and descriptions* of minors engaging in obscene acts or sexual conduct. Specifically, the bill makes it a felony to depict or describe, by means of a computer, a minor engaged in an obscene act or sexual conduct." (Emphasis added.)

Thus, the 1996 addition of the computer-related language with filming and photography reasonably can be understood as a recognition by the Legislature that the computer was a new technology which could be used to create child pornography.

_____**CASE END**

Case Questions
Moore v. State

1. How is the First Amendment implicated in this case?
2. How have Maryland's child pornography laws evolved over the last several decades?
3. Do you agree that based on Moore's actions he could only be charged with a misdemeanor and not a felony? Why or why not?

Additional Crimes to Consult

The Legislature has prohibited many other weapons offenses in addition to those discussed in this chapter. For example, possession of assault pistols is prohibited (Md. Code. Ann., Crim. Law §§ 4-301 et. seq.); persons must register ownership of machine guns (§§ 4-401 et. seq.); possession and making of destructive devices, such as missiles, flamethrowers, bombs and poison gases, are prohibited (§§ 4-501 et. seq.); and a person previously convicted of a violent crime or drug trafficking must have a permit to wear body armor (§ 4-107).

Aside from weapons offenses, the Maryland General Assembly has legislated a host of other crimes against morality. These crimes can be found at Title 10 of the Maryland Annotated Code Criminal Law Article, "Crimes Against Health and Public Safety." Such offenses include hate crimes (subtitle 3), disturbance of human remains (subtitle 4), crimes against marriage including adultery (§10-501) and bigamy (§10-502), animal cruelty (subtitle 6), and flag mutilation (subtitle 7).

Please also see *Miller v. California*, 413 U.S. 15 (1973), for an explanation of how the Supreme Court has defined obscenity and a balancing of First Amendment free speech rights with the government's interest in preventing the making, distribution, possession and sale of obscene materials. For more recent discussions regarding obscenity in the digital age, *see United States v. American Library Ass'n*, 539 U.S. 194 (2003), and *Ashcroft v. Free Speech Coalition*, 535 U.S. 234 (2002).

HYPOTHETICAL #1

Beth, Susan, Bobby and Michael were sitting around Beth's house. To overcome their boredom, Beth suggested that they play poker. Beth got out the poker table and chips. Everyone put $10 in a pile and received chips in exchange. Beth dealt hands of Texas Holdem, a variation of poker. Everyone bet with their chips and the winner of each hand took the pot of chips. In the middle of a game, the police entered Beth's house with a search warrant and seized the table, chips and pile of money.

MAIN ISSUE

Did Beth Gamble by Keeping and Dealing at a Poker Table Where Bobby, Susan, and Michael Bet Poker Chips, Which Had a Monetary Value, on Texas Holdem, a Game of Chance?

ISSUE	THESIS	RULE	ANALYSIS	CONCLUSION
Did Beth keep, deal at or manage a gaming table or have an interest in or share profits in the gaming table WHEN she dealt hands of poker in which chips were earned by the winner of the hand?	Beth dealt at, kept and/or managed a gaming table WHEN she dealt hands of poker in which chips were earned by the winner of the hand.	Maryland law prohibits gambling. There are two prohibited acts, either of which may be proven to establish that the defendant is guilty of gambling. One may not KEEP, MANAGE, OR DEAL AT a gaming table or other place of gambling. HAVING AN INTEREST IN A GAMING TABLE OR PROFITS from a gaming table is also prohibited. A gaming table is a table or device where any game of chance is played for money or at which money is bet or wagered.	Beth gambled BECAUSE she kept a poker table in her house. Beth also dealt hands of poker at the gaming table. The poker table was a table at which people played poker, a game of chance, for money. Money was bet by using chips that were purchased and represented money. While there is no evidence to show that Beth had an interest in or profited from the gaming table, this is not essential to a gambling conviction, as the law only requires that one deal at, keep or manage a gaming table.	Beth gambled by keeping and dealing at a poker table where money was wagered.

CONCLUSION

Beth gambled by keeping and dealing at a poker table where Bobby, Susan, and Michael bet poker chips, which had a monetary value, on Texas Holdem, a game of chance.

HYPOTHETICAL #2

Ripley, Jordan & Ches were members of the K-9 gang. They undertook various nefarious activities to make big profits. They planned one big "working" day full of criminal activities.

At 9:00 a.m. Ches purchased a shotgun from a local drug dealer. No one saw Ches bring the gun home, but at 10:00 a.m., his mother found the shotgun under his mattress and called the police. The police arrested Ches and he was out of the picture for the rest of the day.

At 11:00 a.m. Ripley walked into a bank with a 9 mm handgun in her purse. When she reached the teller, Ripley placed her purse on the counter and opened it wide enough for the teller to see the gun. As the teller's eyes widened at the sight, Ripley said "You know what to do." The teller brought out five large stacks of $100 dollar bills and set them on the counter. Ripley stuffed them in her purse and left the bank. She was apprehended a block away by the police.

At noon, Jordan set out to hijack a large shipment of video games that she knew were in a tractor trailer at the local truck stop. Jordan was well prepared with a handgun under the seat, a shotgun in the trunk, and a machine gun on the back seat. Jordan also had a small amount of plastic explosives with a detonator. She planned to use the small charge to break open the lock on the back of the tractor trailer without damaging the goods inside. Jordan was a little nervous and got extremely intoxicated prior to leaving her house. After having ingested enough alcohol to get a small elephant intoxicated, she got behind the wheel and headed to the truck stop. On the way, she drove head on into incoming traffic, colliding with a woman in an SUV and killing her. Jordan was outraged when she realized that if she was delayed the truck with the video games would likely leave the stop. So, she walked up to a Mustang, shot the Mustang driver with her handgun, pulled the dead driver out of the vehicle, and sped off in the Mustang. The Mustang proved too much for Jordan. About a mile down the road, she lost control and ran the vehicle into a ditch. It was here the police apprehended her.

➲ List the crimes with which each defendant may be charged.

DEFENDANT	CRIMES
Ches	
Ripley	
Jordan	

➲ For EACH crime identified, complete an Analysis Chart assessing the possibility of conviction for each defendant.

DISCUSSION QUESTIONS

1. Why has the Legislature imposed enhanced penalties for crimes committed with weapons?

2. Is it illegal in Maryland to make pipe bombs?

3. Are "Nunchaku," tools used in martial arts, weapons? Could someone's hands be considered a deadly weapon?

4. What makes a crime a hate crime? What is the effect of being convicted of a hate crime?

5. If Gary burns down a church because he does not approve of the religion, can he win an acquittal by asserting that he cannot be convicted of a hate crime with enhanced penalties because to do so would violate his First Amendment free speech and freedom of religion protections?

6. Is Maryland's prohibition against flag mutilation (Md. Code Ann., Crim. Law § 10-704 (West 2002) constitutional? Why or why not? *See Texas v. Johnson*, 491 U.S. 397 (1989).

7. John views pornography in his own home. The pornography depicts adults having sexual intercourse. Is this a crime in Maryland? *See* Md. Code Ann., Crim. Law §§ 11-101, 11-202(a) (West 2002).

8. Do you think that Maryland's laws making it a crime to simply possess certain types of weapons or requiring licenses and background checks to purchase, possess and/or carry certain kinds of weapons violate the Second Amendment? Explain why or why not.

9. Assume that the City Paper publishes a single cartoon depicting two people engaged in sadomasochistic abuse. The balance of the paper covers local news, arts, music and politics. Would this edition of the City Paper be considered obscene? *See Woodruff v. State*, 11 Md.App. 202, 273 A.2d 436 (1971).

10. Do you think that the Supreme Court's ruling that free speech prohibits a child pornography conviction for virtual child pornography, in which no real children are used to generate the materials, is a good ruling? Why or why not? *See Ashcroft v. Free Speech Coalition*, 535 U.S. 234 (2002).

11. In your opinion is pepper spray a dangerous or deadly weapon? Mace? Why or why not? *See Handy v. State*, 357 Md. 685, 745 A.2d 1107 (2000).

TEST BANK

True/False

_____ 1. Brass knuckles are considered dangerous weapons under Maryland law and may not be carried or concealed.

_____ 2. One may not carry a pocket knife in one's pocket because to do so would be considered the crime of carrying a concealed dangerous weapon.

_____ 3. Beth uses a handgun in the commission of a homicide while involuntarily intoxicated. She is convicted of manslaughter. She can also be convicted of using a handgun in the commission of a felony or a crime of violence.

_____ 4. Jake and Josh are on their way to a martial arts class. On their way down the street to the martial arts studio, they practice their moves with their nunchaku. They may be guilty of carrying a dangerous weapon openly with intent to injure.

_____ 5. Josh carried a baseball bat down the street to Jake's house. Josh intended to kill Jake with the bat. Josh cannot be convicted of any weapons crimes because a baseball bat is not per se a weapon.

MULTIPLE CHOICE

6. Which of the following is not, per se, a weapon?

   A. Dirk knife

   B. Bowie knife

   C. Star knife

   D. Penknife without a switchblade

   E. Razor

7. Laurie had a handgun tucked in her waistband with her shirt covering it while riding on a boat. Laurie intended to use the gun to shoot Ashley once Laurie got to the other side of the bay. Laurie may be guilty of all of the following except:

   A. Carrying a dangerous weapon openly with intent to injure

   B. Carrying a concealed dangerous weapon

   C. Carrying a handgun concealed or openly

   D. Transporting a handgun in a vehicle

8. The New London Volunteer Fire Department sponsored bingo every Friday night. The fire department kept 50% of the proceeds and the balance was distributed to the winners. The New London Volunteer Fire Department may be:

   A. Guilty of gambling because it had an interest in the gaming

   B. Guilty of gambling because it managed the bingo

   C. Not guilty of gambling if it had a permit

   D. Not guilty of gambling because bingo can never be considered gambling

9. Pornography may be illegal to possess if it:

   A. Involves children

   B. Is obscene

   C. Both A and B

   D. None of the above

10. Depictions of sexual conduct may be protected from prosecution by the First Amendment if such depictions are for the purposes of:

   A. Sexual arousal or gratification

   B. Monetary profit

   C. Art or literature

   D. Science

   E. Both A and B

   F. Both C and D

chapter ten

Force-Based Criminal Defenses

Introduction

The final two chapters of this book collectively deal with criminal defenses, sometimes referred to as "affirmative defenses." The best way to understand an affirmative defense is to remember the phrase "I did it *but* . . ." In other words, the perpetrator admits to the criminal agency ("I did it") yet offers some legal excuse ("but . . .") that she hopes will absolve her from criminal responsibility. Keep in mind that an alibi is not an affirmative defense. In fact, an alibi is the antithesis of an affirmative defense because the perpetrator is denying criminal agency altogether ("I didn't do it"). The five defenses discussed in this Chapter are force-based defenses, *i.e.*, when the actor uses some form of physical force or aggression to defend someone or something. The remaining five defenses discussed in Chapter 11 will focus on situations in which the actor's intent or capacity to commit a crime is affected.

Focus Defenses

Self Defense, *Dykes v. State*, 319 Md. 206, 571 A.2d 1251 (1990); MPJI-Cr. 5:07.

Defense of Others, *Alexander v. State*, 52 Md. App. 171, 447 A.2d 880, *aff'd*, 294 Md. 600, 451 A.2d 664 (1982); MPJI-Cr. 5:01.

Defense of Habitation, *Crawford v. State*, 231 Md. 354, 190 A.2d 538 (1963); MPJI-Cr. 5:02.

Defense of Property, *Sydnor v. State*, 365 Md. 205, 776 A.2d 669 (2001); MPJI-Cr. 5:02.1.

Duress, *State v. Crawford*, 308 Md. 683, 521 A.2d 1193 (1987); MPJI-Cr. 5:03.

Objectives

Upon completing this chapter you should be able to:

⊃ Explain the concept of an affirmative defense and distinguish that from alibi;

⊃ Analyze the distinction between self-defense and defense of others;

⊃ Analyze the distinction between defense of habitation and defense of property;

⊃ Analyze the distinction between duress and necessity;

⊃ Analyze the distinction between a "perfect" versus an "imperfect" defense;

⊃ Recognize when an individual has a duty to retreat before using force as a defense; and

⊃ Recognize when, if ever, an individual may use deadly force.

CASE LAW	*Lambert v. State*, 70 Md. App. 83, 519 A.2d 1340, *cert. denied*, 309 Md. 605, 525 A.2d 1075 (1987)

A jury in the Circuit Court for Harford County, presided over by Judge Albert P. Close, convicted appellant, William Lee Lambert, of assault and battery, assault with intent to murder, carrying a weapon openly with intent to injure another, and attempt to commit murder. Appellant was sentenced to prison terms of three years for the assault and battery, twenty years for assault with intent to murder, and three years for the weapons offense. For the attempted murder conviction he received a sentence of life imprisonment, with all but twenty years suspended. All sentences were concurrent.

The issues in this appeal are as follows:

1. Whether the trial judge erred in refusing to instruct the jury on the doctrine of self-defense;
2. Whether the trial judge erred in failing to instruct the jury on the doctrine of imperfect self-defense.

For the reasons set forth below, we answer both questions in the negative and, therefore, affirm the convictions.

Facts

All of the charges against appellant stem from the stabbing of Thomas Malone on April 14, 1985. Malone was stabbed with a knife some 26 times in the face, arms, chest, abdominal region and right flank.

The victim and some of his friends, Kevin Kahoe, Charles Offney and Michael Snyder, left a party which appellant and his friends, Mark Rodano, Jeffrey Hoffman and Glen Nealy, had also attended. Appellant's version of the incident, as testified to at trial, is as follows. A car in which the victim was riding pulled up to the place where appellant and his companions were standing and someone yelled something at the victim's group. Kevin Kahoe and the victim asked appellant and his group if they had a problem. Appellant replied in the negative. The car then pulled away. Shortly thereafter, however, the victim and several others ("four or more") returned and approached appellant's group. The victim and appellant's friend Rodano had a verbal confrontation, but appellant testified it was peaceably terminated.

The events subsequent to the termination of the verbal confrontation between the victim and Rodano were described by appellant, on direct examination, as follows:

[APPELLANT]: I felt as if Tom Malone was getting pretty uptight. He was playing with his hands and everything. I didn't know what he was doing. He was just upset. And I felt like things were getting pretty boring. So I said, "if you guys are going to end it, let's end this." And I took off my jacket and laid it on the car.

[COUNSEL FOR APPELLANT]: What happened then?

A. At that time Tom Malone made a remark to me.

Q. What did he say to you?

A. I can't remember what the remark was.

Q. Who advanced to whom, if anyone?

A. I turned around and faced Thomas Malone and we faced each other.

Q. And then what happened?

A. I remember falling against the car.

Q. How did you fall against the car?

A. Thomas and I made contact with each other. I was knocked back.

Q. When you hit the car, did you hit anything?

A. I remember my body hitting the door side of the car, and I fell to the ground, hitting my head and everything.

Q. You hit your head on what?

A. Against the body of the car.

Q. What happened next?

A. I just remember as I was starting to get up, Tom came at me and we started confronting each other.

Q. What happened then?

A. We were swinging. I just remember getting hit. We were swinging. Fighting. I can't picture anybody that was around me. I felt really light-headed.

Appellant recalled fighting with the victim and being hit in the head from behind by someone other than the victim. He also remembered having a knife with him on the night in question, to open beer cans. He testified, however, that he could not recall using the knife on the victim or throwing it away in an effort to conceal it. He attributed his inability to recall using the knife to his hitting the car when the victim pushed him, to the blow he received on the head, and to his intoxication. On cross-examination, appellant proffered that he had not taken off the jacket because he was "bored" but because "I know for a fact when you do drink you get very hot. And I had a thick wool sweater on that night."

Several pre-trial statements that appellant had made to the police were admitted into evidence. A police officer, Sergeant Walter G. Shultz, testified to their content. In appellant's first statement, made to Sgt. Shultz on the scene immediately after the incident, he denied stabbing the victim and claimed he never carried a knife. He made no statement respecting how the fight was initiated or his state of mind during the fight.

In appellant's second statement, made in the early morning hours after the incident, he said he noticed the victim "putting on a ring or something on his right hand" after the disagreement between the victim and Rodano. Appellant then said to the victim, "What are you, a tough guy?" and the victim replied affirmatively. The two had "words" and the victim "punched [appellant] with his right hand on the left side of [his] head." Then somebody hit him in the back of the head and dazed him. Appellant remembered punching the victim, but said it was in "self-defense." He denied owning a knife and could not recall stabbing the victim.

In his third statement to the police on August 1, 1986, appellant admitted having a knife with him on the night in question to "torpedo" (open) beer cans. He stated the victim and about six persons walked toward him and his group as if they wanted to fight. The victim, according to appellant, was acting belligerently and challenging Rodano. When it was apparent Rodano would not fight, the victim badgered appellant and then charged toward appellant and knocked him on the ground. Appellant admittedly went into a rage and started punching the victim while the knife was in his hand. He claimed he did not realize what he had done until after the fight was over and then he became scared and threw the knife into the yard. On cross-examination, Sgt. Shultz was asked whether appellant then told him he was scared of the crowd. The sergeant replied, "he may have made that statement. I don't have it anywhere in my notes to indicate that."

Mark Rodano, one of appellant's group, admitted he and the victim had resolved their differences when appellant threw his jacket off and set it on the car. He testified the victim then said, "that's right, you better take off your jacket." At that point, appellant and the victim "just met coming right at each other." He also said "they both hit and it's just like they went back against the car and went down to the ground." The fight looked "pretty even" to Rodano. He saw the victim's friend Charles Offney hit appellant once in the head and then Offney "just stopped." He said appellant did not appear dazed. Although Rodano did not see the knife during the struggle, he had seen it earlier at the party, and he saw appellant throw his hands up after the fight and what appeared to be "a flash of something that must have been the knife."

Jeffrey Hoffman, another of appellant's friends, admitted the victim and his companions were not intimidating appellant and his group. He could not recall who initiated the struggle between appellant and the victim and said, "they just came together at the same time, and I saw Bill [appellant] fall back" against the car. Appellant then "caught himself and started punching." He remembered Offney trying to intervene and hitting the victim and "everyone just said let him go, let them get it out of their system . . . " He said the fight was "fairly even" and "no one was slacking off" or yielding. Hoffman did not see the knife being used during the altercation although appellant had shown him the knife earlier, outside the party.

In his testimony at trial, the victim portrayed appellant as the initial aggressor. The testimony of Charles Offney and Michael Snyder essentially corroborated the victim's testimony. Offney testified that during the fight appellant and the victim were "in a huddle position. They almost had their heads together, their upper shoulders together." He added that after he saw the victim fall, and then stand up, he wondered why the victim was weak. He saw appellant thrust a long sharp object into the victim several times and then Offney struck appellant on the right side of his face with his fist to get appellant away from the victim. Appellant then stabbed Offney in his left hand. Offney yelled, "he's fighting with a knife," at which point appellant raised his hands and threw the knife behind him. Appellant then said, "I'm not using a knife. I'm using my hands."

Snyder also corroborated Offney's testimony respecting the latter's efforts to get appellant off the victim. He also testified that after Offney hit appellant, "that's when everything stopped." While he did not see the knife during the fight, he heard Offney yell that appellant had a knife. He then saw appellant step back and throw his hands up.

Corporal James Reinhart, an officer of the Maryland State Police, who lived in the immediate vicinity, was awakened by screaming and shouting in the street. He testified the victim and appellant "were like two bulls. They had their heads together and their bodies were humped over." In response to a question as to which of the two combatants was the aggressor, he testified he saw appellant "pushing the other person [the victim] backwards." Reinhart pulled the boys apart. The officer estimated that a crowd of about 30 persons had gathered during the fight. When asked whether, in view of the size of the crowd, he was "beginning to fear a little bit for [his] own safety," Reinhart replied affirmatively. Nevertheless he also stated, "It was two people fighting and the other people were not involved in the fight . . . ."

Appellant, who is 5'11" tall, weighed 185 pounds, was on the varsity wrestling and football teams at his high school and won several Harford County wrestling titles. The victim's height was 5'9" and he weighed 170 pounds at the time of the incident.

I

Appellant's first contention is that the trial court erred in refusing to instruct the jury on the doctrine of self-defense.

> It is incumbent upon the trial court, when requested in a criminal case, to give an instruction to the jury on every essential question or point of law supported by the evidence. *Smith v. State,* 302 Md. 175, 179, 486 A.2d 196 (1985); *Dillon v. State,* 277 Md. 571, 584-85, 357 A.2d 360 (1976); *England and Edwards v. State,* 274 Md. 264, 275-76, 334 A.2d 98 (1975); *Bruce v. State,* 218 Md. 87, 97, 145 A.2d 428 (1958); *see also* Rule 4-325(c)), Md. Rules of Procedure. To generate the issue of self-defense the accused must produce evidence establishing a *prima facie* case of self-defense. *Cunningham v. State,* 58 Md.App. 249, 255, 473 A.2d 40 (1984); *Street v. State,* 26 Md.App. 336, 338-39, 338 A.2d 72, *cert. denied,* 275 Md. 756 (1975). The record below must demonstrate that:
>
> 1. The accused . . . had reasonable grounds to believe himself in apparent imminent or immediate danger of death or serious bodily harm from his assailant or potential assailant;
> 2. The accused must have in fact believed himself in this danger;
> 3. The accused claiming the right of self-defense must not have been the aggressor or provoked the conflict; and
> 4. The force used must not have been unreasonable and excessive, that is, the force must not have been more force than the exigency demanded.

State v. Faulkner, 301 Md. 482, 485-86, 483 A.2d 759 (1984). *See also Tichnell v. State,* 287 Md. 695, 718, 415 A.2d 830 (1980); *DeVaughn v. State,* 232 Md. 447, 453, 194 A.2d 109 (1963), *cert. denied,* 376 U.S. 927, 84 S.Ct. 693, 11 L.Ed.2d 623 (1964); *Guerriero v. State,* 213 Md. 545, 549, 132 A.2d 466 (1957). It should be noted, additionally, that it is the duty of the defendant, when defending himself outside the home, to retreat or avoid the danger if the means to do so are within his power and consistent with his safety. Where, however, the peril is so imminent that he cannot retreat safely, he has a right to stand his ground and defend himself. *DeVaughn, supra,* 232 Md. at 453, 194 A.2d 109; *Bruce, supra,* 218 Md. at 97, 145 A.2d 428.

Even when the evidence is viewed in the light most favorable to appellant, *Jacobs v. State,* 32 Md.App. 509, 510, 363 A.2d 257 (1976), it does not make out a *prima facie* case of self-defense. Appellant used deadly force against the victim. The law is clear that a person may defend himself even to the extent of taking life to repel the attack of an aggressor when he *reasonably* and *actually* believes both 1) that the other is about to inflict death or serious bodily injury upon him and 2) that it is necessary to use deadly force to prevent it. *Shuck v. State,* 29 Md.App. 33, 38, 349 A.2d 378 (1975). *See also Guerriero, supra,* 213 Md. at 549, 132 A.2d 466; *Ware v. State,* 3 Md.App. 62, 65, 237 A.2d 526 (1968); *Tipton v. State,* 1 Md.App. 556, 562, 232 A.2d 289, *cert. denied,* 247 Md. 742 (1967). One is not privileged to use deadly force in defending oneself against non-deadly force. *Shuck, supra,* 29 Md.App. at 37, 349 A.2d 378. It has been said that the rule generally "precludes the use of a deadly weapon against an unarmed assailant." W. La-Fave & A. Scott, *Criminal Law,* at 456-57 (2d ed. 1986). This is not inevitably the case for "account must be taken of the respective sizes and sex of the assailant and defendant, of the presence of multiple assailants, and of the especially violent nature of the unarmed attack. Past violent conduct of the assailant known by the defendant is also relevant in assessing what the defendant reasonably believed was the quantum of risk to him." *Id.* at 457. *See also Wharton's Criminal Law,* at 318-19 (C.E. Torcia 14th ed. 1979). Appellant contends that the following evidence indicates appellant had reasonable grounds for believing he was in imminent peril of death or serious bodily injury and needed to use deadly force to prevent the harm: 1) at the outset of the struggle, appellant was pushed back forcefully against a car by the victim; 2) the victim never backed down from the fight and the match was fairly even in nature; 3) appellant was struck in the head by Charles Offney, a member of the victim's group; and 4) the police officer's affirmative response to the question whether he "feared a little bit for [his] safety" because of the size of the crowd that gathered.

With respect to the first blow struck by the victim, we note that under similar circumstances we have upheld the finding of a trial judge that the defense of self-defense was unavailable. *Ware, supra,* 3 Md.App. at 64-65, 237 A.2d 526 (appellant not entitled to acquittal on basis of self-defense although he was hit with such force that he fell to the ground immediately prior to stabbing the deceased). In *Shuck, supra,* we held that the evidence did not generate the issue of self-defense where the appellant used deadly force in circumstances similar to those involved here. We noted:

Even granting that the appellant and his companion were mere victims . . . the brawl or scuffle which was taking place was non-deadly in character . . . The appellant and his companion were good-sized and healthy men who were by no means outclassed physically. There had been several blows struck with fists and the appellant's companion had been wrestled to the ground. It was at this point that the appellant himself escalated the combat to the deadly level by ⋯ taking out a baseball bat and introducing that weapon into the fray.

29 Md.App. at 37, 349 A.2d 378. The use of deadly force against non-deadly force in these circumstances precluded an instruction on self-defense.

While the first blow struck by the victim may have afforded a reasonable basis for a conclusion that the victim intended to inflict *some* harm, it did not provide a reasonable basis for the belief he intended to inflict serious bodily harm or death or that deadly force was needed to prevent such harm. As in *Shuck*, appellant was by no means outclassed physically by the victim. He was both taller and heavier than the victim and acknowledged at trial that he was a champion wrestler.

The testimony as to the fairly even nature of the match would tend to support the conclusion that deadly force was not needed to repel the attack. While the victim did not back down, neither did appellant. The evidence does not suggest that appellant was under attack or threatened with attack by any members of the crowd at the time he chose to use deadly force on the victim. In fact, uncontradicted testimony indicated that by the time Offney, the victim's friend, hit appellant, multiple stab wounds had already been inflicted on the victim, and the fighting between appellant and the victim stopped after Offney hit appellant. Under Maryland law, Offney was in fact entitled to intervene in defense of the victim. *See* art. 27, sec. 12A, Md. Ann. Code (1982 Repl.Vol.); *Alexander v. State*, 52 Md.App. 171, 175-77, 447 A.2d 880, *aff'd*, 294 Md. 600, 451 A.2d 664 (1982). *Cf. Jacobs, supra*, 32 Md.App. at 510-11, 363 A.2d 257 (jury instruction of self-defense appropriate where appellant testified he feared for his life and fired a weapon after multiple assailants had approached him with bats, clubs and tire iron).

The police officer's statement that he feared a little bit for his safety because of the size of the crowd does not provide a reasonable ground for believing deadly force was necessary. The police officer testified that the only people involved in the struggle were the victim and appellant. With the exception of Offney's intervention, *after* deadly force had been employed, appellant was not threatened or attacked by any members of the crowd.

There was no evidence to demonstrate that appellant reasonably believed the victim to be armed. We do not equate with such belief his pre-trial statement that he saw the victim "putting a ring or something on his right hand." The evidence reveals only that the victim fought with his fists and wrestled with appellant. There was nothing to indicate the unarmed attack involved especially violent force. Finally, there was no testimony respecting appellant's awareness of any prior violent conduct on the part of the victim which might reasonably have led him to believe he was in danger of grievous injury or death. *Cf. Gunther v. State*, 228 Md. 404, 407-09, 179 A.2d 880 (1962).

While the question whether the force used in a given case was unreasonable is usually one for the trier of fact, *Falcon v. State*, 4 Md.App. 467, 472, 243 A.2d 631 (1968), *cert. denied*, 251 Md. 748 (1969); *Brown v. State*, 4 Md.App. 261, 268, 242 A.2d 570, *cert. denied*, 251 Md. 747 (1968), we believe the level of force employed by appellant was so grossly excessive that the court properly determined as a matter of law, that he was not entitled to a self-defense instruction.

In light of the above conclusion, we need not consider whether appellant presented sufficient evidence to establish the other elements of self-defense. We note, however, that appellant could similarly have been denied an instruction as to self-defense for the further reason that the evidence did not establish that he subjectively believed in the necessity of employing deadly force (*see infra*, section II).

II

Appellant's second contention is that the trial court erred in refusing to instruct the jury on imperfect self-defense.

Whereas perfect self-defense requires not only that the accused "subjectively believed that his actions were necessary for his safety, but objectively, that a reasonable man would so consider them," imperfect self-defense "requires ⋯ a subjective, honest belief on the part of the [accused] that his actions were necessary for his safety, even though, on an objective appraisal by a reasonable man, they would not be found to be so." *Faulkner v. State*, 54 Md.App. 113, 115, 458 A.2d 81 (1983), *aff'd*, 301 Md. 482, 483 A.2d 759 (1984). An accused may be entitled to invoke the doctrine of imperfect self-defense even where he subjectively but unreasonably believed he needed to escalate a non-deadly combat to the deadly level. *Shuck, supra*, 29 Md.App. at 43, 349 A.2d 378. One who is the aggressor in an encounter, however, is not entitled to invoke the imperfect self-defense doctrine, even though he honestly (but unreasonably) believed that he was required to use the level of force employed in order to defend himself. *Cunningham, supra,* 58 Md.App. at 255-57, 473 A.2d 40; *see also Simmons v. State,* 66 Md.App. 629, 632, 505 A.2d 577 (1986). Only where evidence has been produced which establishes both elements is the accused entitled, on request, to an imperfect self-defense instruction. *Simmons, supra,* 66 Md.App. at 632, 505 A.2d 577.

Where successfully invoked, the imperfect self-defense doctrine does not completely exonerate the accused; it merely serves to negate malice. *Faulkner, supra,* 301 Md. at 486, 483 A.2d 759. Thus, it would operate to reduce the offense of murder to manslaughter and the offense of assault with intent to murder to simple assault, at most. *Id.* at 486, 504, 483 A.2d 759. Appellant did not testify at trial that he used deadly force against the victim because of any subjective fear that he was in imminent peril of death or serious bodily injury. Nonetheless, he contends that the existence of such a belief may be inferred from the evidence presented. Before examining his specific contentions, we note, initially, that the record is not utterly devoid of evidence respecting appellant's state of mind. At trial, appellant testified that his mind was a complete "blank" during the incident. He was "dazed," "lost" and "light-headed" as a result of his state of intoxication and the blow he received to his head. In pre-trial statements appellant said he went into a rage after the victim knocked him down and insisted he did not realize what had happened until after the fight was over and *then* became scared and threw the knife away. He claimed that, not realizing the knife was in his hand, he punched the victim in "self-defense." He did not state he felt it necessary to stab the victim to defend himself. The evidence leads to the conclusion that appellant subjectively experienced various emotions during the fight, but fear was not one of them. Moreover, appellant's repeated assertions that his mind was a "blank" during the incident are inconsistent with and belie a fearful state of mind.

We have previously noted that in determining whether mitigating circumstances exist in a given case to reduce murder to manslaughter we generally find that the accused is the only one who can attest to the fact that he committed the homicide while in a heat of passion. *Tripp v. State,* 36 Md.App. 459, 469, 374 A.2d 384 (1977); *Bartram v. State,* 33 Md.App. 115, 175, 364 A.2d 1119 (1976). While it is not inconceivable that without testimony from the accused as to a state of fear, other evidence might be sufficient to permit an inference as to an accused's subjective beliefs, we do not believe the evidence in this case was sufficient to raise such an inference.

Appellant contends that his subjective although unreasonable belief in the need to use deadly force may be inferred from the very same evidence which we previously found failed to provide basis for a reasonable belief on his part that the victim intended to inflict grievous injury or death. We disagree.

That the police officer, breaking up a fight with a crowd of people around him, may have feared a "little bit" for his safety says nothing respecting whether appellant feared *far more* than a little bit for his safety. With respect to Offney's blow to appellant's head, we have already noted that Offney's uncontradicted testimony was that appellant had already knifed the victim before Offney intervened. Appellant's state of mind *after* the use of the deadly weapon is not relevant to whether he subjectively believed during the fracas that the use of deadly force was necessary. Again, the fact that the match was "fairly even" would only tend to support the inference that appellant did not fear for his safety. If the victim did not yield, neither did appellant. The initial blow suffered by appellant when knocked against the car does not, when viewed in context with all the other evidence, give rise to any reasonable inference that appellant, the larger of the combatants and a successful wrestler, honestly believed it was necessary to use deadly force to defend himself.

While someone in appellant's position might have entertained an honest but unreasonable belief that he needed to use deadly force to defend himself, the evidence furnishes no indication that appellant did, in fact, so believe. *Cf. Simmons, supra,* 66 Md.App. at 632-34, 505 A.2d 577. As a matter of law, therefore, he was not entitled to an instruction on imperfect self-defense.

JUDGMENTS AFFIRMED; COSTS TO BE PAID BY APPELLANT.

CASE END

Case Questions

Lambert v. State

1. Describe the facts of the case. What were the inconsistencies among the various witness accounts of what occurred?

2. What requirements did Lambert have to meet before the trial judge would instruct the jury on the issue of self-defense?

3. When is the use of deadly force appropriate for defending oneself? Why was Lambert not justified in using deadly force?

4. What is the difference between a "perfect" and an "imperfect" self defense? Explain in detail. Did either defense apply in this case?

Additional Defenses to Consult

In the civil context, the Maryland General Assembly has provided that certain individuals who come to the aid of another in need are protected from civil liability for their actions. For example, individuals such as volunteer fire-fighters, police, or persons certified by the American Red Cross in first aid are protected from liability when rendering aid to another during an emergency as long as individual is not grossly negligent in performing that aid. All other individuals (*i.e.*, Good Samaritans) are also protected from liability as long as the aid was rendered in a reasonably prudent manner and that individual relinquishes care of the victim if and when licensed medical personnel arrive on the scene. Md. Code Ann., Cts. & Jud. Proc. § 5-603 (2006). The law was designed to protect the "Good Samaritan" from any legal consequences in seeking to help another and, implicitly, to encourage individuals to "get involved" and help another individual in need when feasible to do so.

For additional non-force based defenses, see Chapter 11, Intent-Based Criminal Defenses.

HYPOTHETICAL #1

Professor Periwinkle was notoriously known as the "Persnickety Old Professor" at the University of Annapolis, Maryland's most prestigious college. In fact, he was such a grumpy and cantankerous old man that he often received death threats from fellow faculty members, students, and even the campus police! One fateful day, as the captain of the campus police was making his usual rounds, he found Professor Periwinkle sprawled on the floor of classroom 217 with a letter opener protruding from his chest. He was as dead as a doornail! After an extensive investigation all evidence pointed to Dean McDevious, the dean of the university who was known as a stern woman willing to do anything to get her way. She was brought into the police captain's office and after several hours of questioning this is what she had to say: "I did it! I killed Professor Periwinkle, but I can explain everything. You see, around 8 o'clock I approached Professor Periwinkle as he was grading exams in Room 217. I told him that I had received all kinds of complaints from students and that he had to shape up his teaching or else. That's when he attacked me—he came running after me with a very sharp pencil raised above his head as if he were going to stab me and I panicked. I thought he was going to poke me to death. So, I grabbed a letter opener that was on the table and stabbed him in the chest. I didn't want to do it, but it was an awfully sharp pencil that he had!" "Hmmmm," replied the police captain, "very interesting. Anything else you'd like to tell me?" "Yes," answered Dean McDevious, "I feel my actions were totally justified! I was protecting myself and I was only trying to rid this wonderful university of such a horrible teacher!" Later that day, Dean McDevious was arrested for the murder of Professor Periwinkle and escorted off the university campus in handcuffs.

MAIN ISSUE

Did Dean McDevious Act in Self-Defense when Killing Professor Periwinkle?

ISSUE	THESIS	RULE	ANALYSIS	CONCLUSION
Did Dean McDevious believe she was in immediate and imminent danger of bodily harm WHEN Professor Periwinkle came running after her with a sharp pencil raised over his head?	Dean McDevious believed she was in immediate and imminent danger of bodily harm WHEN Professor Periwinkle came running after her with a sharp pencil raised over his head.	For a valid claim of self defense the actor must believe she was in IMMEDIATE AND IMMINENT DANGER OF BODILY HARM.	Dean McDevious believed she was in imminent and immediate danger BECAUSE she explained that Professor Periwinkle came running after her with a pencil raised overhead; she said it was her perception that he was going to "poke her to death." Self-defense may be generated from the actor's testimony and beliefs.	Dean McDevious believed she was in immediate and imminent danger of bodily harm.
Was Dean McDevious' belief that she was in immediate danger of bodily harm reasonable WHEN Professor Periwinkle came running after her with the pencil?	Dean McDevious' belief that she was in immediate danger of bodily harm was not reasonable WHEN Professor Periwinkle came running after her with the pencil.	The belief of being in immediate and imminent danger of bodily harm must be REASONABLE under the circumstances.	Dean McDevious' belief was probably not reasonable under the circumstances BECAUSE Professor Periwinkle only had a pencil (not considered a dangerous weapon); he issued no verbal threats and he did not actually harm her. Additionally, she had an avenue of retreat available (leaving the room).	Dean McDevious' belief she was in immediate danger of bodily harm was probably not reasonable.
Did Dean McDevious use no more force than was reasonably necessary to defend herself in light of the threatened harm WHEN she stabbed Professor Periwinkle in the chest with a letter opener?	Dean McDevious used more force than was reasonably necessary to defend herself in light of the threatened harm WHEN she stabbed Professor Periwinkle in the chest with the letter opener.	In defending oneself the actor must USE NO MORE FORCE THAN IS REASONABLY NECESSARY TO DEFEND HERSELF IN LIGHT OF THE THREATENED OR ACTUAL HARM.	Dean McDevious used more force than was reasonably necessary to defend herself BECAUSE she used deadly force (letter opener to the chest) whereas Professor Periwinkle was apparently threatening her with only a pencil.	Dean McDevious used more force than was reasonably necessary to defend herself in light of the threatened harm.

CONCLUSION

Dean McDevious did not act in self-defense when killing Professor Periwinkle because she probably did not have a reasonable belief that she was in immediate danger of bodily harm and because she used more force than was reasonably necessary in defending against the threatened harm.

HYPOTHETICAL #2

One sunny afternoon, Andrew took his friends Bob, Marty, Susan, and David, for a boat tour of the Chesapeake Bay. But suddenly a violent storm came upon them, and they found themselves stranded on a mysterious island smack in the middle of the bay with no method of communication to the outside world whatsoever. Not only did they find an island that had never before been discovered, but they also found a tribe of savage islanders who gave them some trouble. Here's what happened. . . .

As the group of friends were gathering straw to make some huts (just in case they were stranded for a very long time), Charlie, the chief of the savages, came up behind Andrew and began beating him over the head with a huge wooden club. Bob, who saw the whole thing, ran over, pulled out his pocket knife, and slit Charlie across the throat. Charlie fell to the ground dead. Andrew turned around and said, "Thanks Bob, you're the best!" "Any time pal," Bob replied. But just then, Bart the savage, who couldn't have been more than 12-years-old and stood only a little over four feet tall, came running toward Andrew. Andrew, who by now assumed that all of the savages were violent, grabbed the wooden club that Charlie had been holding and smashed Bart over the head with the club. Bart too was dead.

Meanwhile, Marty and Susan had already built their hut and were inside taking a nap when Marty awoke to a strange noise. He then saw Sally the savage rummaging through the couple's belongings. "Stop you thief!" he shouted. Upon realizing that Marty was awake, Sally ran out of the hut. As Sally ran through the brush, Marty noticed that Sally had in her hand a very expensive necklace that he had given Susan. Marty ran after Sally. He soon caught up with her, tackled her, and beat Sally unconscious until she let go of the necklace. Little did Marty know that Sally was more than just unconscious—she was dead.

After Marty realized that he had killed Sally he became very distraught and had this terrible feeling of guilt come over him. He ran up to David and with his bare fists began pounding David on the chest, sobbing "What have I done? What have I done?" Andrew, afraid that Marty might really hurt David, ran up to Marty and successfully subdued him by grabbing Marty's arms and pinning them behind his back. Bob, who saw the whole thing happen and was so angry that Marty had just beaten up on David and wanted to help David, ran over to Marty and began repeatedly punching Marty in the face. Somehow Marty managed to break free of Andrew's grip. Marty immediately lunged at Bob, took the pocket knife out of Bob's pocket, and slashed Bob across the throat with his own knife. Bob fell to the ground dead.

Meanwhile, Susan was becoming very stressed out that they were all stuck on this island that had hardly any food. She soon became convinced that the only way to survive would be to kill everyone on the island so she wouldn't have to share the meager supply of berries with them and she could survive longer. So, Susan grabbed a large branch of a tree, sharpened the end into a point and stabbed David, Andrew, and Marty to death. Only moments after her rampage, Susan spotted a Coast Guard cutter in the distance. She managed to signal for help and soon she was rescued. She then explained the horrid tale of how the savages killed all of her best friends and she alone managed to survive by spearing the savages to death.

➲ List the crimes with which each defendant may be charged and list any possible defenses each defendant may raise.

DEFENDANT	VICTIM	CRIME(S)	DEFENSE(S)
Bob	Charlie		
Andrew	Bart		
Marty	Sally		
Bob	Marty		
Marty	Bob		
Susan	David, Andrew & Marty		

➲ For EACH crime and defense identified, complete an Analysis Chart assessing the possibility of conviction.

DISCUSSION QUESTIONS

1. Tim is walking down the street one day when he sees something that troubles him: A woman is lying face down on the sidewalk kicking and screaming while a very large man dressed in jeans and a sweatshirt is straddling the woman, struggling with her in an apparent attempt to gain control of the woman's flailing hands. Tim, thinking the woman is in serious danger, runs over and punches the man in the face as hard as he can, knocking the man to the ground and letting the woman free. As it turns out, the man was an undercover police officer and the woman was a notorious drug dealer whom the police had been trying to catch for months. The police, obviously, are less than thrilled that Tim let their suspect get away. Does Tim have any good defenses to his battery of the police officer? Explain.

2. Why does the law permit the use of deadly force under certain circumstances when defending your habitation yet the law never permits the use of deadly force when defending your property? Why is that not contradictory? Explain.

3. Bert is sleeping one night when he is awakened by a strange noise downstairs. He lies in bed for a few moments and, after hearing several other strange noises, he is convinced that an intruder is in his home. So, Bert grabs a loaded hand-gun he keeps for protection in his dresser drawer and he quietly tiptoes down the stairs. When he reaches the bottom step he flips on the lights and sees a very large man, dressed all in black with a ski cap on. The man has his back facing Bert with his rear end inside Bert's house, one leg in the living room and one leg swung out the window. Bert shouts "What are you doing?" The man turns towards Bert when Bert opens fire and shoots the man once in the buttocks. Was Bert justified in using deadly force? What arguments can you think of on behalf of Bert? What arguments can you think of that deadly force was inappropriate? Explain.

4. Research challenge: In 1964 a 28-year-old woman by the name of Kitty Genovese was brutally murdered in New York City. The tragic facts of the case quickly garnered national attention and outrage. How did her death impact laws throughout this country regarding coming to the defense of another person in peril?

5. Jerome throws Megan to the ground and forcibly rapes her. Immediately after the rape Megan grabs a kitchen knife and stabs Jerome to death. Will Megan be able to argue self-defense? Why or why not? *See Souffie v. State*, 50 Md.App. 547, 564, 439 A.2d 1127 (1982).

6. What is the distinction between the defenses of duress and necessity? Can you think of an example for each?

7. Research challenge: Tony and Matt Geckle owned and operated the Back River Supply concrete plant in Owings Mills. In March of 2001 their business had been burglarized on two sequential nights. Numerous items had been stolen, including saws, drills, a fax machine, and a rifle. The brothers contacted the police each morning and reports were filed but nothing else was done. The brothers also bought a video surveillance camera but had difficulty installing it. The third night the brothers decided to sleep at their business to protect their belongings, including computers with financial data on them. Both brothers brought rifles with them. On the third night, shortly after 1 a.m. they awoke to noises. The brothers encountered three burglars, and Tony yelled "Freeze! Don't move, I have a gun!" According to their version of events, the three burglars ran directly towards the brothers, and Tony opened fire. All three men were wounded, and 24-year-old Jonathan Steinbach was killed. None of the three burglars was armed. What, if anything, do you think Tony and Matt Geckle should be charged with? What defenses do they have? How was the actual case resolved, both criminally and civilly?

8. Is the right to defend another individual absolute, regardless of who that individual might be? For example, would the right to defend another who reasonably appears to be in immediate danger apply to a prison inmate defending another inmate from being assaulted by a correctional officer? *See Alexander v. State*, 52 Md.App. 171, 447 A.2d 880 (1982).

9. Explain in detail the distinction between a "perfect" defense and an "imperfect" defense as discussed in the Lambert case you read.

10. Ron looks out his bedroom window and sees a strange man attempting to break into his neighbor's car. Ron runs outside and grabs the man's arm so forcefully he breaks the man's arm. If Ron is charged with battery of the man, do you think Ron can argue defense of property even though the property he was defending belonged to his neighbor?

TEST BANK

True/False

_____ 1. In Maryland, you must always attempt to retreat before using deadly force to defend yourself, regardless of the circumstances.

_____ 2. Defense of habitation and defense of property are essentially the same thing.

_____ 3. The amount of force you may use when defending yourself depends to some extent on the amount of force being used against you.

_____ 4. You may never use deadly force when defending another person.

_____ 5. You may never use deadly force when defending your property.

MULTIPLE CHOICE

6. Mary puts a gun to Connie's head and says to Connie, "You either kill Jane or I'll hurt you." Connie reluctantly kills Jane. Connie's best defense would be:
   A. Defense of habitation
   B. Defense of others
   C. Duress
   D. Connie has no good defenses

7. In which of the following situations do you NOT have a duty to retreat before using force to defend yourself?
   A. In your own home
   B. If there is no avenue of retreat
   C. Both A and B
   D. You must always retreat before using force to defend yourself

8. Which of the following statements is TRUE:
   A. A perfect defense will result in a not guilty verdict; an imperfect defense will result in a lesser crime
   B. A perfect defense will result in a lesser crime; an imperfect defense will result in a not guilty verdict
   C. Both a perfect and an imperfect defense will result in a not guilty verdict
   D. Both a perfect and an imperfect defense will result in a lesser crime

9. Billy was walking down the street one day when he saw Butch beating Kurt up. Although Billy didn't particularly like Kurt and could care less if Kurt got beaten to a pulp, Billy and Butch were arch enemies. So, Billy figured this was his chance—he ran up to Butch under the pretense of coming to Kurt's aid and beat Butch until he was unconscious. Can Billy claim he was acting in defense of another?
   A. Yes, because he actually came to Kurt's aid regardless of his motive
   B. Yes, because he did not know whether Kurt was the initial aggressor or not
   C. No, because his actions were not for the purpose of aiding Kurt but rather his intent was to harm Butch
   D. No, because defense of others can only be used if a homicide occurs

10. Which of the following is NOT an element of self-defense?
    A. The defendant must believe she is in danger of bodily harm either immediately or at some point in the future
    B. The defendant's belief must be reasonable
    C. The defendant must have used no more force than was reasonably necessary to defend herself in light of the threatened or actual harm
    D. All of the above are elements of self-defense

Intent-Based Criminal Defenses

Introduction

The final chapter of this book deals with criminal defenses whereby the perpetrator's capacity or ability to appreciate the criminality of her actions is in some way hampered. Some of the defenses discussed in this chapter, if successful, will completely negate criminal responsibility, while others may serve only to diminish punishment. With any of the defenses, it is first the burden of the state to prove beyond a reasonable doubt that the underlying crime was committed by the defendant. The focus then shifts to whether the defendant has a viable defense. The burden remains on the state to prove the absence of a defense beyond a reasonable doubt with all defenses except insanity. If the defendant asserts insanity, she bears the burden of proving insanity by a preponderance of the evidence.

Focus Defenses

Entrapment, *Bowser v. State*, 50 Md.App. 363, 439 A.2d 1 (1981); MPJI-Cr. 5:04.

Mistake of Fact, *Garnett v. State*, 332 Md. 571, 632 A.2d 797 (1993); MPJI-Cr. 5:06.

Intoxication, *Shell v. State*, 307 Md. 46, 512 A.2d 358 (1986); MPJI-Cr. 5:08.

Insanity, Md. Code Ann., Crim. Proc. § 3-109 (West 2002); MPJI-Cr. 5:01.1.

Infancy, *Adams v. State*, 8 Md.App. 684, 262 A.2d 69, *cert. denied*, 400 U.S. 928 (1970) (infra).

Objectives

Upon completing this chapter you should be able to:

- Analyze the impact of a successful intent-based defense on crimes charged;
- Analyze the requirements to successfully assert mistake of fact;
- Analyze the applicability of intoxication as a defense to various crimes;
- Analyze the availability of insanity as a defense and the impact that such a defense will have on the nature of the trial proceedings and the resultant penalty or punishment; and
- Analyze the availability of infancy as a criminal defense based upon relevant factors, including the perpetrator's age and the crime committed.

> **CASE LAW**   *Adams v. State*, 8 Md.App. 684, 262 A.2d 69, *cert. denied*, 400 U.S. 928 (1970)

A life sentence was imposed upon a 13-year-old boy, Ronnie Adams, after his conviction of first degree murder in a non-jury trial in the Criminal Court of Baltimore.

The record discloses that sometime before midnight on the evening of June 1, 1968, Charles A. Snyder, while operating a Baltimore Transit Company bus, was shot and killed in the course of a holdup. Two days later, appellant was surrendered to the police by his mother who also gave them a .32 caliber revolver which was later proven to be the murder weapon. Ronnie Adams gave a written statement to the police, which was introduced into evidence without objection, in which he admitted that he had taken his mother's gun from their home earlier in the evening of the crime, joined his friend Ryor Mills, aged sixteen years, and both met up with another friend, Earl Hill, in front of a shop at the intersection where the crime occurred; and that just prior to the holdup he had given the gun to a girl whom he had seen across the street and that immediately thereafter "I heard Earl say to Ryor, 'Do you want to hold up a bus?' and Ryor said to Earl, 'If you want to,' and this is when Ryor got the gun from the girl." His statement continued: "The girl gave Ryor the gun and as she was handing the gun to Ryor the mumber [*sic*] bus was coming up Fayette Street and caught the light at the corner of Fayette and Fremont. After this I started to walk over towards the Dixie shop and as I was doing this, I saw Earl and Ryor get on the bus. After Earl and Ryor got on the bus I saw Ryor through the front window pulled [*sic*] the gun from out of the waist of his pants and point it at the bus driver who was sitting in the driver's seat. And then the bus driver swung at hand that Ryor had the gun in and then Ryor shot him. Then Ryor reached down on the floor of the bus beside the driver and Earl reached into the shirt pocket of the bus driver. After this they both came off of the bus. Earl first. And Earl ran up Fayette Street towards the Dixie shop and Ryor ran up Fremont Avenue towards the projects. At this point Frank Harper, who was standing at the dixie shop with me, said to me, 'Let's follow Ryor.' So then me and Frank ran behind Ryor and we caught up with him on Mulberry Street. * * * And then Ryor opened a little green box which he had taken off of the bus and in the box was some little papers and some Kennedy half dollars. He gave Frank two of them and me two of them and some other boys some of them. After this I went home and he went towards the Dixie shop. But, before I went home, Ryor gave me the gun back. After I got home, I put the gun in some newspaper and put it in the kitchen table drawer. I haven't seen Ryor or Earl since."

Frank Harper, the first of three witnesses called by the State, testified that while he was looking out the window of the Dixie shop he observed Adams, Mills and Hill playing with a revolver and "saw them walk across the street toward the bus stop and saw a bus approaching." According to him, he saw nothing more until he heard a shot, ran out of the shop and saw "the bus driver slumped in the chair" and saw Earl Hill running "through the projects" with a "shiny object" which appeared to be a money changer.

George McCullum testified that he observed Mills and Hill standing together at the bus stop and Adams standing approximately ten to twelve feet away. He next heard a shot and saw Mills and Hill running from the direction of the bus and when asked about Adams, he stated, "* * * I ain't seen him run nowhere."

Detective George Montgomery testified that he went to appellant's home where he was given a gun which appellant's mother took from a kitchen drawer and that tests at the police crime laboratory disclosed that the bullet recovered from the victim's body was fired from that gun. It is first contended that the motion for judgment of acquittal should have been granted since, it is argued, the State failed to adduce evidence legally sufficient to overcome the common law presumption that a child under the age of fourteen years is incapable of committing a crime.

Since the Code of Hammurabi (circa 2250 B.C.) and down through the ages, society, under the law, has viewed and treated offenders of tender years in a light differently and more favorably than that accorded adults accused of breaching the law. Over the centuries and during the evolution of the common law of England, there emerged a rule of law governing "the responsibility of infants" under which an individual below the age of seven years cannot be found guilty of committing a crime; an individual above fourteen years charged with a crime is to be adjudged as an adult; and between the ages of seven and fourteen there is a rebuttable presumption that such individual is incapable of committing a crime. In the absence of any pertinent legislative enactment in this State, the common law principles, as stated above, would appear to govern in Maryland and we so hold.

In the case at bar, the appellant was shown to be thirteen years, ten and a half months of age at the time the crime was committed. It was, therefore, incumbent upon the State to produce sufficient evidence to overcome the presumption that the appellant was doli incapax, an expression ordinarily employed by the text writers. The proof necessary to meet this burden has been variously phrased: It must be shown that the individual "had discretion to judge between good and evil"; "knew right from wrong"; had "a guilty knowledge of wrong-doing"; was "competent to know the nature and consequences of his conduct and to appreciate that it was wrong." Perhaps the most modern definition of the test is simply that the surrounding circumstances must demonstrate, beyond a reasonable doubt, that the individual knew what he was doing and that it was wrong.

It is generally held that the presumption of doli incapax is "extremely strong at the age of seven and diminishes gradually until it disappears entirely at the age of fourteen * * *." Since the strength of the presumption of incapacity decreases with the increase in the years of the accused, the quantum of proof necessary to overcome the presumption would diminish in substantially the same ratio.

Judged by these precepts, and on the record before us, we cannot say that the trial judge was clearly erroneous in concluding that the State had met its burden. The judge below, as appears in the record, made a specific finding that "the State has rebutted the presumption * * * with evidence which would convince me beyond a reasonable doubt that this defendant is capable of understanding the nature of his acts and is, therefore, such a person to whom guilt could attach or responsibility could attach for his acts." This conclusion was not precipitously reached by the lower court but was made at the conclusion of the entire trial. It was arrived at only after the trial judge had weighed the demeanor, conduct and comprehension of Adams while being interrogated on the witness stand, prior to trial by both the court and his counsel concerning his understanding of the right to a jury trial. As announced by the judge, his conclusion that Adams understood the nature of his acts was fortified by analyzing the written statement given by him to the police in which he described, in narrative form, the events surrounding the commission of the crime. After carefully scrutinizing the record before us, we cannot disagree with the conclusion of the lower court that the evidence demonstrated, beyond a reasonable doubt, that Adams, who would have reached his fourteenth birthday in two and a half months, was doli capax.

* * *

JUDGMENT AFFIRMED.

_____**CASE END**

Smith v. State, 69 Md.App. 115, 516 A.2d 985 (1986)

A Baltimore County jury convicted appellant, Merlin Sherrill Smith, of assault with intent to murder, shooting with intent to disable, unlawful use of a handgun in the commission of a felony, unlawful carrying of a handgun, and assault. The conviction for assault was merged into the conviction of assault with intent to murder. He received a sentence of 25 years for the assault with intent to murder, imposed under Maryland's Subsequent Offender Law, Md. Ann. Code art. 27, section 643B, and concurrent sentences of five years for each of the other convictions. We will reverse as to the convictions for assault with intent to murder, shooting with intent to disable, and use of handgun in the commission of a crime of violence, but affirm as to the other convictions.

Facts

At approximately 2:00 a.m. on June 20, 1985, Kenneth Munshower was shot while carrying a six-pack of beer to a car in the parking lot of his employer, the Seagull Inn. Witnesses to the incident identified appellant, Merlin Sherrill Smith, as the assailant. Testimony at trial indicated that Smith approached Munshower and demanded the beer, asserting that Munshower had purchased it on Smith's behalf. When Munshower refused to hand over the beer, Smith produced a handgun and shot Munshower in the head.

Appellant's counsel requested the court to give the jury an instruction concerning the effect of voluntary intoxication on the ability of the accused to form the necessary *mens rea* to commit the specific intent crimes with which he was charged. The court refused to do so, finding there was insufficient evidence of intoxication to warrant the requested instruction. Smith's counsel also objected to certain remarks by the State's Attorney during closing arguments.

Issues

Appellant raises the following issues: I. Whether there was sufficient evidence of intoxication to warrant the trial court to give a jury instruction concerning voluntary intoxication as a defense to the crime of assault with intent to murder? . . .

I

Appellant argues that the evidence adduced at trial was sufficient to require the court to instruct the jury on voluntary intoxication as a defense to the specific intent crime of assault with intent to murder. We agree.

Although it has been stated that voluntary intoxication is no defense, *Saldeveri v. State,* 217 Md. 412, 143 A.2d 70 (1958), Maryland has long recognized that voluntary drunkenness can negate the *mens rea* element of specific intent crimes. *See Spencer v. State,* 69 Md. 28, 13 A. 809 (1888). The Court of Appeals in *State v. Gover,* 267 Md. 602, 298 A.2d 378 (1973), described the level of intoxication necessary to constitute a defense. After stating that the defendant "is criminally responsible so long as he retains control of his mental faculties sufficiently to appreciate what he is doing," *id.* at 607, 298 A.2d 378 (quoting *Beall v. State,* 203 Md. 380, 385-86, 101 A.2d 233 (1953)), the Court concluded:

> The degree of intoxication which must be demonstrated to exonerate a defendant is great. Evidence of drunkenness which falls short of a proven incapacity in the accused to form the intent necessary to constitute the crime merely establishes that the mind was affected by drink so that he more readily gave way to some violent passion and does not rebut the presumption that a man intends the natural consequences of his act.

267 Md. at 607-08, 298 A.2d 378

Dictum in *Johnson v. State,* 292 Md. 405, 439 A.2d 542 (1982) implied that the circumstances in which voluntary intoxication negates *mens rea* are more narrow than the language of *Gover* indicates. Citing to *Gover,* in a footnote, the Court in *Johnson* stated that the degree of intoxication necessary to negate *mens rea* is "comparable with that degree of mental incapacity that will render a defendant legally insane." *Id.* at 425 n. 10, 439 A.2d 542. In *Shell v. State,* 307 Md. 46, 512 A.2d 358 (1986), however, the Court expressly stated that *Johnson* was not intended to overrule *Gover. Shell,* at 64, n. 14, 512 A.2d 358. *Gover,* therefore, continues to express the Court's view of the degree of intoxication required to constitute a defense to a specific intent crime in Maryland. A trial judge, when requested to do so, is obligated to instruct the jury on every essential point of law supported by the evidence. *Waddell v. State,* 65 Md.App. 606, 613, 501 A.2d 865 (1985), *cert. denied,* 305 Md. 622, 505 A.2d 1342 (1986); *Tripp v. State,* 36 Md.App. 459, 463, 374 A.2d 384, *cert. denied,* 281 Md. 745 (1977). We believe there is sufficient evidence, "if deemed weighty and credible by the trier of fact," *Fisher v. State,* 28 Md.App. 243, 248-49, 345 A.2d 110 (1975), *cert. denied,* 276 Md. 743 (1976), to support a finding that Smith was so inebriated at the time of the shooting that he was incapable of forming a specific intent to kill Mr. Munshower.

Smith had consumed a large quantity of alcohol and drugs during the afternoon and evening prior to the shooting, which occurred around 2:00 a.m. on June 20, 1985. Between 3:00 and 4:30 p.m. on June 19, Smith ingested three beers, three shots of schnapps and six ten-milligram valium pills. He then traveled to his mother's house where he consumed an additional two beers and three or four valium pills. Smith proceeded from his mother's to a bar, the Main Event. Although there was no evidence as to what, if anything, Smith ingested at the bar, there is a reasonable inference that he consumed some additional inebriants, for it may be "presumed he saith not a *pater noster*" there. In any event, there was direct evidence that Smith had at least ninety milligrams of valium, five beers and three shots of liquor over a relatively short period of time.

Testimony concerning Smith's demeanor would also support a determination that he was highly intoxicated. A person with whom Smith rode from the Main Event to the scene of the shooting described Smith as acting "strange," "slurring," "down, drunk, unbalanced when he was walking." Moreover, the victim himself testified that Smith rendered his repeated demands for the beer in a "dull monotone" without raising his voice. This would appear to be a most unusual way for a person to make a demand of another. Smith's girl friend testified that when he arrived at her house about 2:30 a.m. (a half hour after the shooting) he was "drunk," "totally out of it," and "falling in the doorway." After she got him into bed, he passed out and slept six hours, after which he was taken to his mother's house where he slept until 11:00 p.m.

Additional significant testimony shedding light on Smith's state of consciousness at the time of the shooting concerns the manner in which he walked as he approached Munshower. Uncontroverted testimony disclosed that Smith had previously suffered an accident that caused him to walk with a definite limp and experience a great deal of difficulty maneuvering, even with a cane. At the time of the shooting, however, Smith was without his cane (having lost it at the Main Event) yet neither the victim nor any of the other witnesses noticed a limp or anything unusual about Smith's gait as he approached the victim. Apparently, Smith literally was "feeling no pain."

The State cites other evidence it asserts generates a different inference as to Smith's state of awareness. For example, the State notes there was no direct testimony that Smith consumed inebriants after the early evening hours. Moreover, Smith successfully traversed a quarter mile to his girl friend's house after the shooting. The State's contentions, however, go to the weight of the evidence, not its sufficiency. We need not choose between conflicting inferences; that is the role of the jury. *Cf. Hounshell v. State,* 61 Md.App. 364, 486 A.2d 789, *cert. denied,* 303 Md. 42, 491 A.2d 1197 (1985). The evidence of intoxication presented by Smith is comparable to that found in other Maryland decisions sufficient to require a jury instruction. The Court of Appeals in *Avey v. State,* 249 Md. 385, 240 A.2d 107 (1967) held that an instruction on voluntary intoxication was warranted when the defendant produced evidence that he and another shared a pint of "moonshine" and 18 or 19 beers five or six hours before the defendant shot two policemen. The *Gover* Court held that a jury instruction was required when the evidence indicated the defendant consumed numerous beers, a large quantity of whiskey and eight amphetamine tablets over a 13-hour period prior to robbing a convenience store. *State v. Gover, supra,* 267 Md. at 603-04, 298 A.2d 378. Moreover, this Court in *Biggs v. State,* 56 Md.App. 638, 468 A.2d 669, *cert. denied,* 299 Md. 425, 474 A.2d 218 (1984), implicitly expressed approval of the trial court's giving a jury instruction on voluntary intoxication when there was "some evidence that appellant was intoxicated at the time of the shooting." *Id.* at 648, 468 A.2d 669.

In contrast, those Maryland cases which hold that a jury instruction on voluntary intoxication was not warranted all involve considerably less evidence of intoxication than appellant produced at this trial. *See Myers v. State,* 58 Md.App. 211, 219, 472 A.2d 1027 (1984) (evidence defendant-conspirator may have been intoxicated on day conspiracy formed, but murder occurred six days later); *Monge v. State,* 55 Md.App. 72, 82, 461 A.2d 21 (1983) (defendant admitted to being sober on day of murder); *Bateman v. State,* 10 Md.App. 630, 637, 272 A.2d 64 (only evidence of intoxication was bartender's testimony defendant consumed two beers over a one and one-half hour period) *cert. denied,* 261 Md. 721 (1971); *Mock v. State,* 2 Md.App. 771, 775, 237 A.2d 811 (defendant testified he was not drunk), *cert. denied,* 250 Md. 732 (1968).

Because we believe that a reasonable trier of fact could conclude Smith was sufficiently intoxicated to lack the ability to form the specific intent to commit the crime of assault with intent to murder, we reverse his conviction for that offense.

Although shooting with intent to disable (shooting, stabbing, assaulting with intent to maim, disfigure or disable, Md. Code Ann., art. 27, § 386) is also a specific intent crime, *see State v. Jenkins,* 307 Md. 501, 515 A.2d 465 (1986), appellant's brief and argument in this Court asserted error in the refusal to instruct the jury on the defense of intoxication only as to assault with intent to murder. Ordinarily, we would decline to address an issue not raised on appeal, but we exercise our discretion to do so in this case in the interest of judicial economy and to avoid an inevitable post conviction assertion of inadequate representation on appeal. Accordingly, we will reverse the conviction for shooting with intent to disable and, since the conviction for use of a handgun in the commission of a crime of violence was necessarily predicated upon guilt of either assault with intent to murder or shooting with intent to disable, Md. Code Ann., art. 27, §§ 36B(d) and 441, we will reverse that conviction as well.

* * *JUDGMENTS REVERSED AND CASE REMANDED FOR NEW TRIAL AS TO CONVICTION FOR ASSAULT WITH INTENT TO MURDER, SHOOTING WITH INTENT TO DISABLE, AND USE OF HANDGUN IN THE COMMISSION OF A CRIME OF VIOLENCE.

CASE END

Case Questions

Adams v. State

1. What are the significant ages of a juvenile when it comes to criminal responsibility? Where did Adams fall within that spectrum?

2. What factors will determine whether a juvenile will stand trial as an adult?

Smith v. State

1. Can voluntary intoxication serve as a defense to all crimes? Explain.

2. Did the facts in this case support an inference that Smith was intoxicated at the time he shot the victim? Explain.

Additional Defenses to Consult

The plea of not criminally responsible by reason of insanity is a complex process. Title 3 of the Criminal Procedure Article of the Code outlines in depth the procedures before and after trial for the insanity plea and discusses the standard for legal insanity in Maryland (*see* Md. Code Ann., Crim. Proc. §§ 3-109–3-123). Additionally, Maryland Rule 4-314 describes the procedure of a bifurcated trial when a defendant enters a plea of not criminally responsible by reason of insanity.

HYPOTHETICAL #1

Paul has been a police officer for over twenty years, but he has never had much ambition or direction in life. In fact, he is known by his fellow officers as "Paul the Putz." One day, Paul figured he'd change his lazy ways and make his family and colleagues so proud of him. Paul met up with his old pal Tom, and he explained to Tom how great it would be if Tom started his own gambling scheme. "Gee, I don't know," said Tom, "isn't that illegal or something?" "Naa," replied Paul, "it's only a little bit illegal, and besides, you'll make a lot of money if you do it!" "I don't think so," replied Tom, "I'm not the gambling type, and besides, I've never committed a crime in my entire life!" However, after lots of persuading on Paul's part, Tom finally agreed. Tom set up the most elaborate gambling scheme in years, and Paul busted him for gambling!! The police department was so ecstatic that Paul got his badge back and was promoted to chief! Tom, however, appeared to be well on his way to jail for gambling.

MAIN ISSUE

Was Tom Entrapped into Committing the Crime of Gambling?

ISSUE	THESIS	RULE	ANALYSIS	CONCLUSION
Did Tom commit the crime of gambling WHEN he set up an elaborate gambling scheme?	Tom committed the crime of gambling WHEN he set up an elaborate gambling scheme.	The State must prove the elements of the offense of GAMBLING beyond a reasonable doubt.	Tom committed the crime of gambling BECAUSE he set up the gambling scheme.	Tom committed the crime of gambling.
Was Tom induced or persuaded to commit the crime by a law enforcement officer WHEN Paul encouraged him to start a gambling operation?	Tom was persuaded to commit the crime by a law enforcement officer WHEN Paul encouraged him to start a gambling operation.	A person must be entrapped into committing the crime by a LAW ENFORCEMENT OFFICIAL OR SOMEONE ACTING FOR THE OFFICER.	Tom was entrapped into committing the gambling offenses BECAUSE Paul was a police officer, even though he may not have been a particularly diligent one.	Tom was induced to commit a crime by a law enforcement officer.
Was Tom induced or persuaded into committing the crime of gambling WHEN Paul encouraged him to start a gambling operation?	Tom was induced and persuaded into committing the crime of gambling WHEN Paul encouraged him to start a gambling operation.	The defendant must be INDUCED OR PERSUADED to commit a criminal act.	Tom was induced or persuaded BECAUSE Paul approached Tom about the gambling agency, said it was only "a little bit" illegal, and said Tom would make a lot of money.	Tom was induced or persuaded to commit the gambling offenses.
Was Tom predisposed to commit the crime of gambling WHEN Paul approached Tom and encouraged Tom to start a gambling operation?	Tom was not predisposed to commit the crime of gambling WHEN Paul approached Tom and encouraged Tom to start a gambling operation.	The defendant must not have been PREDISPOSED TO COMMIT THE CRIME prior to the time the officer makes initial contact.	Tom was not predisposed to commit gambling offenses BECAUSE he first expressed doubt ("Gee, I don't know . . ."), he said he wasn't the "gambling type," he had never committed a crime before, and he needed a lot of persuading before he agreed.	Tom was not predisposed to commit the gambling offenses.

CONCLUSION

Tom was entrapped into committing the gambling offenses by Paul.

HYPOTHETICAL #2

Brandon was a thirteen-year-old student in middle school, and he was known throughout the school as "Brandon the Bully." Brandon had been in trouble in some way or another from the time he was old enough to walk. One day, Brandon decided he would wreak havoc on his middle school and the elementary school right next door. First he enlisted the help of Charlie, a first grader who was going to turn seven in just one month. "Hey Charlie," Brandon said in his devilish voice, "Why don't you put a smoke bomb in one of the toilets in your school bathroom?" "Wow, what a cool idea!" Charlie exclaimed with excitement. Charlie took two weeks to painstakingly make the smoke bomb, he planned out which bathroom of the school would be the best one to "hit" so he would get away with it, and he waited for the perfect time when everyone was in class to plant his smoke bomb. Just as planned, Charlie's bomb exploded in the bathroom and completely destroyed two bathroom stalls. The cost would be at least $8,000 to repair. But, Charlie wasn't so smart after all, because he left his very favorite baseball cap with his name written inside at the scene of the crime.

Brandon, meanwhile, wanted to have some "fun" of his own. Early one morning before school started, Brandon drank a pint of Jack Daniel's while he contemplated all of the crimes he would commit. He made his way to school and once there he set the gymnasium on fire, beat up his long-time enemy Edgar, and broke into the principal's office in order to steal a plaque on her wall she was given for being "Principal of the Year." Brandon was feeling pretty woozy at the time from the alcohol, so he staggered out of the principal's office and into the hallway where he had left his backpack full of cherry bombs, cigarettes, and comic books. But, he mistakenly picked up an identical backpack on the chair next to where his backpack sat, which unbeknownst to him belonged to "Beatrice the Brown Noser," the middle school's most outgoing student. Beatrice, who was paranoid that everyone was trying to steal her notebooks and reports, put a tracking device in her backpack. As soon as she noticed that the backpack was gone she notified the police, who quickly made their way over to Brandon's house. As the police were walking up to Brandon's front door, Mrs. Pevis, the principal of the school, came tearing up the front steps like a mad woman screaming "You'll never take my award for Principal of the Year, I will always reign as the best principal ever!" Mrs. Pevis flailed her hands, began foaming at the mouth, and shoved all of the officers out of the way. She ran into Brandon's house and as soon as she found him she beat him to within an inch of his life. Then she calmly recovered her plaque, fixed her hair, and smiled warmly at the officers, who were all staring at her in utter disbelief.

Once at the house the officers retrieved Beatrice's prized backpack along with handwritten notes detailing Charlie's plan to put a smoke bomb in the toilet and a floor plan of the school with a star marked on Mrs. Pevis' office.

⮕ List the crimes with which each defendant may be charged and list any possible defenses each defendant may raise.

DEFENDANT	CRIME(S)	DEFENSE(S)
Brandon		
Charlie		
Mrs. Pevis		

⮕ For EACH crime and defense identified, complete an Analysis Chart assessing the possibility of conviction.

DISCUSSION QUESTIONS

1. Do you agree with the sentence imposed upon thirteen-year-old Ronnie Adams by the court in *Adams v. State*, 8 Md.App. 684, 262 A.2d 69, *cert. denied*, 400 U.S. 928 (1970)?

2. Could long-term addiction to drugs and/or alcohol and the effects of such an addiction render an individual legally insane? Why or why not?

3. Do you think the defense of mistake of fact should apply to the commission of any crime? What about, for example, selling alcohol to a minor or statutory rape? *See Garnett v. State*, 332 Md. 571, 632 A.2d 797 (1993).

4. Do you agree that the burden should rest on the defendant to persuade the fact finder by a preponderance of the evidence that he was insane at the time of the crime? Why or why not?

5. What is a "bifurcated trial"? Why is a bifurcated trial used in insanity cases? What other types of criminal cases make use of the bifurcated trial? *See* Maryland Rule 4-314.

6. In your opinion, is a successful insanity plea in a criminal case an "easy way out" for the defendant? Explain.

7. Revisit Hypothetical #1: What if Tom had argued that he wasn't the one who set up the gambling ring. Would his defense of entrapment succeed? Why or why not?

8. Revisit Hypothetical #1: Suppose at the time of the occurrence Paul had been placed on indefinite suspension pending an internal investigation due to inappropriate conduct while on duty. Would Paul still qualify as a "law enforcement officer" if the rest of the scenario occurred as described?

9. John and Mary had been married for ten years. One day, Mary went out alone on their boat but she never returned home. Two days later the boat was found in the middle of the Chesapeake Bay, but Mary was nowhere to be found. Five years later there is still no sign of Mary, and John is convinced she drowned. Therefore, John remarries Jane. The next month, Mary turns up alive and well. John is charged with bigamy. John asserts mistake of fact as his defense— he claims he reasonably believed Mary to be dead. Do you think his defense should be successful? Why or why not? What if instead of being dead, John thought that he and Mary had obtained a valid divorce prior to his marriage to Jane, when in fact he hadn't? *See Braun v. State*, 230 Md. 82, 185 A.2d 905 (1962).

10. Jenna wants to break into her neighbor's house to steal her neighbor's prized collection of antique dolls, but Jenna doesn't have the guts to do it. So, Jenna buys a twelve pack of beer, drinks them as fast as she can, and once the effects of the alcohol kick in she quickly gets up the nerve to break into her neighbor's house and take the dolls. Can Jenna argue intoxication as a defense? *See State v. Gover*, 267 Md. 602, 298 A.2d 378 (1973).

11. David has been charged with first-degree murder. David's defense attorney is convinced that David is legally insane, but David refuses to enter a plea of not criminally responsible by reason of insanity. May David's defense attorney enter a plea of insanity over David's objection? Why or why not? *See Treece v. State*, 313 Md. 665, 547 A.2d 1054 (1988).

12. What is "temporary insanity"? Does Maryland recognize it as a defense?

TEST BANK

True/False

_____ 1. Insanity can be a defense to any crime.

_____ 2. Intoxication can serve to negate the intent of any crime.

_____ 3. Mistake of fact and mistake of law are identical.

_____ 4. A person under the age of ten may never be held criminally responsible for her actions.

_____ 5. The burden of persuasion rests on the defendant for any of the intent-based defenses.

MULTIPLE CHOICE

6. In order to be found not criminally responsible by reason of insanity, the defendant must have been legally insane:
   A. Throughout his entire life
   B. At the time the crime was committed
   C. At the time the defendant was arrested
   D. At the time trial was set to begin

7. Buddy and Billy are cellmates in prison. Carl the cop forces Buddy to talk Billy into attempting to escape from prison one day. Although reluctant to do so, Billy finally agrees after much persuading. Billy is apprehended while trying to escape and charged with attempted escape. Can Billy argue entrapment as a defense?
   A. No because Buddy was not a cop
   B. No because Billy wasn't successful in his escape from prison
   C. No because by definition Billy had a predisposal to commit a crime because he was already in prison in the first place
   D. Yes

8. Kimberly goes on a crystal meth binge one night and while high on the drug she murders her grandmother. At trial she argues she was legally insane because she was under the influence of drugs. Will her defense succeed?
   A. No, because intoxication from drugs or alcohol does not qualify as a mental disorder
   B. No, because she was not under the influence of the drug at the time her trial began
   C. Yes, if she can persuade the jury that her capacity was impaired by the drug while she committed the murder
   D. Yes, if the state fails to persuade the jury that her capacity was impaired by the drug while she committed the murder

9. Valerie is eating lunch one day in a cafeteria when she sees her friend across the room and goes over to talk to her. Valerie inadvertently leaves her purse on the table. When Valerie leaves, however, she picks up a purse on another table and proceeds to exit the cafeteria. Before she can look inside the purse she is arrested for theft. Will Valerie succeed in arguing mistake of fact?
   A. Yes, assuming the purse Valerie picks up is similar in appearance to her purse
   B. Yes, assuming the purse she picked up is at a table near the one in which she was originally sitting
   C. Both A and B
   D. No, she will not be able to argue mistake of fact under any circumstances

10. The presumption that a juvenile lacks the ability to appreciate the wrongfulness of her conduct generally disappears once that juvenile has reached the age of:
    A. Eighteen
    B. Fourteen
    C. Ten
    D. Seven

Test Bank

CHAPTER ONE
Parties to a Crime

1. T	6. A
2. T	7. A
3. F	8. B
4. F	9. D
5. F	10. A

CHAPTER TWO
Inchoate Offenses

1. T	6. B
2. T	7. B
3. F	8. B
4. F	9. D
5. F	10. A

CHAPTER THREE
Homicide

1. F	6. D
2. T	7. B
3. T	8. C
4. T	9. A
5. T	10. C

CHAPTER FOUR
Rape and Sexual Offenses

1. T	6. A
2. F	7. B
3. F	8. D
4. T	9. A
5. F	10. D

CHAPTER FIVE
Other Crimes Against Person

1. F	6. A
2. T	7. B
3. F	8. D
4. F	9. C
5. T	10. C

CHAPTER SIX
Hybrid Crimes

1. T	6. D
2. F	7. C
3. F	8. A
4. F	9. C
5. F	10. C

CHAPTER SEVEN
Crimes Against Property

1. F	6. D
2. F	7. A
3. T	8. B
4. F	9. B
5. F	10. D

CHAPTER EIGHT
Drug and Alcohol Offenses

1. T	6. B
2. F	7. D
3. F	8. C
4. T	9. D
5. F	10. C

CHAPTER NINE
Crimes Against Morality

1. T	6. D
2. F	7. A
3. T	8. C
4. F	9. C
5. F	10. F

CHAPTER TEN
Force-Based Criminal Defenses

1. F	6. C
2. F	7. C
3. T	8. A
4. F	9. C
5. T	10. A

CHAPTER ELEVEN
Intent-Based Criminal Defenses

1. T	6. B
2. F	7. D
3. F	8. A
4. F	9. C
5. F	10. B